HIDDEN CULTURES
IN
CLINICAL PSYCHOLOGY

Fielding University Press is an imprint of Fielding Graduate University. Its objective is to advance the research and scholarship of Fielding faculty, students, alumni and associated scholars around the world, using a variety of publishing platforms. For more information, please contact Fielding University Press, attn. Jean-Pierre Isbouts, 2020 De la Vina Street, Santa Barbara, CA 93105. Email: jisbouts@fielding.edu. On the web: www.fielding.edu/universitypress.

Library of Congress Cataloging-in-Publication data
Hidden Cultures in Clinical Psychology by Henry V. Soper and
K. Drorit Gaines (Eds.)
1. Modern Psychology-Social Diversity

HIDDEN CULTURES IN CLINICAL PSYCHOLOGY

Sensitivity to Diversity in Culture

EDITED BY

HENRY V. SOPER, PhD AND K. DRORIT GAINES, PhD

FIELDING UNIVERSITY PRESS

KATRINA S. ROGERS
PRESIDENT, FIELDING GRADUATE UNIVERSITY

MONIQUE L. SNOWDEN
PROVOST, FIELDING GRADUATE UNIVERSITY

KRISTINE M. JACQUIN
CHAIR, DEPARTMENT OF PSYCHOLOGY

MARILYN FREIMUTH
PROGRAM DIRECTOR, CLINICAL PSYCHOLOGY

JEAN-PIERRE ISBOUTS
EDITOR, FIELDING UNIVERSITY PRESS

MONOGRAPH VOLUME 13

EDITORS
HENRY V. SOPER
K. DRORIT GAINES

CONTRIBUTORS
SCOTT CURRY
RACHEL RUGH FRASER
SAMANTHA F. HILL
PAVEL LITVIN
MARGARET LOO
ANGELINA J. PRINCE-JEFFERS
WHILLMA QUENICKA
LAURA RIEFFEL
IYA RITCHIE
HEATHER SORENSEN

TABLE OF CONTENTS

Foreword

Hidden Culture and Clinical Psychology

Arthur MacNeill Horton, Jr., EdD
Chief, Neuropsychology Section
Psych Associates of Maryland LLC

Definitions of culture are like toothbrushes: everyone has one but no one wishes to use another's. Perhaps the first author who used the term "culture" with regards to learned human behavior was the pioneering English anthropologist Edward B. Tylor in his book, *Primitive Culture*, published in 1871. Taylor defined culture as "that complex whole which includes knowledge, belief, art, law, morals, customs and any other capacities and habits acquired by man as a member of society." Of course, in our current society the proper term would be "human beings" rather than "man," as both men and women are more appropriately referred to as "human beings" because both men and women acquire culture as members of society. Put more specifically, perhaps we could see culture in a (grossly simplified) psychology context as socially learned human behavior, rather than nature or genetic inheritance.

There are, in fact, theoretical models for conceptualizing culture from a psychological point of view. One is the Cultural-Historical theory of Lev Vygotsky, which he developed with Alexander Luria, better known for his contributions to Clinical Neuropsychology. What Vygotsky tried to do is develop a universal integrative theory of the human mind and social development that was distinct from Freudian and behavioral psychology. In other words, he tried to conceptualize human beings as more than pure reflexes and biology.

Vygotsky described his theory as involving "cultural", "historical," and "instrumental" mechanisms by which society organized higher cognitive processes in human beings. For example:

• The "cultural" mechanisms "involved the socially structured ways in which society organizes the kinds of tasks that the growing child faces and the kind of tools, both mental and physical, that the young child is provided with to master those tasks" (Luria, 1979, p. 44). Vygotsky argued that the key tool in the organization and development of such thought processes was language (Luria, 1979).

• The "historical" mechanism referred to the tools by which human beings master their environments and behavior. These tools, such as language, writing, and arithmetic were developed over time and promoted the development of higher cognitive processes.

• The "instrumental" mechanism "referred to the basically mediate nature of all complex psychological functions" (Luria, 1979, p. 44). Vygotsky also postulated (1979) that higher cognitive processes incorporated auxiliary stimuli that were self-produced, for example, the idea of tying a string around one's finger to remember more effectively.

In order to develop empirical scientific support for Vygotsky's theories, his colleague Luria performed a study that examined cultural differences in thinking (Luria, 1931). Grossly oversimplified, groups that differed in education (illiterate vs. graduates of teacher colleges) were assessed regarding higher cognitive processes. To describe one example, subjects were asked to characterize several drawings of a hammer, a saw, a log, and a hatchet. Illiterates saw the hatchet, saw, and log as related functionally, as one would use the hatchet to cut down a tree and then the saw to cut the log into firewood. By contrast, graduates of teacher training colleges would group the hatchet, saw, and hammer as tools and leave out the log.

In other words, illiterates would characterize objects in a functional-graphic way, based on their personal real-life experiences. By contrast, graduates of the teacher training colleges grouped the drawings in an abstract-categorical fashion. As noted by Luria (1979),

> "...categorical thinking is not just a reflection of individual experience but a shared experience that society can convey through its linguistic system. This reliance on society wide criteria transforms functional-graphic thinking process to a scheme of semantic and logical operations in which words become the principal tool for abstraction and generalization." (p. 68).

The point, of course, is that the cultural history of learned behavior as transmitted by educational experiences (graduates of teacher training colleges vs. illiterates) through the instrument of language profoundly impacts the higher cognitive processes of human beings.

The implication is that any attempt to understand a culture from a psychological point of view should consider the cultural-historical heritage by which this culture was created over time, and realize the mutability and importance of accurate cultural understanding. The hope and expectation is that these thoughts will be of assistance to the readers of this book in better understanding the psychology of various cultures.

About the Author

Arthur MacNeill Horton, Jr., received his Ed.D. Degree from the University of Virginia in 1976. He also holds Diplomates in both Clinical Psychology and Behavioral Psychology from the American Board of Professional Psychology (ABPP) and in Neuropsychology from the American Board of Professional Neuropsychology (ABN) and in Pediatric Neuropsychology from the American Board of Pediatric Neuropsychology (ABPdN). Dr. Horton is the author/editor of 17 books, 47 book chapters, and over 130 journal articles. He is a past-president of ABN, the National Academy of Neuropsychology (NAN), and the Maryland Psychological Association (MPA). In addition, Dr. Horton was a member of the State of Maryland Board of Examiners of Psychologists for two four-year terms. Previously, Dr. Horton was a Program Officer with the National Institute of Drug Abuse (NIDA) of the National Institutes of Health (NIH) with responsibilities for neuropsychology and child development. Currently, Dr. Horton is in independent practice as Chief of the Neuropsychology Section at Psych Associates of Maryland in Towson, Columbia and Bethesda, Maryland. He is also the current Editor in Chief of both *Applied Neuropsychology-Adult* and *Applied Neuropsychology-Child.*

References

Luria, A. R. (1931). "Psychological expedition to Central Asia." *Science, 74*(1920), 383-384.

Luria, A. R. (1979). *The Making of Mind.* Harvard University Press, Cambridge, MA

Introduction
Henry V. Soper, PhD

I suppose it is fair to say that cultures other than our own can make us feel uncomfortable because they present us with something that we are not used to, something different. When individuals from other cultures have psychological difficulties, it should be obvious that therapy work should be done in or with the background of the client's culture, and for several reasons. First, perhaps, this client will return to that culture and have to function successfully within it. This also means that it behooves the therapist to try to see the world through the eyes of this person from the other culture, and understand what makes sense to him or her. Otherwise, therapy will likely be fruitless. One sometimes hears that the reason the person has psychological difficulties means that their culture is not working for them. Would you say that for someone from your own culture?

Of course, there are many things that can go wrong that have nothing to do with culture. Also, one's position within the culture may have an effect, whether male or female, married or single, aged or young. It has been said that there are as many cultures as there are people within that culture, and that everyone has slightly different forces acting on them. Although one could argue this, it is not clear how useful it is. And it would be impossible to know everything about a given culture. However, developing a sensitivity to the various aspects within a client's culture is undoubtedly very important.

Another way to put this is that once therapists have identified a culture, they should next identify what aspect of that culture their patients represent. Someone from a South Seas culture who works the telephone line may live in quite a different culture than someone from the same culture who runs a restaurant or a dental laboratory. Identifying the major culture is certainly important, but then one should probably identify those aspects of diversity within that culture that are particularly important to the patient or the psychological problem. Understanding the diversity within a culture is just as important as understanding the major tenets of that culture.

When the authors in this book were assigned (or chose) their chapters they were given as little guidance as possible, only enough so that the final objective could be obtained. This is why these chapters vary in form. Some are more informal, discussing culturally inappropriate topics, whereas others are more academic, with more of an emphasis on presenting data for their conclusions. We believe that all of these methods of presentation are appropriate as long as they get the message out. Certainly, the fact that someone is very familiar with a particular culture does not qualify that person to serve as a therapist. We don't have to be experts in order to be able to listen to the client and find out what is going on in this client's world. But one has to be open to the diversity within that culture. These diversities may or may not be related to the presenting problem, but appreciating them is exceedingly important for the effective therapist.

Section I

The first section of this book approaches the hidden cultures of clinical psychology from a number of perspectives. The chapter on prejudice argues that prejudice itself is not a result of "bad" thinking but a result of normal cognitive processes that can create a picture of the world, or of peoples, that is inaccurate and has been developed from inadequate or false data. Under normal circumstances these inaccurate prejudices might become corrected, but this discussion goes on to present the impedimenta to correcting these false impressions or false thinking.

One chapter is devoted to gender-based cultural biases. This is a popular topic, and books could be written on the factors involved. One such is domestic violence and battered women, about whom, try as we might, it has proven very difficult to get the message out, especially through the judicial system. One of the intentions of this chapter is to point out sensitivity to areas where the other gender may not have knowledge because of a lack of personal experience.

Another "hidden" group are those with medical conditions, especially those that manifest physically. Although these people are not mentally disabled and have relatively normal minds, their behaviors tend to make them rejected, which can interfere with living a normal social life. In many ways, the elderly are treated as if they have disabilities, though only some do, and it has become clear that the difficulties faced by the elderly are not at all understood by those who are younger.

The author of the chapter on transgender has spent years working with this group and conducting research on attitudes toward them. This is a very complex area to try to sort out. Indeed, the first question to address is not as easy as it seems: What does the term "transgender" refer to, especially because it has been used in various ways.? The author also mentions the horrible treatment such individuals have received in our supposedly enlightened society, and discussions about the various forms of sexual identity. As such, the chapter paints a compelling picture of the transgender person to whom one can provide effective therapy. For example, it stresses the importance of identifying the problem the client wants to address in his or her culture, not the one you would want to address in *your* culture.

One of the more difficult chapters to write was the one on aging, especially if one is not very old oneself. I suggested the authors talk to old people about the topic, and they all turned to talk to me! One insight of this chapter is that the psychology of the elderly is substantially different than that of those who are younger, and that these younger people have difficulty guessing what the stresses of the elderly are. These stress factors themselves can be very different than what one would expect, and that working with the elderly is different than working with other groups where the stresses may be more obvious.

The last chapter in this section is focused on the role of Jewish culture in therapy, which discusses the diversity of cultures within Judaism. Unlike many other religious identities, the Jewish culture is exceedingly varied and actually could be said to contain many major subcultures, some of which are discussed here. Both religious and cultural identities are discussed, with an emphasis on diversity (e.g., dress codes and the influences of the ancestral and current homelands on the culture). There are discussions of Orthodox Judaism (as well as the various streams of thought within Orthodox Judaism), Conservative Judaism, the Sefaradi/Mizrachi Jew versus the Ashkenazi Jew, the American Jew, and the Israeli-American Jew. After a brief discussion on antisemitism, we provide some recommendations for working with Jewish people.

Section II

The second section of this book shows how such cultures can develop. One chapter is written by two women of "Asian" descent, one of whom came to this country relatively recently. It includes several excellent examples of culturally inappropriate behavior from which one can gain a sensitivity to what is offensive and clinically ineffective with this population. The second part of the chapter is written by someone whose family has been in the United States for several generations, and whose close relatives had to suffer through the interment of the Second World War. She shows how the effects of not only the interment but of their treatment for generations before can affect generations that follow. She gives a good picture of the ambient background with which many of Japanese live, which must be respected by the therapist.

There is also a study from within the United States where variables in culture are so different that many students were baffled by the report. By way of comparison, the development of cultures in non-human primates is discussed, in which three different groups of primates substantially changed their way of living due to unusual circumstances. Within this chapter are discussions of diversity and culture and race, which seems to be a biologically null term, despite its popular use.

One chapter was written by a member of the First Nations Peoples, and this chapter is particularly valuable because it presents us with many areas of misunderstanding that can be offensive to these peoples, even though there is great diversity among their cultures. It provides us with a great feel, or sensitivity, for many of these peoples and the individuals within these cultures. The author describes a strong sample of many different phenomena, so that the therapist can have a greater appreciation for the problems that are presented by this population. In fact, although this chapter covers a lot of ground, one could argue that if it were written by a woman 20 years older, or a grandfather of the tribe, the emphasis might well be on quite different things. For example, one man about 70 years old read the chapter and said he could relate to little that the author mentioned. His chapter would have been quite different, although it would still be about First Nations Peoples.

A chapter on working with Hispanic clients was written by an excellent clinical and neuropsychologist with over 25 years of experience in the field. She has also spent years supervising non-Hispanic interns working with Hispanic clients. "Hispanic clients" refers to a very diverse group of people, many with little in common except the language. However, the author has done a great job of presenting areas of diversity within cultures, so as to develop a greater sensitivity to these factors and make therapy more effective. She discusses the generational effects of relatively newly arrived people and the related level of acculturation, as well as the difficulty of living in two cultures simultaneously, and some of the cultural barriers to treatment. For example, while this woman is from Colorado, and one can imagine the differences with a Hispanic from, say, San Diego or Miami.

As such, each of the chapters serves as an example of what one person views as his or her culture, and how this relates to effective therapy. In other words, these chapters are intended to develop a sensitivity to the cultures they address, not tell us everything about them. They can assist the therapist in knowing what to look for, but would hardly cover the whole diversity of that culture. Developing a sensitivity to differences between and within cultures is exceedingly important for effective therapy. Sometimes, as we will see with the example of the Portuguese women, there may appear to be little consistency within aspects of a culture.

In the next chapter we discuss the development of culture and some of the forces involved in changing it, especially among monkeys. We will also talk about two American women who identify as having and living in a Portuguese culture. Somehow the cultures described developed quite differently and resulted in what could be called quite different cultures. Looking at these two cultures together one can easily see how they can develop quite differently, somewhat like those of the different baboons described shortly afterward. After the monkeys, we discuss a (Texan) culture that is so different from that of most America that at least some people had difficulty believing it.

It is good to understand and appreciate the major cultures one deals with, but it is also important to appreciate the diversity within those cultures and the unique circumstances of a client within a given culture. Of course, every client is unique, or at least should be presumed to be. However, a knowledge of the culture he or she lives in and an appreciation for the diversity within that culture are essential for maximal therapeutic outcomes. It behooves the therapist to view the world through the eyes of the client, including respecting the experiences of that person and the cultures and beliefs he or she has or holds.

One danger in not taking into account the diversity of patients within a culture is that we can experience the danger of one-size-fits-all ("This is how you treat clients from Long Island"). This kind of response often occurs in drug and alcohol therapy, where some people believe you have to have been an addict and recovered in order to be an effective therapist. The song goes on that "this worked for me, and so it will work for you if you apply it appropriately." Therefore, if the therapy does not work, it is the client's fault. One example is the low-back pain syndrome. "I have low back pain and this exercise or medication worked for me, so it will work for you." Yes, each of our clients is an individual and can have a diverse number of factors within his or her culture causing him or her psychological problems. Much as with any other client, the job of the therapist is to find out exactly what is going on and then correct the consequences.

Again, these chapters should be viewed as expressing important factors for some members of a culture, but more toward developing a sensitivity to what else may be involved. One can get an idea of what to look for in an elderly Hispanic man with epilepsy, but his stresses are unique and not just the sum of what was captured in those chapters. Developing a sensitivity to those stresses and looking for the relevant ones through engaging the client will vastly improve the success of the therapy.

Section I
Hidden Cultures in Clinical Psychology

1.

THE DEVELOPMENT OF PREJUDICE

Angelina Prince-Jeffers, MA and Henry V. Soper, PhD

Just what is prejudice? It has different meanings to different people. One way to look at it is to break the word down into pre- and judge, possibly making a decision or judgement before all the relevant information is used to make the decision. This is, perhaps, sadly, the way our minds work when we are learning. When we lift a pencil and let it go, it drops, so we may make the judgment that pencils which are let go drop. But then someone lets a pencil go in a bucket of water, and now it rises. Then we can refine our judgment to "pencils dropped in air fall", and maybe add "pencils dropped in water rise." As we gain knowledge from our experiences we can come out with a more reasonable understanding of the situation.

When we see someone who acts or looks different than those in our culture, it is natural for our minds to ask: In what ways, other than skin color and texture of hair, does this person differ from me and those in my culture? An African American student was admitted to one of our upper-class Western prep schools, and on hearing this the basketball coach made room for the expectant trophy for winning the league the next year. However, this student did not even try out for the basketball team, but he did play a very good trombone in the school band.

Prejudice, the word often, but not always, refers to members of a certain culture and it usually, but not always, has a negative connotation or an excuse for failure. ("I know I did not do well in math, but I am a girl.") We, as people, use what information we have to draw conclusions, and it would seem likely that the more information we have the more accurate our conclusions would be. Sometimes we reject information that runs contrary to our beliefs. In other words, we have prejudged what we will accept as true. I have met many "jungle" people, known as Montagnards, in Vietnam, none of whom had ever had any formal education. So my prejudicial position may be that any Montagnards I meet will be uneducated. I am sure there are some who have more education than I, but I do not think of this when I meet someone new from this culture. One could say that prejudice reflects erroneous conclusions from information about a given subject or culture. However, when it rained, the Montagnards took their clothing off to keep it dry, which seems like a very sensible thing to do.

Some say stereotypes are beliefs, prejudice is an attitude, and discrimination is an act. All three are related and imbedded in everyday life. Repeated exposure to positive stereotypes about a group of people, such as the stereotype that Asians are intelligent, contributes to the development of feelings and attitudes about that group of people. In a similar fashion, repeated exposure to negative stereotypes about Black people can lead to the development of negative attitudes about this group of people. Many people are unaware that they may be prejudiced and consequently unaware of how the prejudice developed. Everyone is prejudiced or has been prejudiced at some point. While many may take offense to this basic statement, it is in fact true and unavoidable. Prejudice can simply be thought of as negative preconceived beliefs or feelings about a particular group of people; in itself prejudice does not entail action. The term prejudice typically carries a negative connotation, is deemed damaging, and is frequently confused with stereotypes and discrimination.

Many people are confused as to what prejudice actually is and many individuals equate prejudice with racism. In reality, racism is one of many types of prejudice. Other well-known types of prejudice include:

- Homophobia
- Nationalism
- Ageism
- Classism
- Sexism
- Religious prejudice
- Ableism
- Colorism

Most do not become aware until the prejudice manifests in a discriminatory act. These actions are more easily observed and documented in research, while the advent of the prejudice is more difficult to assess and examine. While stereotypes may form unknowingly, some purport that prejudice occurs when an individual is consciously aware of these stereotypes. In reality, we are prejudiced because we prejudge people, places, and events based on the information that we already have. This information is often limited and often inaccurate. The act of prejudging is automatic and does not always involve negative stereotypes.

Ehlrich (1973) and Allport (1954) were proponents of the notion that prejudice emerges somewhat naturally as a result of the ordinary categorization of information. In other words, stereotypes are a normal part of human thinking. Allport (1954) firmly states that human thinking relies on the formation of categories and that these categories form the basis for normal prejudgment. He puts forth the notion that this necessary and unavoidable process assists us all in making sense of the world around us.

Devin (1989) outlines the viewpoint that prejudice is inevitable:

The basic argument of the perspective of the inevitability of prejudice is that as long as stereotypes exist, prejudice will follow. This approach suggests that stereotypes are automatically (or heuristically) applied to members of the stereotyped group. In essence, knowledge of (or belief in) a stereotype is equated with prejudice toward the group.

In accordance with Allport's view, the advent of prejudice is simply a mental error that occurs during the categorization process. Allport (1954) notes that the average human is bombarded with countless bits of information daily and that it is impossible to actively sort through this information in a thorough, methodical manner. Our ability to categorize information makes the world much easier to understand and aids in quick interpretations and reactions. In accordance with Allport's perspective, prejudice is simply an accidental, unwanted byproduct of a very essential categorization process.

Another view on the development of prejudice does not agree with the notion that knowledge of a stereotype automatically denotes prejudice. Devin (1989) outlines an alternative view that separates stereotypes and personal beliefs as distinctly different cognitive structures. This perspective directly refutes the automaticity of the development of stereotypes and prejudice and indicates that people can have knowledge of stereotypes and still have personal beliefs that directly contradict these stereotypes. As you read this, you may think of a number of stereotypes that you are familiar with that you simply do not believe and that therefore do not shape your attitudes toward specific groups of people. Being consciously aware of the existence of stereotypes makes way for the active rejection of stereotypical thinking. Does this apply to prejudice as well? If this cognitive model of prejudice holds true, then the answer is yes. We are usually cognizant of our attitudes toward other people, even if the origins of the attitudes are unknown.

Culturally Transmitted Prejudice (CTP)

In searching for the root source of prejudice, it is posited that the development of prejudice is imbedded in culture. Famous anthropologist Margaret Mead (1937) described culture as follows:

> Culture means the whole complex of traditional behavior which has been developed by the human race and is successively learned by each generation. A culture is less precise. It can mean the forms of traditional behavior which are characteristics of a given society, or of a group of societies, or of a certain race, or of a certain area, or of a certain period of time (p.17).

Mead's critical differentiation between culture in general and individual cultures is necessary to understand how each individual culture differs in beliefs, behavior, and lifestyle. Because beliefs differ across cultures, it makes sense that prejudicial attitudes also differ across cultures.

Can culture explain the existence of prejudice? This notion is not farfetched, in the sense that we are all cultural beings and influenced by culture in ways that we do not think of. Consider a fish swimming in the ocean; the ocean is likened to culture and the fish is largely unaware of being completely and totally immersed in the ocean. We are all like fish in the ocean that are steadily influenced by the environments that we are immersed in—our cultures. We are so heavily influenced by culture that some cite culture as the origin of prejudice. This culture theory, or cultural transmission theory, simply posits that children learn stereotypes that contribute to the development of prejudice. This behavior is learned from the society or culture in which a person is surrounded. By this logic, culture is responsible for the existence of prejudice and the behaviors that stem from prejudicial beliefs. A fish in water is influenced by everything from the quality of the water to the other fish that surround it. In a similar fashion, people are influenced by society, culture, and the people they coexist with.

Think of the behaviors you deem acceptable when meeting someone for the first time. Where did you learn these norms? Think of the people you find the most attractive or unattractive. What influences these views? Think of the ways in which you react to individuals of diverse backgrounds. What shapes these reactions? Culture.

Culture shapes our attitudes, our views of normalcy, and even our expectations. This includes our expectations of the world and the people we encounter. As people encounter, interpret, and attempt to make sense of the world, information is categorized into schemas. Most will agree that we need schemas in order to integrate new information into meaningful components. The formation of categories is not unlike the formation of stereotypes. They are developed based on exposure, experience, and expectations. This cultural explanation of the development of prejudice does not differ from the basic components of Allport's viewpoint that stereotypes and prejudice emerge somewhat naturally as we try to make sense of our daily surroundings. However, this viewpoint puts forth the notion that the very way that we go about categorizing and interpreting the world is culturally influenced. We consciously and unconsciously place people into mental groups based on appearance, age, race, gender, and several other factors. However, culture influences the categories that actually exist.

Consider the following examples:

Children in Suburbia

Four-year-old Becca and her five-year-old brother Alfred are children of the only people of color in their suburban southern California neighborhood, coming from a Hispanic and African American family. One morning they walk toward the children who live next door as they play in an outdoor tent. Janay, a four-year-old Caucasian girl, is playing enthusiastically with her brothers Jonathan and Taylor, ages six and eight respectively. As Becca and Alfred approach, Janay greets them with a smile and wave. Taylor immediately says, "My mom says you

25

can't play with us." Becca inquisitively asks, "Why?" A brief silence follows and Jonathan suddenly blurts out, "because you're black." Janay chimes in by saying, "She's not really black; she's just tan like us. She can play with us, but he can't. Momma won't be mad." Alfred gently grasps Becca by the elbow and guides her home.

Homeboys

While flipping through a magazine on his flight to Los Angeles, a 38-year-old law professor comes across an article. The image immediately catches his attention. Two tattooed Hispanic men are standing outside of a building called Homeboys. The professor takes in their white undershirts, loose fitting jeans, and earrings and begins shaking his head in dismay. He thinks, "Men like them are the reason there's so much violence. They fill the jails." The professor continues to focus on his dislike for men like those portrayed in the magazine. The professor was unaware that the men were actually volunteers at an organization called Homeboys, where they worked with young, at-risk children in order to promote engagement in training and productive activities. After reading the article, the professor was embarrassed at his error in thinking and began to wonder how he came to his initial conclusion.

Prejudice is evident in each example. While the origin may not be clear, it is posited that these prejudicial beliefs were derived from culture. In the first example, the mother of the Caucasian children transmitted negative thoughts about people of color to her children. This prejudice manifested in an act of discrimination where the children told their neighbors they would not play with them simply because of the color of their skin. These beliefs did not stem from personal interactions; instead they were transmitted via family, one of the most influential cultural components. The second example also reflected the manifestation of a stereotype. The professor placed Hispanic males who dressed in certain attire and had tattoos into a category of individuals who commit crimes. Prejudice emerged as his negative feelings toward these individuals became apparent.

Culture dictates a great deal of the existence of prejudice simply because culture dictates what is deemed normal and acceptable. Culture, in many ways, also shapes our perceptions of individuals who belong to different groups. Following 9/11, there were countless incidents in which individuals who appeared to be Middle Eastern were discriminated against and feared. September 11th was such a culturally and historically significant event that many Americans began to develop prejudicial attitudes about individuals whom they thought fit into their schema of what a Middle Eastern person looked like. The development of these attitudes was arguably culturally transmitted because the prejudice emerged through a nation's response to a major incident.

While cultures may have many shared experiences in common, there are also culturally bound experiences that are unique to each culture. These unique experiences shape worldviews. This helps to explain why prejudice varies across cultures. If prejudice is indeed culturally transmitted, then the prejudicial manifestations should reflect these cultural differences. Consider the cross-cultural manifestation of colorism. Colorism can be defined as "the allocation of privilege and disadvantage according to the lightness or darkness of one's skin" (Burke, 2008, p. 17). In many cultures, such as Hispanic/Latino, there are attitudes that have prevailed across generations that reflect preference for more light-skinned people. Quiros and Dawson (2013) assert that within many Latino communities within the U.S. power and privilege are often given to Latinos who appear more White and that individuals of darker skin tones often distance themselves from being identified as Black because there is a tendency to experience marginalization and discrimination. Colorism is a social phenomenon that has predominantly been observed in African Americans and has also transcended generations. Hannon (2014) traces the roots of colorism in the African American community back to the slavery regime when African Americans with more Eurocentric features were given less cruel treatment and more privileges than their darker counterparts. Eventually, the preference for lighter-skinned individuals permeated the family unit and the attitude of superiority and preference for lighter-skinned people developed.

Consider cross-cultural differences in how the elderly are viewed. In American culture, aging is often associated with weakness and fragility, and aging is typically not viewed as a desired occurrence. Many Americans may prejudge an elderly woman as being incapable and a financial burden on society. However, in many Asian cultures aging is celebrated and the aged are typically viewed with great respect. These cross-cultural differences in perception alter the attitudes that develop surrounding the elderly and the aging process. Furthermore, it also consequently shapes the way that individuals are treated.

Perhaps blaming culture for the advent of prejudice and all that follows is a simple way to remove blame from the prejudiced individual. Indeed, culture does dictate a great deal of our perceptions, and we develop within the bounds of the culture that we are immersed in. It's fair to say that culture does heavily influence the way in which we perceive and prejudge the world.

Why is the Development of Prejudice Important in Psychology?

If prejudice is defined as attitudes, then what is the rationale to investigate the root cause so extensively? After all, beliefs and attitudes are relatively harmless, right? The fact is that our attitudes and beliefs shape our daily interactions and heavily influence the way that we relate to other people. Prejudice seldom exists in isolation. With prejudice there is typically bullying, discrimination, unfair treatment that can ultimately impede the quality of life of groups of individuals.

An entire subset of study in psychology has been dedicated to the influence that culture has on psychological and behavioral functioning. Understanding prejudice in the psychology field is relevant to clinical practice, research, organizational development, and collectively understanding the human experience.

Reducing Prejudice

Researchers, clinicians, and policy reformers alike are keenly aware of the potentially damaging effects of prejudice. The research examining why prejudice may occur is abundant and there is also ample research on ways to reduce prejudice at the individual and societal level. Across history, there is evidence of laws, rules, regulations, and common practice that promoted prejudice, but recent history has focused more on promoting fair, equal treatment of people of varying groups. Exposure is also critical to reducing prejudice. A lack of exposure to diverse groups is a large contributor to prejudicial beliefs because there is no basis to compare beliefs with actual experience. Consider the following example:

Beth, a 21-year-old student at an Ivy League school, grew up in an affluent community on Staten Island. She went to costly prep schools and her family only socialized with people in their neighborhood and individuals from other affluent communities. Her family traveled the world frequently. Beth and her siblings each had their own bank accounts and their parents often purchased expensive gifts for them. During her junior year in college, Beth overheard her classmate Maria's phone conversation, "I don't know how I will be able to finish school. I still have a balance for this semester, and it's really hard to balance my class load with the job that I do have. Mom, there's no way I can work more hours; I already work over 40 hours a week. You really can't help me out at all?"

As Beth listened to the conversation, she observed her department store clothing from last season and took note of her Spanish accent.

Beth was immediately disgusted with her classmate's situation and wondered why people did not take better care of their finances so that their children did not end up in bad situations like her classmate. Beth thought, "I could never end up in a situation like Maria. I wonder if her family is even here legally. Isn't she Mexican? They just come to our country, use free services that we have to pay for, and don't work for what they want in life. Maria probably doesn't even belong here."

In the above example, Beth's prejudicial attitudes are readily apparent and it is clear that her negative outlook on Maria's situation is based on a number of assumptions that she has made based solely on Maria's belonging to a minority ethnic group and to a lower socioeconomic status. There is also a clear disconnect. Beth's upbringing limited her experiences with individuals from different cultural groups and different economic classes.

Reducing prejudice can be challenging at the individual and societal level. At the individual level, people can be made aware of inconsistent beliefs and widen their experiences with other groups by increasing contact with individuals outside of the groups that they identify with. At the public level, public education campaigns can be useful in the dissemination of material that supports anti-prejudice norms. Public policy can shape laws that dictate fair treatment of individuals from all groups.

Prejudice: A Double-Edged Sword

Widespread prejudice transcends personal attitudes and beliefs and manifests at the societal level. When prejudice permeates public policy and practice, then the very notion of social justice is threatened. Prejudice creates the foundation for discrimination and largely contributes to social injustice. With colorism, for example, the attitudes that have developed based solely on the color of an individual's skin alter their life experiences and the way that others view and treat them. The results of a study by Hannon (2014) revealed that Hispanic participants with the lightest skin tone were viewed as being more intelligent when compared to those with the darkest skin-tones. When a society holds preconceived beliefs about an individual's ability based solely on a physical attribute, it can influence the experience of those individuals at school, work, and even in basic social settings. It may influence the opportunities or lack of opportunities allotted and it may ultimately influence the way that people treat each other.

Prejudice, in itself, is not a negative entity. As mentioned earlier, we rely on the ability to prejudge in order to make sense of the world around us. We need to be able to place people, places, and events into meaningful categories. This bright side of prejudice may be helpful in making swift decisions and in guiding judgments. The dark side of prejudice largely contributes to the unfair treatment of many.

Prejudice has a bad reputation and this may explain the emphasis on attempts to eradicate prejudice. Attempts to combat prejudice at the individual and societal level can be thought of as a major component of the social justice movement. We firmly believe that the pursuit of social justice, or the concept of fairness and justness between the individual and society, is heavily contingent upon the understanding and acknowledgment of how prejudice manifests in society. We, the fish swimming in our cultural waters, must begin to more thoroughly comprehend our waters and how they shape us.

References

Allport, G. W. (1954). *The nature of prejudice*. Reading, MA: Addison-Wesley.

Devine, P. G. (1989). Stereotypes and prejudice: Their automatic and controlled components. *Journal of Personality and Social Psychology, 56,* 5-18.

Ehrlich, H. J. (1973). *The social psychology of prejudice*. New York: Wiley.

Hale, L. (2014). Globalization: Cultural transmission of racism. *Race, Gender & Class, 21*(1/2), 112.

Hannon, L. (2014). Hispanic respondent intelligence level and skin tone: Interviewer perceptions from the American National Election study. *Hispanic Journal of Behavioral Sciences, 36*(3), 265-283. doi:10.1177/0739986314540126

Mead, M. (1937). *Cooperation and competition among primitive peoples*, McGraw-Hill Book Company. doi:10.1037/13891-000

Quiros, L., & Dawson, B. A. (2013). The color paradigm: The impact of colorism on the racial identity and identification of Latinas. *Journal of Human Behavior in the Social Environment, 23*(3), 287-297. doi:10.1080/10911359.2012.740342 .1

Uhlmann, E., & Nosek, B. (2012). My culture made me do it lay theories of responsibility for automatic prejudice. *Social Psychology, 43*(2), 108-113. doi:10.1027/1864-9335/a000089

2.

Those Golden Years

**Pavel Y. Litvin, MA, Rachel Rugh Fraser, MA, MAEd,
and Iya Ritchie, MA**

Although we spend much of our lives setting up for retirement, we know very little about the culture of our retirees. For instance, John and Martha were found with bullets in their heads. Martha was severely demented and would not let anyone but her husband care for her; John was facing repeat serious surgery in the near future. It was quite clear that John did not want to go through that again, and he could not leave his wife alone without him to comfort her. This situation and John's resolution are not all that uncommon among the elderly, especially in retirement communities. Many feel they do not want to become demented, spend their life savings in that state, and prevent their children from getting all that they had saved throughout their lives. There are "pacts" that are made. Namely, if they start to "go," a friend or a spouse will put a pillow over their face and save their kids all that money. The police and physicians are fully aware of these situations, but not many young psychologists are.

Perspectives on Aging and Diversity

Generally, diversity examines the shared differences of a group that may affect a group member's life experiences and how they are viewed and treated by others. Like other domains of diversity, older adults are a heterogeneous group, and scholars have provided a number of salient insights (for a review, see Mehrotra & Wagner, 2013); however, the approach of this chapter is to provide a supplementary perspective on the aging population, specifically on older adults over the age of 64.

First, let us consider the metaphor of three blind men attempting to describe an elephant (Cianciolo & Sternberg, 2004). With all three never having seen an elephant, the first describes the animal as a tree, shortly after holding the elephant's thick legs. The second blind man exclaims that the elephant is snake-like, while touching the trunk. The third blind man, feeling the animal's side, argues that the elephant is more akin to wall. That is, as clinicians and researchers, we are the blind men, sizing up this aging elephant, and the more perspectives we acquire, the greater our understanding of the greater Gestalt.

Consider Leopold Bellak's (1986) work on the Thematic Apperception Test from the time of its developers, Henry Murray and Christiana Morgan, to the modern day. He also developed the Children's Apperception Test, but he had a lot of difficulty with the Senior Apperception Test, which he initially developed on the basis of what he thought were the stressors of senior society (e.g., moving to a nursing home, loneliness, uselessness, illness, helplessness, withdrawal, denial, projection, somatization, lowered self-esteem). Only 16 of the original 44 cards proved useful, even after modifications, and there were some surprises. Death, it turns out, was not one of the great concerns among the aged. In addition, and perhaps surprisingly, finances, despair, and loss of motor control were also not major emerging themes among the elderly. Although it would make sense that these latter might be major concerns of the elderly, in fact they appear not to be. Conversely, themes that did emerge were a longing for connectedness and activity and, more surprisingly, relative to younger adults, the elderly generated narrative outcomes that were more positive or neutral (Bellak, 1986).

In contrast, while empirical studies have suggested that concerns about death are higher in middle-aged participants than in the elderly, institutionalization (i.e., independent living versus nursing home), physical and psychological problems, and religiosity all appear to play an important role in the presence of death anxiety (Fortner & Neimeyer, 1999). Moreover, review studies have revealed that the elderly in care institutions have high levels of fear for others and of the dying process; furthermore, fear for significant others was related to poor physical health, and fear of the dying process was correlated to low self-esteem, little purpose in life, and poor mental well-being (Missler et al., 2012).

In a similar vein, Erik Erickson's psychosocial theory posits that the increased awareness of death precedes old age, and this awareness is a likely contributing factor to the generativity versus stagnation crisis in the midlife years (Fortner & Neimeyer, 1999). During the ego integrity versus despair crisis (over the age of 65), productivity tends to slow and one begins a process of life reflection, especially as it relates to attaining life goals. If life is viewed as unproductive, despair surfaces, frequently leading to depression and hopelessness; success during this crisis, characterized by considering one's being full of meaning, leads to a sense of closure and acceptance of death without fear.

Conceptually, these insights provide perspectives from several "blind" men who provide explanations of the data they have collected; the uniqueness of our approach lies in the methodology from which our descriptions emerge—clinical experience with this population. We are well aware of the limitations or "blindness" of such an approach, but we also understand the value it may bring to clinicians who may want to gain a glimpse of what major themes can be expected in the elderly.

In the next section we will discuss some of the relevant literature in becoming older, some of the predictors of a healthy elder life. This includes discussions on living longer, life expectancies, and aging factors as well as the roles of factors such as mood, affect, and resilience as positive effects on aging.

Human Aging, Resilience, and Biopsychosocial Perspective

Human development, including the latest stages of life, is a simultaneous occurrence of stability and change (Bronfenbrenner & Morris, 2006) that emerges at the intercept of biopsychological, sociocultural, and temporal domains (Lerner, Easterbrooks, Mistry, & Jayanthi, 2012). Two main trends have emerged in the last decades of the 20th century. Biological neuroscience and multicultural perspective have advanced the field of developmental psychology to include genetic and contextual-interactive components in the modern conceptualization of human development. Since then, it has been accepted that genetic and epigenetic factors interact with psychobiological, contextual elements, contributing to phenotypic variations in individual abilities, personality, maturation, and aging (Lerner et al., 2012). As the world population is growing older, whether the additional years will be lived in good or poor health is questioned (Christensen, Doblhammer, Rau, & Vaupel, 2009). Given the impact of diversification, as well as the aging fabric of industrial societies, contemporary understanding of what constitutes successful development is important, as processes that preceded old age provide the foundation of well-being and functioning across the lifespan, promoting nonpathological aging (Freund & Riediger, 2012). Psychological resilience, as an ability to response to stressors in adaptive ways, has emerged as an important antiaging factor. However, a reinterpretation of resilience from the bio-social-ecological systems perspective suggested that adaptive functioning in the face of adversity is better explained by individual characteristics, as well as processes and interactions that arise from the immediate and distal sociocultural environments (Ungar, Ghazinour, & Richter, 2013).

Aging Is a Human Phenomenon: Modern Concerns and Controversy

Very few animal species in a natural environment are affected by senescence, faced with disease, predation, drought, starvation, and, more recently, pollution (Holiday, 2006). This evolutionary observation offered a viewpoint that aging is a human phenomenon, with life expectancy (LE) drastically varying, especially across generations. The increased longevity and advances in population health experienced by developed countries have substantially destabilized assumptions on what aging and old age are (Johns & Higgs, 2010). Many Westerners are living a life that is very different in character from the one experienced by their predecessors. Previous beliefs and expectations of a natural life course originated in predictable and culturally normative stages concluding in infirmity and, ultimately, death, have been challenged by biomedical, environmental, and social developments. Together, all of this has also proposed that our constructs of natural, abnormal, or successful life paths have been challenged, requiring attention and amendment (Cosco, Prina, Perales, Stephan, & Brayne, 2014). At the same time, there is no compelling evidence for the use of existing cures to decelerate aging or extend lifespan in humans (Tosato, Zamboni, Ferrini, & Cesari, 2007). Nevertheless, extended LE, an artifact of human civilization, is at our doors, demanding attention to matters for which we were teleologically (Hayflick, 2006), economically, and ideologically ill-unprepared (Benedikter & Siepmann, 2016).

Findings from animal studies demonstrated the possibility of modification in aging rate and LE, fueling the transhumanistic movement, as well as debates about whether striving for immortality and disease-free old age should be embraced or abandoned as unrealistic and degrading (Benedikter & Siepmann, 2016). Transhumanism moved beyond the idea of aging, proposing that technology and biomedicine can help individuals to become cyborgized neohumans to transcend the limitations of their bodies (Benedikter & Siepmann, 2016). The argument that aging requires intervention was founded on the idea that getting old is undesirable (Tosato et al., 2007). In the West, where independence and productivity are fundamental values, old age has grown to be synonymous with deterioration, pathology, decay, and death (Hayflick, 2004).

Various public figures, including psychologists, urge the public and scientists to reconsider the disease-like approach to maturation and learn to appreciate old age to the same extent as we celebrate youth (Tosato et al., 2007). In their view, the destigmatized approach would allow for more favorable evaluation of oneself and others, facilitating the diminution of ageism, lightening the burden on aging individuals and their family members who assume caretaking roles. Moreover, aging is negatively associated with fitness and the capacity to respond to stress but positively linked to homeostatic balance and the occurrence of pathology (Tosato et al., 2007). Following this argument, since we all will be joining the stigmatized group of elderly at some point, what we should continue to strive for, and what is both advantageous and attainable, is the prevention and resolution of various illnesses (Hayflick, 2004). While caring for the elderly is expensive, the latest findings on the leveling off in disability after the ninth decade of life strongly suggest that care cost per person does not increase for centenarians (Christensen et al., 2009). From the societal perspective, a practical strategy to deal with the economic implications of widespread population aging is to modify the workforce environment (e.g., a shorter workday) and raise the established age of retirement. Moreover, while assistive technology will continue to reduce the need for some types of personal care, our eldest need help not just from healthcare providers, but also from the service sector and families, as machines cannot substitute for human interactions (Christensen et al., 2009).

Stages of Development, Age, and Life Expectancy

Age-associated concepts require some elucidation. From a medical perspective, aging is characterized by a progressive physiological deterioration, leading to impaired function and increased vulnerability to death (López-Otín, Blasco, Partridge, Serrano, & Kroemer, 2013).

This cumulative loss is the fundamental risk factor for of survival from age 80 to 90 years, with an average of 15% to 16% for women, and 12% for men. The same analysis in 2002 revealed these values at 37% and 25%, for women and men, respectively (Rau et al., 2008). Research on aging has experienced unparalleled progress in recent years, discovering that the rate and processes of aging are predetermined, at least to some extent, by genetic and biochemical pathways preserved in evolution (López-Otín et al., 2013). However, people from different cultures, religious backgrounds, and generations may have their own unique interpretation of what is aging (Lerner et al., 2012).

In addition, what constitutes "old" for lay people, administrators, and researchers can vary dramatically. Traditionally, human development was seen through three major periods of life: childhood and adolescence; adulthood; and old age (Lerner et al., 2012). In gerontological studies, such as one carried out by Volkert, Kreuel, Heseker, and Stehle (2004), elderly individuals are generally stratified into young-old (65-74), old-old (75-84), and oldest-old or very-old (>85-99), although variations in classification were noted, with oldest-old describing any people who are older than 90 (Siegler, Elias, & Bosworth, 2012). While the prospects for healthy longevity were seen as poor, a fourth stage, of extremely old, was added for centenarians (Siegler et al., 2012).

To further clarify, the concept of lifespan defines the furthest temporal boundary of life—a maximum number of years a person could live (Dong, Milholland, & Vijg, 2016). The total number of years that a human is expected to live on average defines the mentioned construct of life expectancy (LE). Although the maximum human lifespan of approximately 125 years has been documented as constant for thousands of millennia (Dong et al., 2016), our LE in the industrialized world has increased in the last two centuries by about 27 to 30 years (Siegler et al., 2012). Moreover, some scholars have advocated a higher 130-year limit to the human lifespan (Newman & Easteal, 2017). They asserted that even a higher age bound is conceivable, and should not be ruled out based on the observed LE limits alone (Newman & Easteal, 2017).

While the boundaries of lifespan are debated, the increased LE trends cannot be ignored. Christensen et al. (2009) predicted that if the high pace of LE growth remains through the 21st century, then the vast majority of children born after 1999 in North America, Europe (e.g., Denmark, the UK, France, Germany, Italy), and Japan will live to celebrate their 100th birthdays. Evaluation of LE data from more than 30 developed countries by Rau, Soroko, Jasilionis, and Vaupel (2008) indicated gender differences in the probability of the best chances of survival. The likelihood of remaining alive from age 80 years to 90 years exceeded 50% for women (Max Planck Institute for Demographic Research, 2009).

Effects of Longer Life Expectancy (LE), Gender, and Culture

How we view older people may not be congruent with how they endure the aging process. The vast majority of the young-old and old-old people reported taking daily medications, and suffering from at least one chronic disease, yet nearly half considered their health to be good, or even very good (Volkert et al., 2004). Evidently, in the eyes of older people, diseases do not stop them from participating in everyday life or compromise their well-being. In Germany, among independently living oldest-old, the majority (i.e., 98%) were cooking their daily meals (Volkert et al., 2004). However, Freund and Riediger (2012) argued that most of the favorable findings are more applicable to young- and old-old, but not oldest-old individuals and centenarians.

In research, the sociodemographic characteristics of the oldest-old, such as age, education, gender, and relational status, when considered alone, were not significantly related to negative affect (Haynie et al., 2001). The experiences of aging and cognitive decline, on the other hand, namely subjective health, daily functioning, and timed performance (i.e., block design), indeed predicted a negative effect, at significant levels. Changes in individual health status may precede changes in cognition, emotions, personality, and social functioning, but the relationship is bidirectional, as changes in health status can be resultant from critical changes in other areas of life—loss of a long-term partner or lack of access to care. However, cognition is arguably the most salient aspect of development that is compromised when health is impaired (Siegler et al., 2012). Dementia can be debilitating at any age, and has been associated with higher rates of ADL impairments, institutionalization, and premature mortality. Thus far, research on the prevalence of all-cause dementia proposed that its presence increases exponentially from ages 65 to 85 for both men and women, but it may stabilize for men in the ninth decade (Corrada, Brookmeyer, Berlau, Paganini-Hill, & Kawas, 2008). In a study of a U.S.-based sample of 903 participants with an average age of 94 (range=90-106), all-cause dementia was more common in women (45%, 95%, CI: 41.5-49.0) than in men (28%, 95%, CI: 21.7-34.2). Not just the gender but individual factors emerged as influential. The prevalence of dementia was doubling every five years, but only for women, not men, with higher education serving as a protective factor, once again, for women but not men (Corrada et al., 2008). Although the stabilization of dementia incidence in men was considered as possible, it is also possible that women may live longer with dementia than men, especially those with higher educational attainment. Corrada et al. (2008) proposed to look at cohort effects as well, as women in their study were pursuing advanced degrees in the 1930s, which implied that these women may have had a variety of risk factors different from the rest of the sample in regard to socioeconomic status, intelligence, access to health care, and better nutrition.

Other gender differences were noted among the elderly. Women and men may cope, share, and even report their experiences differently

41

(Haynie et al., 2001). In the German sample, many more oldest-old women were widows than widowers (85% vs. 53%), but sustained independent living in 76% of cases, whereas only 40% of men lived without a family, wife, or companion (Volkert et al., 2004). Whereas men acknowledged depression less frequently than women (25% vs. 36%), and consumed much more alcohol (39% vs. 10%), the subjective experience of health by both genders was comparable (Volkert et al., 2004).

More interesting and contradictory findings were reported in studies of oldest-old and centenarians—one of the fastest growing populations worldwide (Pierce & Kawas, 2017). Baltes and Smith (2003), for example, saw centenarians as a group affected by a substantially reduced sense of identity, personal control, and psychological autonomy. Reaching this juncture, in their view, marks the period of "biocultural incompleteness, vulnerability and unpredictability" (Baltes and Smith, 2003, p. 123). Forette (1999) concluded that centenarians are the extremely heterogeneous group, and estimated that a third of them remain independent and reside in community dwellings; another third showed functional impairment; and the remaining third became extremely frail and disabled. Centenarians may not be more disable than the oldest-old, and individual variability is significant. For instance, in a study of 32 American supercentenarians (i.e., 110-119 years), 41% were independent or needed little assistance (Schoenhofen et al., 2006). This and similar findings suggested that while the ontogenic losses may outnumber gains at the fourth age, the drastic view of Baltes and Smith (2003) are too sweeping. In the mentioned American supercentenarians study, men were underrepresented (16%), which is proposed as typical (Schoenhofen et al., 2006). The investigators suggested that a low male-to-female ratio is likely to accurately reflect the proportion of surviving men in the industrialized world. However, those men who live beyond 100 years of age tend to be more functionally fit, increasing their chances in research participation (Schoenhofen et al., 2006). While cancer affected one-fourth of the sample, at some point reports of cardiovascular disease and stroke were rare among American supercentenarians, probably because these illnesses would otherwise hinder participants' survival to extreme age (Schoenhofen et al., 2006).

Similarly to cross-gender research, the cross-country comparisons captured variability in participants' reports. Chinese centenarians describe better physical functioning than Danish centenarians, for example (Christensen et al., 2009). Studies in France, Germany, and Belgium concluded that gains in LE over the last three decades added more years of experiencing moderate difficulties but not years with severe disabilities. Karasawa et al. (2011) noted that experiences of well-being are linked with high levels of autonomy, self-efficacy, uniqueness, and self-motivation in more independent cultural contexts, such as the United States. By contrast, attainment of social relational factors, such as relational goals, perceived emotional support, and harmony with significant others, as well as socially engaging emotions, predicted experiences of well-being in interdependent cultural contexts, such as Japan (Karasawa et al., 2011).

Trends among high-income populations could be more promising than among middle- and low-income individuals (Zeng, Feng, Hesketh, Christensen, & Vaupel, 2017). One of the largest studies conducted by Zeng et al. (2017) included 19,528 Chinese elderly, among them 7,288 octogenarians (i.e., 80-89 years), 7,234 nonagenarians (i.e., 90-99 years), and 5,006 centenarians, documenting very high mortality in individuals from low- to middle-income backgrounds, with only 2.8% of participants interviewed in both 1998 and 2008. The study recruited volunteers from randomly selected communities, targeting an equal number of females and males of 65 years of age and up, who resided near the centenarians, to establish determinants of healthy longevity across age and gender groups, in view of a shared environment.

Study results proposed that there are benefits and costs of longer living, whereas temporal life experiences and environmental conditions play an important role in aging (Zeng et al., 2017). On the one hand, advances in care, socioeconomics, and lifestyle appeared to mitigate and compress disability associated with activities of daily living (i.e., ADL) and, as such, represent benefits for survival. On the other hand, the lifespan extension was linked with higher rates in physical and cognitive impairments, as frailer elderly, incapacitated by health problems remained alive, signifying the costs of surviving into old age (Zeng et al., 2017). Moreover, gerontologists noted that reports of ADL are subjective, and participants judged their abilities more favorably, in comparison to their objectively assessed functional capacity. In addition, cross-cohort differences were established for educational attainment and childhood experiences (e.g., feeling hunger), with the earlier cohorts (i.e., from 1893 to 1902) performing significantly better on cognitive measures than the later cohorts (i.e., from 1903 to 1928). Zeng et al. (2017) hypothesized that the increase in domestic hostilities, during the critical developmental periods for later cohorts, could explain their poorer educational achievement, adverse childhood conditions, and ensuing lower socioeconomic status in adulthood, and therefore, their lower cognitive function scores in old age. Finally, although the scores measuring self-reported ADL, with objective physical and cognitive performance dropping from ages 80 years to 100 years or older, the number of the oldest-old participants describing satisfaction and good health remained nearly unchanged, and even slightly increased, across these ages (Zeng et al., 2017). These findings were parallel to those in Danish research on the elderly (Engberg, Jeune, Andersen-Ranberg, Martinussen, Vaupel, & Christensen, 2013), suggesting that personal characteristics, such as ability to maintain a positive outlook on life, may influence the chance of living longer.

While the objective predictors of LE, such as physical function and health status, have been well studied among the oldest-old, only a few investigations have been published on the effect of personality traits such as optimism, on longevity. Results from a longitudinal nationwide survey that included all individuals born in Denmark in 1905 (N=2,411) indicated that optimism was a significant predictor of survival among the oldest-old female participants (Engberg et al., 2013). The association between optimistic outlook and lower risk of death was also noted for men, but the effect was non-significant, likely due to the small male sample size (Engberg et al., 2013). The same Danish cohort of oldest-old was evaluated as a sub-sample in the larger longitudinal study that included two other population-based surveys, with a total of 11,307 participants aged 45 years and older (Vestergaard, Thinggaard, Jeune, Vaupel, McGue, & Christensen, 2015). This investigation evaluated the relationship between happiness, depression, and functioning (i.e., cognitive and physical), across different ages. In this investigation, older cohorts performed more poorly on objective tests than the youngest individuals, with a greater decline in physical (i.e., mobility), then mental abilities, especially after 70 years (Vestergaard et al., 2015). Scores on depression were successively higher with older age, but the gradient was much steeper, and somatic complaints were more prominent than affective. Interestingly, researchers reported that scores on happiness remained largely unchanged, regardless of the noted age-related gap between the youngest and oldest age cohorts on measures of physical and mental abilities (Vestergaard et al., 2015). However, closer evaluation uncovered significant gender differences, while in-group (i.e., individual) differences were not evaluated. Here, women had better immediate and delayed recall, and overall cognitive composite scores than men ($p<0.001$). Conversely, men were able to name more animals, and reported lower symptoms of depression, with lesser affective and somatic complaints ($p<0.02$). Despite better general mental functioning in women, they reported being less happy than men, perhaps due to problems with physical functioning, as more males than females could walk 400 meters, run 100 meters, and manage stairs (p<0.001). It must be noted that the findings could be somewhat misleading, as the concept of happiness was not described, and was assessed via a single question: "Do you feel happy and satisfied with life at present?" (Vestergaard et al., 2015, p. 3). To summarize, as we can see, the same sample can be used to produce different, and perhaps contradictory findings, whereas imprecision in reporting may create a biased perception of the elderly.

Research with the elderly, especially with centenarians, captured a large within-group variation, reflecting both diversity and range in functioning and health, suggesting that old age should be seen on a continuum, that is, some individuals do extremely well, and some not so well.

Main Theories of Aging and Stress

Research on aging has experienced an unparalleled progress over recent years, discovering that the rate and processes of aging are predetermined, at least to some extent, by genetic and biochemical pathways preserved in evolution (López-Otín et al., 2013). By the 1990s, more than 300 theories of aging have been noted, but none has yet been generally accepted by gerontologists (Nowotny, Jung, Grune, & Höhn, 2014). At least nine tentative hallmarks emerged to represent common denominators of aging. Among them are genomic instability, epigenetic alterations, telomere attrition, cellular senescence, loss of proteostasis, deregulation in nutrient-sensing, mitochondrial dysfunction, stem-cell exhaustion, and changes in intercellular communication (López-Otín et al., 2013). A medical model attempts to investigate the interconnectedness between the tentative markers and their contribution to aging processes, with a goal of creating pharmaceutical objectives to enhance human health through aging with the fewest side effects (López-Otín et al., 2013). A global view of the nine tentative hallmarks of aging proposed three categories: primary; antagonistic; and integrative. The cardinal feature of the primary markers (e.g., DNA damage, mitochondrial DNA mutations, loss of telomeres, epigenetic drift, deficient proteostasis) is that they are all negative. The antagonistic markers (e.g., senescence, mitochondrial and nutrient-sensing dysfunctions) have opposite effects based on their intensity: at low levels they negotiate benefits, but at high levels they become harmful. The last category includes the integrative hallmarks (e.g., stem-cell exhaustion, problems in intercellular communication) that directly affect homeostasis and function (López-Otín et al., 2013). On the one hand, there is an interconnectedness between all hallmarks, but on the other hand, each of the markers exemplifies a distinct theory. Nonetheless, organismic reaction to stress came forth as one of the most prominent and recurring themes. As such, aging can be seen as the outcome of the decreased capacity to survive stress—the main detriment to human longevity (Nowotny et al., 2014).

Factors Known to Positively Influence Executive Functions and Aging Processes

Various determinants emerged as protective against premature aging, functional limitation, and disability, such as early diagnosis, improved treatment, and amelioration of endemic and chronic illnesses (Freund & Riediger, 2012). Also, access to supportive technology, public transport, and housing, advances in health and diversity-promoting social policies, shifts in gender roles, and disability biases have emerged as active contributors. Other factors, such as improved early childhood experiences, higher levels of educational attainment, higher income, as well as a growing number of couples and close companions among the elderly, also emerged as reasonable safeguards against late-life disability and functional impairment (Christensen et al., 2009). Familial and general support and involvement in social activities have frequently been mentioned by researchers as influential in well-being in older adults (Learner et al., 2012).

The examination of risks and protective factors suggests that human longevity and survival is affected by two main factors—absence of pathology and ability to respond to stress (Freund & Riediger, 2012). Rowe and Kahn (1987) put forward a notion of successful aging and described possible developmental trajectories. The first trajectory, unsuccessful aging, is characterized by disease and disability. The second possible path, or usual aging, was defined by the absence of manifested pathology but some decline in normative function. The last trajectory, which they termed "successful aging," would lead to minimal physiological deterioration and an absence of pathology. They proposed several mechanisms of successful aging, such as endurance of normal function and plasticity, counteractive restorative function, and treatments to supplant deficiencies in function (Rowe & Kahn, 1987). Three important mechanisms were identified as disease prevention, modification of risk profiles, and strengthening of social support and interactions. The last three devices can be targeted at individual, organizational, and societal levels, promoting and supporting functional transformation and influencing and fortifying organismic systems (e.g., neuroendocrine, immune) that can counteract the impact of stress. Rowe and Kahn (1987) emphasized the importance of resilience, which they conceptualized as an ability to return to levels of premorbid stable functioning, quickly and efficiently, following exposure to stress, such as forced retirement, assaults, physical injury, and personal loss (Rowe & Kahn, 1987). They considered low variability in blood pressure as one of the tentative measurable indicators of individual resilience and called for further research. In recent years, the notion of successful aging was popularized, but heterogeneous interpretations of the concept indicated the multidimensionality of the concept, and disputes surrounding what constitutes usual and natural or successful aging continue to persist

(Cosco et al., 2014). While the majority of interpretations revealed a biomedical focus, later research increasingly incorporated idiosyncratic and psychosocial components, such as resilience (Freund & Riediger, 2012). In research, the positive relationship between health behaviors and successful aging has been established: lower body mass index; not having addictions (e.g., smoking); exercising; and moderate/social alcohol consumption or full abstinence. Subjectively experienced physical and mental health in the elderly was linked to better social support and stronger religious affiliations. In some studies, low levels of education and a history of incarceration had an inverse relationship with successful aging, whereas adaptive, healthy changes in mid- and later life showed a positive correlation with the reported well-being in later years.

Relationship Between Resilience and Aging

The concept of resilience typically captures a personality characteristic that moderates the adverse effects of stress and fosters adaptation (Wells, 2012). Resilient individuals are thought of as able to identify and rely on protective factors that help with the adjustment to acute or enduring stress. Richardson (2002) developed a comprehensive resiliency model, positing that when individuals experience life disruptions, they employ a particular set of internal protective factors, such as self-reliance and good health practices, as well as external safeguards, such as technology and social networks, to restore life homeostasis. This process of self-restoration was identified as resilient reintegration (Richardson, 2002). However, more than one definition of resiliency exists, with other theorists seeing resilience as a process or outcome. Conceptual discrepancies impede the evaluation and comparison of resilience across study findings, obstructing meta-analytic research, and operationalization of the construct for assessment purposes (Davydov, Stewart, Ritchie, & Chaudieu, 2010).

Nonetheless, the primary contribution of Richardson (2002) is that his model explains resilience as a complex process—a conception that is congruent with the modern bioecological approach to human development (Bronfenbrenner & Morris, 2006).

The bioecological model is a contextual, epigenetic, and systemic approach to human life, introduced by Bronfenbrenner (1979). In its latest variant, the Process-Person-Context-Time (PPCT) model of Bronfenbrenner and Morris (2006), human development is seen in the context of multiple environments, or ecological systems, at the micro (i.e., individual), meso (i.e., immediate surroundings), exo (i.e., interconnecting), macro (e.g., group and societal level), and chrono (i.e., time) levels. At birth, individuals simultaneously join a multi-membership of several systems, and humans emerge from interactions with various systems. From the PPCT perspective, genetics do not offer definitive traits, but rather the background and materials for interplay. Instead early and enduring interactions between the evolving human organism, the environment (i.e., exo-, meso-, macro-ecosystems), as well as time (e.g., cohort, event, aging), responsible for the emergence of the physiological and psychological characteristics that we understand as phenotypic expressions (Bronfenbrenner, 1999). More supportive, nurturing, and stimulating environments foster optimal development in individuals, positively influencing their abilities, educational attainment, and functional and social skills (Bronfenbrenner & Ceci, 1994). Conversely, early childhood adversity (e.g., poverty, illness, malnutrition), high levels of environmental instability, and severe neglect of the child's needs reduces the chances of healthy development (Bronfenbrenner, 1995). That is to say, the lack of exposure to a consistent opportunity to progress impairs the individual's ability to actualize his or her genetic potential, leading to possible deficiencies in emotional control, social relationships, psychological independence, resilience, and general well-being (Bronfenbrenner & Ceci, 1994).

Returning to the concept of resilience, Richardson (2002) saw it as a process that begins with a state of bio-psycho-spiritual homeostasis, where the individual is balanced and in harmony with his or her environment. Per Richardson (2002), disruption of this homeostatic state occurs if the person has insufficient protective factors (i.e., resources, abilities) to protect him or her against stress, adversity, and significant life events. Over time, the individual who has endured disruption adjusts and reintegrates. In this model, Richardson (2002) proposed one of four outcomes. First, resilient reintegration, when disruption results in the adaption, or attainment of new or additional protective factors, and a higher level of homeostasis. Second, homeostatic reintegration, when disruption leads to the maintaining of the comfort zone, guided by the goal to pass through stressful circumstances. Third, reintegration with loss, when disruption occasions the loss of safeguards, and a new, lower level of homeostasis. Lastly, when exposure to stressors triggers self-destructive behaviors, such as substance abuse, social withdrawal, or suicidality, Richardson (2002) explained individual deterioration by dysfunctional reintegration.

In research, much more complex relationships emerged between well-being, resilience, positive and negative emotions. Studies of widows, conducted by Ong, Bergeman, Bisconti, and Wallace (2006) produced results that converged on several key findings: (1) the adaptive gains of positive affect were greatest when the elderly were under stress; (2) positive affect was more common among highly resilient elderly; (3) participants low in resilience exhibited difficulties with regulating negative emotions and showed heightened reactivity to daily stressors; (4) in the context of stress, positive affect has been particularly salient for low-resilient elderly; and (5) positive affect moderated individual abilities to rebound from adversity for elderly people who were highly resilient. In conclusion, resilience emerged as both process and personality trait, with a key defining feature of emotional complexity, rather than positive outlook on life (Ong et al., 2006). The authors warned that resilience might not generalize across all domains, with previous results showing ontogenic variability, whereas investigations on the chronic mobilization of psychological resilience and positive emotions affecting various aspects of allostatic load are scarce (Ong et al., 2006).

Bringing together ideas of PPCT and the resiliency model, we can hypothesize that an individual's psychobiological factors, together with their experience and reactions to contextual and stressful interactions, give them a unique perspective and guide their actions, choices, and motivation which, in turn, impact their ability to resist stress, and access resources and social interchange (Bronfenbrenner & Morris, 2006). Meanwhile, health and life trajectories are also contingent on modification of risk profiles—improvements in elderly individuals' lives, with the foundation for disease prevention and the ability to participate in medical restorative processes established upon familial origin, cultural values, and living conditions of early life (Pruchno, Wilson-Genderson, Rose, & Cartwright, 2010). According to the researchers, from the point of view of successful aging, it appears, individuals are primarily responsible for their health and aging. They are the agents who chose lifestyles that impact their body (i.e., function and plasticity) and social interactions. Individuals are in charge of decisions about education and career paths that enable them to access modern restorative and remedial interventions, as well as assistive technologies. Industrial society and even families seemed to be unaccounted for in this model of aging, with the theorists throwing the last stone, resilience, at the elderly, expecting them not just to persevere but to transcend the last moments of their lives on their own. While resilience is indeed a protective factor, it is supposed to emerge from the environment in which individuals are born and raised. Moreover, both the experience of well-being and the ability to exercise resilience in old age can be greatly influenced by objectively irremediable factors, such as terminal illness, extreme poverty, geographical isolation, inability to access better health care, and elderly abuse.

Conclusion

The experience of very old age is a fairly new phenomenon that posited many questions that are awaiting further investigations and ongoing discussions. In view of a few developmental gains and many losses in late adulthood, especially for the oldest-old, the term "successful aging" was regarded as an oxymoron by many gerontologists (Freund & Riediger, 2012). Findings from the Pruchno et al. (2010) study provided support for the fact that mid- to late-life can be positive and productive, suggesting that successes in old age are not implausible, although what constitutes happiness or wellness cannot be easily defined. This notion has led to arguments about how to redefine successful aging in the future, with one possible option being to conceive success as a function of objective, quantifiable criteria, as well as individual value judgments of gain and losses (Pruchno et al., 2010). Considering the inherent nature of these value judgements required for establishing benchmarks of successful aging, and sociocultural variability in interpretations of old age and aging, the universally accepted criteria for this concept do not exist. While various perspectives on aging may seem at odds, each theory has the particular understanding of cause-effect relationships and offers valuable insights into age-related physiological and psychological changes. As such, a global and integrative view is required, as the quest for a single source of aging has been outdated and replaced by the perspective that human development, including aging, is an exceptionally elaborate and multifactorial process. Although we have acquired new knowledge on short- and long-term adaptation across the lifespan, the concept and the role of resilience remained elusive and understudied, especially in late adulthood. Finally, significant methodological drawbacks shared by numerous studies on aging, such as culturally insensitive samples, lack of experimental control over various confounding variables, as well as unreliable measuring systems that don't permit comparison or generalization, represent some of the significant concerns, and therefore, warrant future investigations.

Clinical Cases

These presented cases are of patients we have been directly treated or evaluated or are combinations of those we have seen in the clinic, presented to show the diversity of responses to growing older and, in some ways, contradicting what the scientists say.

In the first case (A), we see a number of themes that frequently reoccur. The primary in this case is concern about one's children. Time and time again, we have been faced with grandparents having to step again into the parental role for their grandchildren, given the high rate of divorce and blended families; sometimes they step in to compensate for their perceived flawed parenting earlier in life. Additionally, there is a postponement of enjoying retirement, given that fixing a broken family becomes a priority and their perceived responsibility. Reminiscence about the "good old times" is often present, especially in relation to the cohesiveness of family and loss of previously held traditions. Divorce in general is more difficult for older adults to fully endorse, as most older adults emerged from an era that discouraged dissolution of marriage in spite of marital difficulties. The case demonstrates a pull for connectedness to family and activity rather than fixation on the finiteness of life, as postulated by Bellak (1986).

Mrs. A is a 68-year-old Caucasian female who presented for psychotherapy to address anxiety symptoms related to an incident where she was run over by a car. Mrs. A grew up in a small town in Wyoming and, after working as a grade school teacher, she married a Vietnam veteran and settled down to start a family, raising a son and a daughter. Mrs. A's husband had a drinking problem until 20 years ago, and he reportedly continues to display symptoms of PTSD (i.e., hypervigilance, social withdrawal, nightmares, flashbacks). They have been married for 43 years, with significant improvement in their relationship since Mrs. A's husband stopped drinking. She explained that they spoiled their children, but generally had a decent life, often going on vacations, participating in various sports, and celebrating holidays joyfully.

Her daughter married into a well-to-do family, but the day after the wedding, her daughter's in-laws brought her daughter back to their home, insisting that Mrs. A take her daughter back and that she was unfit to be their son's spouse. Since then, her daughter has dated intermittently, had no children, and has mostly lived alone.

Her son married and had two children. Approximately six years prior to Mrs. A's presentation, her son's spouse began showing signs of a mental disorder, frequently going on shopping sprees, engaging with other men, and displaying indifference to her children. The divorce between her son and his wife was finalized three years prior, which Mrs. A described as a "nightmare." Since the divorce, her son's ex-wife has had numerous boyfriends, but of most distress to Mrs. A was an unstable home environment that her grandchildren (a girl age 13 and a boy age 10) were enduring. Specifically, her son and his ex-wife had 50/50 custody and neither was reportedly providing a good environment for her grandchildren. Since the divorce, her son began drinking heavily and his ex-wife has had four boyfriends, another divorce, and was dating an ex-convict. Notably, over the past six years, the family has not had a Christmas or Thanksgiving dinner together, which was particularly disheartening for Mrs. A.

Mrs. A and her husband have retired, but she continues to substitute teach to stay active.

While the initial focus of therapy was to address her anxiety related to driving, motor vehicles, and gas stations, treatment shifted to address some of the depression and sadness related to the absence of unity within her family. She tearfully explained, "I feel my granddaughter is heading to a dark place. . . It's only a matter of time until her mother starts taking her to bars. . . This is on my mind every day. . . I feel hopeless. . . Where did we go wrong?" She finds herself trying to facilitate an environment for her grandchildren that would instill family values and protect them from the turmoil present in their lives. She explained that she would often attempt to reevaluate what she could have done differently in raising her own children. She noted feeling that she is unable to truly enjoy her retirement because of these familial troubles; however, she described finding considerable comfort in attending a veteran's group geared toward women of veterans with PTSD.

In the next case (B) we can observe concern regarding the loss of one's mental functioning, which is particularly an issue in cultures where independence and self-reliance are valued. Getting older means acknowledging that compete independence may no longer be feasible, which can elicit anguish and embarrassment, although in cultures that facilitate interconnectedness, dependence in old age is not immensely dissimilar to dependency during other life phases. Simply saying the word "Alzheimer's disease" instills fear, given that there is no currently available treatment and the disease has a projective progressive loss of functionality. In 2010, of older adults in the United States with dementia, Alzheimer's disease accounted for 70% of all dementias and affected approximately 4.7 million individuals aged 65 years or older. However, the media has contributed to portraying Alzheimer's disease as more prevalent than it truly is, given that only 13.9% of the total adult population over the age of 70 is diagnosed with this neurodegenerative disorder (Plassman et al., 2007). The fact is, most older adults (i.e., 86%) are unaffected by Alzheimer's disease, and some memory loss may be part of normal aging or the result of other medical or psychiatric etiology.

The current case is one such example of an older male who expressed concern about developing Alzheimer's disease and the functional decline associated with it. The results of his neuropsychological evaluation suggested a vascular contribution given his medical history (i.e., hypertension, hyperlipidemia, multiple documented falls without obvious loss of consciousness, obstructive sleep apnea, carotid artery plaque, and a 10-year history of tobacco use), possibly a consequence of long-term use of a psychostimulant, and mood symptoms. However, evidence for a progressive neurodegenerative condition was not found.

Mr. B is an 84-year-old Caucasian male who presented for a neuropsychological evaluation to address a gradual decline in his cognitive abilities (i.e., memory, attention, processing speed, language) over the past one to two years in the context of a long-standing ADHD diagnosis. Mr. B was born and raised in Chicago, Illinois, but his parents immigrated from the Russian Empire during the Russian Revolution. When queried about his elected ethnicity, Mr. B reported a "kinship" with the Russian people. After graduating from high school, Mr. B completed two years of college prior to being drafted into the military. Following the completion of his four years of service in the military, Mr. B found college course work difficult, failing a number of classes, which led to a period of depression. He noted receiving a diagnosis of ADHD approximately 20 years ago, at which time he was prescribed Adderall, which he reported taking since his diagnosis.

Despite his academic difficulties in college, Mr. B completed a number of engineering courses and obtained an associate's degree. He was eventually grandfathered into an engineer career and was employed by a number of aerospace companies. He reported retiring in 1975. He does not have children. Mr. B currently lives in California with his wife of 45 years, and described his marriage as based on "mutual respect," although he stated that his spouse often gets frustrated with his memory difficulties.

During this evaluation, he described forgetting doctors' appointments and other important events, misplacing items, occasionally forgetting to take his medication, and forgetting where he parked his car. Mr. B reported three instances of forgetting to display his disabled person parking placard while parking (resulting in a total of $1,300 in fines including penalties) and another instance when he forgot to register a vehicle as non-operative, resulting in a total of approximately $3,500 in fines. He reported that he keeps a calendar on his bedroom wall, but stated that he is inconsistent in terms of recording upcoming events and appointments. Mr. B did not report difficulty recalling conversations or remote events. He did report difficulty concentrating, stating that his mind frequently wanders, especially while reading. Mr. B also described noticing a decline in processing speed approximately one year ago, when he began having difficulty keeping up with the pace of television captions. In regard to language, Mr. B reported word-finding difficulty, decline in his ability to express his concerns to his doctors, and occasional difficulty following conversations and narratives, but he did not report word finding difficulties. Mr. B further reported no difficulty in navigation, stating that he has historically has relied on maps and GPS devices.

Mr. B noted current anxiety, depression, and apathy that have developed gradually following the increase in ADHD symptoms two years ago. He reported that he has lost confidence in his ability to control his ADHD, stating, "I'm worried that I won't be able to be back to normal", "I'm afraid I have Alzheimer's disease," and "I don't want to end up in a home." Current psychosocial stressors included a decline in ability to concentrate and financial strain (i.e., credit card debt and legal fines secondary to forgetfulness). Mr. B stated that he fears becoming an "invalid" or a "couch potato." He described depressive symptoms including dissatisfaction with life, dropping activities and interests, not feeling happy most of the time, feeling helpless, feeling worried about the future, having difficulty starting new projects, and having problems with concentration.

The following case (C) highlights a masculine perspective on aging and coping with a neurodegenerative process. While not exclusive to men, our clinical work with older men has revealed a more stoic and unmoving attitude with regard to men being poised to remain the same person in spite of health or cognitive decline. Generally, masculinity encompasses values of resilience, industriousness, independence, physical and cognitive strength, courage, and fortitude, which all contribute to aligning men in a position of dominance within many, although not all, societies. Illnesses that compromise those values pose a significant challenge to these values, especially a neurodegenerative process such as Alzheimer's disease. In conducting qualitative interviews with men with dementia, Tolhurst and Weicht (2017) found several emerging themes, which included remaining unmoved, fighting back, emphasizing social contributions, and redefining services. Tolhurst and Weicht explain that by remaining unmoved and dismissing concerns about health-related matters, men are able to preserve themselves as the same person in the face of an illness such as dementia and may believe they are able to sustain their status within the social fabric of their culture and family. Fighting back, or taking on an active and problem-solving role, similarly affirms a non-passive, more masculine role in facing dementia head-on. In emphasizing social contributions, Tolhurst and Weicht discuss the continued effort to maintain a reciprocal system of support, often by acknowledging the assistance individuals with dementia receive from others, along with the value they provide. The final emerging theme is redefining services, during which men seek services with a sense of purpose of engaging with professionals, again, to be an active player in their treatment instead of being a passive victim of the illness. The case below illustrates an Hispanic man who aims to retain his sense of masculinity despite acknowledging decline.

Mr. C is a 65-year-old Puerto Rican male who was referred by his geriatrician to evaluate his current cognitive functioning and assist in diagnostic and treatment planning. He was accompanied by his wife, who served as an ancillary historian. Mr. C was born in Puerto Rico and moved to New York when he was six years old. He described himself as a "good student" and completed the 10th grade in New York. He began working at a medical college, where he held a number of positions (custodian, patient escort, and kitchen staff). He relocated to the greater Los Angeles area approximately 40 years ago and became employed at a university within the housekeeping department. Mr. C worked as a patient escort before taking a position as a hazardous material worker at the university's environmental services. He retired from this employment six years ago. Mr. C has been married three times. His first marriage lasted for approximately 10 years and the couple had three children (two daughters and a son). The second marriage lasted approximately 12 years, and the couple had two children from that marriage (one son and one daughter). He married his current wife 27 years ago and they have one daughter (age 26). He reported having good social support and indicated that he enjoys having breakfast with fellow retirees on a daily basis. Mr. C reported enjoying frequent trips to the local swap meet, taking walks, and watching television, especially *Jeopardy!*.

In regard to current stressors, Mr. C reported experiencing stress related to his relationship with his wife, particularly pertaining to his wife's "reminders" and "nagging." At the time of the interview, Mr. C denied having any cognitive symptoms, stating that all of his peers have some memory complaints. However, his wife stated that she noticed gradual declines in her husband's memory beginning approximately two years ago, with a worsening of symptoms over the last year. More specifically, with regard to his memory, Mr. C's wife reported that he has experienced a gradual decline in short-term memory, including difficulty recalling details of conversations, being repetitive in conversation, and forgetting where he places things. Additionally, his wife has reportedly started to manage his upcoming events and medical appointments. Mr. C's wife further reported a recent change to an automated bill payment system due to Mr. C's being late in making payments, which is highly atypical for him. Notably, his wife described Mr. C as having difficulty with executive function (i.e., tasks that require more complex planning such as finances and projects around the house). Specifically, she described the patient as having a difficult time installing lights in their home—a task he had no problem completing years before. His reduced ability to problem solve was previously reported as a source of frustration. Throughout the interview, Mr. C appeared annoyed with his wife's descriptions, and his wife at times submissively agreed with her husband's denial of symptoms appearing not to want to antagonize him further. In the absence of his wife, Mr. C stated,

> There isn't anything you can do about it. I think something is wrong, but why should she or I worry about it? I exercise, stay active, help around the house, eat healthy, do what the doctors tell me to do, and stay positive.

His performance on the neuropsychological evaluation suggested a diagnosis of Alzheimer's disease with an early onset, as he demonstrated impaired performance on a cognitive screener, all verbal and non-verbal memory tasks, and on tasks involving language, processing speed, visual spatial functioning, and executive functioning.

61

The following two cases (D and E) illustrate two women with dementia who presented for a neuropsychological evaluation, one who is African American and the other who is a European-born Caucasian. While both came from similar socioeconomic status and were similarly impaired in the instrumental activities of daily living (e.g., managing daily affairs), there were several noteworthy differences, including attitudes regarding their dependency, the attitudes of their families, and their living arrangements.

The first case describes an African American female whose son is the primary caregiver. Her son implemented a system that permitted his mother to stay within his home and live a relatively enjoyable residence over the past three years, with frequent visits from family. There was no pretense of independence, as her son actively managed all of her daily affairs (e.g., finances, medication, appointments).

The second case describes a Caucasian female who lives in an upscale assisted living facility, where she is surrounded by various activities, social events, and is also frequently visited by family. In contrast to the first case, however, in the second case, there is an expressed desire for the individual to maintain some sense of independence, to which the family caters.

The important aspect to consider here is not ethnicity, but the psychosocial history. The first case centers on closeness primarily with immediate family, while the second employs additional socialization, interests (i.e., the arts), and activities outside the family. Furthermore, there is a fundamental difference in attitudes toward psychotherapy and assessment, as the second case appeared to be unwilling not only to access feelings of loss related to the recent suicide of her daughter, but also her decline in cognition.

Mrs. D is an 81-year-old African American female who presented for a neuropsychological evaluation to assess her current cognitive functioning and assist in diagnostic and treatment planning. She was accompanied by her son, who served as an ancillary historian. Mrs. D was born and raised in Missouri. She completed high school and she noted a "good" academic performance. She relocated to California shortly after completing high school and worked in a necktie store while completing course work in electronics. She completed an associate's degree in electronics and obtained a certificate that allowed her to be employed as a specialist in the laboratory testing of electronics. Her longest employment was 30 years as an inspector. She retired from this employment 12 years ago. Mrs. D has been married twice. Her first marriage lasted for five years, from which she had her son (age 57) and daughter (age 55). She remarried 34 years ago and was widowed three years ago. Since the passing of her husband, Mrs. D has been living with her son, who is financially well off and who has been supporting his mother for the past three years. Mrs. D mentioned that she particularly enjoys visits from her grandchildren and going on biweekly outings with her son's and daughter's families. Notably, Mrs. D reportedly engaged in talk therapy for six months when she was in her mid-30s, to assist in coping with her brother's psychiatric diagnosis of schizophrenia, and stated that with the help of her psychotherapist, she was able to accept that "the mind could get sick just like the body."

Concerning her cognitive complaints, Mrs. D and her son described difficulty with memory (i.e., details of conversations, names of people, taking medication, tracking appointments), attention (i.e., increased distractibility), processing speed (i.e., thinking more slowly), and language (i.e., word-finding difficulty). Mrs. D was reportedly independent in her basic activities of daily living (e.g., eating, bathing, dressing, and hygiene); however, she depended on her son to manage her medication, medical appointments, bills, shopping, cooking, cleaning, and transportation. Mrs. D's son had reportedly implemented a system for managing aspects of his mother's care, including setting up a routine, organizing her medication, and setting alarms throughout the house as reminders to perform certain tasks. He stated that he could not imagine putting his mother into an assisted living facility. During the evaluation, Mrs. D would often make light of and joke about the errors she made on tests. The results of the neuropsychological evaluation revealed a neurodegenerative dementia called posterior cortical atrophy.

Mrs. E is an 84-year-old Caucasian female who presented for a neuropsychological evaluation at the request of her treating neurologist to evaluate her current cognitive functioning for her clinical care. She was accompanied by her brother, who served as an ancillary historian. Mrs. E was born and raised in Belgium. Her brother reported that she had "aced everything" academically. She completed college-level coursework in art in London at age 19. She taught art in London prior to relocating to New York at age 21, where she became employed as an art instructor. She moved to Los Angeles at age 27, and continued working as an art instructor and artist until retiring 11 years ago. She has been widowed for 12 years and had two children. Mrs. E's son (age 60) visits her daily; her daughter committed suicide two years ago. Mrs. E was voluntarily hospitalized for one week following the suicide and she was avoidant in discussing the details of her daughter's suicide. Mrs. E is currently taking an antidepressant, and psychotherapy was discontinued after several sessions, as she reported that the sessions were unhelpful in improving her mood. Mrs. E currently lives in an upscale assisted living center, where she has resided for the past year. She is independent in all basic activities of daily living but requires assistance in managing her finances, medications, and calendar. The assisted living staff administer her medications, while her brother and his wife manage her finances, calendar, and appointment scheduling. Her brother noted that they are very careful to not make her feel dependent on them, as Mrs. E reportedly appears to want to maintain a sense of independence.

Mrs. E's daily routine varies as a function of the activities arranged by the assisted living facility staff and she described fully enjoying the various recreational activities (i.e., drawing, listening to music, watching television, and attending weekly art classes). She expressed notable enjoyment from conversations with other residents at the assisted living center, art activities, regular visits from her son, and outings with her grandchildren. Concerning her cognitive difficulties, Mrs. E demonstrated poor insight into her deficits, appearing genuinely surprised by her brother's description of recent events and her cognitive symptoms, including short-term memory difficulties (e.g., being repetitive in conversation). Mrs. E admitted to no longer reading heavy books, describing a loss of interest in reading lengthy literature.

Following the interview, Mrs. E was informed of the approximate time required for the testing, to which the she responded that she would not be able to fully complete the testing in one sitting. She then expressed hesitation in wanting to know the results of the evaluation and the value it will bring to her quality of life. With encouragement from the examiners, the patient agreed to attempt to complete as much testing as she could. After answering seven items on a cognitive screener, the patient requested that the evaluation be discontinued because she felt that she was unable to provide her best effort.

The client seemed aware of not answering some of the items correctly and appeared embarrassed. Despite empathic encouragement from the examiner, the patient stated that she did not want to continue testing. She again reiterated that she really did not want to know how badly she was performing and would rather live as she had been. She stated that testing would not enrich her life and had the potential to only dampen her enjoyment of life.

Summary and Closing Remarks

Although in no way comprehensive, the selected cases capture some of the frequently occurring themes that have emerged in our clinical work with older adults. The story of the blind men and the elephant echoes many of the prior findings, given that we are describing the same elephant. Similar to Bellak (1986), we more often encounter older adults longing for affiliation, connectedness, familial cohesiveness, and socialization, rather than fixating on death or despair. Notably, within Western culture, the loss of one's cognitive functioning is a common concern observed during our clinical work; however, it is important to note that some decline in cognition is expected and that most older adults are unaffected by neurodegenerative processes, such as Alzheimer's disease. For those diagnosed with dementia, the symptoms appear to significantly impact values that underlie masculinity for men, and while they appear stubborn or unconcerned by their diagnosis, it may be worthwhile to conceptualize the stoic unmovingness of older men as a method for maintaining a masculine identity within their cultural and social circles. The decision for institutional care of older adults with dementia versus in-home care is dependent not only on one's ability to manage day-to-day life, but also on the person's psychosocial history and the family's perceptions of what institutionalization means to the family as a whole.

Older adults are a heterogeneous group and making clinical assumptions based on just one man's blind account is unwise. Alternatively, we encourage young clinicians to interact respectfully with older adults in a way that utilizes older adults' needs for affiliation, connectedness, and socialization. With men dealing with medical or cognitive decline, it may be best to keep in mind the shift in traditional masculine values (independence, physical and cognitive strength) to preserve a masculine identity by remaining emotively unmoved, fighting back (i.e., being proactive), or emphasizing other social contributions (i.e., recognizing their ability to continue to contribute).

References

Baltes, P. B., & Smith, J. (2003). New frontiers in the future of aging: From successful aging of the young old to the dilemmas of the fourth age. *Gerontology, 49*(2), 123-135. doi:10.1159/000067946

Benedikter, R., & Siepmann, K. (2016). "Transhumanism": A New Global Political Trend? *Challenge, 59*(1), 47-59. doi:10.1080/05775132.2015.1123574

Bronfenbrenner, U. (1999). Environments in developmental perspective: Theoretical and operational models. In S. L. Friedman & T. D. Wachs (Eds.), *Measuring environment across the life span: Emerging methods and concepts* (pp. 3-28). Washington, DC: American Psychological Association.

Bronfenbrenner, U., & Ceci, S. J. (1994). Nature-nurture reconceptualized in developmental perspective: A biological model. *Psychological Review, 101*, 568-586.

Bronfenbrenner, U., & Morris, P. A. (2006). The bioecological model of human development. In W. Damon & R. M. Lerner (Eds.), *Handbook of child psychology: Theoretical models of human development* (6th Ed., Vol. 1, pp. 793-828). New York, NY: Wiley.

Christensen, K., Doblhammer, G., Rau, R., & Vaupel, J. W. (2009). Ageing populations: the challenges ahead. *The Lancet, 374*(9696), 1196-1208. doi:10.1016/S0140-6736(09)61460-4

Cianciolo, A. T., & Sternberg, R. J. (2004). *Intelligence: A brief history.* Malden, MA: Blackwell.

Corrada, M. M., Brookmeyer, R., Berlau, D., Paganini-Hill, A., & Kawas, C. H. (2008). Prevalence of dementia after age 90: Results from the 90+ study. *Neurology, 71*(5), 337-343. doi:10.1212/01.wnl.0000310773.65918.cd

Cosco, T. D., Prina, A. M., Perales, J., Stephan, B. C., & Brayne,

C. (2014). Operational definitions of successful aging: a systematic review. *International Psychogeriatrics, 26*(03), 373-381. doi:10.1017/s1041610213002287

Davydov, D. M., Stewart, R., Ritchie, K., & Chaudieu, I. (2010). Resilience and mental health. *Clinical psychology review, 30*(5), 479-495. doi: 10.1016/j.cpr.2010.03.003

Dong, X., Milholland, B., & Vijg, J. (2016). Evidence for a limit to human lifespan. *Nature, 538*(7624), 257-259. doi:10.1038/nature19793

Engberg, H., Jeune, B., Andersen-Ranberg, K., Martinussen, T., Vaupel, J. W., & Christensen, K. (2013). Optimism and survival: does an optimistic outlook predict better survival at advanced ages? A twelve-year follow-up of Danish nonagenarians. *Aging Clinical and Experimental Research, 25*(5), 517-525. doi: 10.1007/s40520-013-0122-x

Freund, A. M., & Riediger, M. (2012). Successful aging. In R. M. Lerner, A. M. Easterbrooks, & J. Mistry (Eds.). *Handbook of psychology: Volume 6. Developmental psychology* (2nd ed., pp. 601-629). Editor-in-Chief: I. B. Weiner. Hoboken, NJ: Wiley.

Forette, B. (1997). Centenarians: Health and frailty. In J. M. Robine, J. W. Vaupel, B. Jeune, & M. Allard (Eds.), *Longevity: To the limits and beyond* (pp. 105-112). New York, NY: Springer-Verlag.

Fortner B. V. & Neimeyer R. B. (1999). Death anxiety in older adults: A quantitative review. *Death studies, 23*, 387-411.

Hayflick, L. (2004). Aging: The Reality "Anti-Aging" Is an Oxymoron. *The Journals of Gerontology Series A: Biological Sciences and Medical Sciences, 59*(6), B573-B578. doi:10.1093/gerona/59.6.B573

Haynie, D. A., Berg, S., Johansson, B., Gatz, M., & Zarit, S. H. (2001). Symptoms of depression in the oldest old a longitudinal Study.

The Journals of Gerontology Series B: Psychological Sciences and Social Sciences, 56(2), 111-118. 10.1093/geronb/56.2.P111

Holliday, R. (2006). Aging is no longer an unsolved problem in biology. *Annals of the New York Academy of Sciences, 1067*(1), 1-9. doi:10.1196/annals.1354.002

Karasawa, M., Curhan, K. B., Markus, H. R., Kitayama, S. S., Love, G. D., Radler, B. T., & Ryff, C. D. (2011). Cultural perspectives on aging and well-being: A comparison of Japan and the United States. *The International Journal of Aging and Human Development, 73*(1), 73-98. Retrieved from http://journals.sagepub.com/doi/abs/10.2190/AG.73.1.d

Lerner, R. M., Easterbrooks, A. M., & Mistry, J. (Eds.). (2012). *Handbook of psychology: Volume 6. Developmental psychology (2nd ed.)*. Editor-in- Chief: I. B. Weiner. Hoboken, NJ: Wiley.

Mehrotra, C., & Wagner, L. S. (2013). *Aging and diversity: An active learning experience.* Taylor & Francis.

Missler, M., Stroebe, M., Geurtsen, L., Mastenbroek, M., Chmoun, S., & Van Der Houwen, K. (2012). Exploring death anxiety among elderly people: A literature review and empirical investigation. *OMEGA-Journal of Death and Dying, 64*, 357-379.

Newman, S. J., & Easteal, S. (2017). The dynamic upper limit of human lifespan. *bioRxiv*, 124800. doi:10.1101/124800

Nowotny, K., Jung, T., Grune, T., & Höhn, A. (2014). Accumulation of modified proteins and aggregate formation in aging. *Experimental gerontology, 57*, 122-131. doi:10.1016/j.exger.2014.05.016

Ong, A. D., Bergeman, C. S., Bisconti, T. L., & Wallace, K. A. (2006). Psychological resilience, positive emotions, and successful adaptation to stress in later life. *Journal of personality and social psychology, 91*(4), 730. doi:10.1037/0022-3514.91.4.730

Pierce, A. L., & Kawas, C. H. (2017). Dementia in the oldest old:

Beyond Alzheimer disease. *PLoS medicine, 14*(3), e1002263. doi: 10.1371/journal.pmed.1002263

Plassman, B. L., Langa, K. M., Fisher, G. G., Heeringa, S. G., Weir, D. R., Ofstedal, M. B., ... & Steffens, D. C. (2007). Prevalence of dementia in the United States: the aging, demographics, and memory study. *Neuroepidemiology, 29*, 125-132.

Pruchno, R. A., Wilson-Genderson, M., Rose, M., & Cartwright, F. (2010). Successful aging: Early influences and contemporary characteristics. *The Gerontologist, 50*(6), 821-833. doi:10.1093/geront/gnq041

Rowe, J. W. and Kahn, R. L. (1987). Human aging: usual and successful. *Science*, 237, 143–149. doi:10.1093/geront/37.4.433

Rau, R., Soroko, E., Jasilionis, D., & Vaupel, J. W. (2008). Continued reductions in mortality at advanced ages. *Population and Development Review, 34*(4), 747-768. doi: 10.1111/j.1728-4457.2008.00249.x

Schoenhofen, E. A., Wyszynski, D. F., Andersen, S., Pennington, J., Young, R., Terry, D. F., & Perls, T. T. (2006). Characteristics of 32 supercentenarians. *Journal of the American Geriatrics Society, 54*(8), 1237-1240. doi:10.1111/j.1532-5415.2006.00826.x

Siegler, I. C., Elias, M. F., Bosworth, H. B. (2012). Aging and Health. In A. Baum, T. Revenson & J.E. Singer (Eds.) *Handbook of Health Psychology,* 2nd Ed., (pp. 617- 633). New York, NY: Psychology Press.

Tolhurst, E., & Weicht, B. (2017). Preserving personhood: The strategies of men negotiating the experience of dementia. *Journal of Aging Studies, 40,* 29-35.

Tosato, M., Zamboni, V., Ferrini, A., & Cesari, M. (2007). The aging process and potential interventions to extend life expectancy. *Clinical interventions in aging, 2*(3), 401.

Vestergaard, S., Thinggaard, M., Jeune, B., Vaupel, J. W., McGue, M., & Christensen, K. (2015). Physical and mental decline and yet rather happy? A study of Danes aged 45 and older. *Aging & mental health*, *19*(5), 400-408. doi:10.1080/13607863.2014.9 44089

Volkert, D., Kreuel, K., Heseker, H., & Stehle, P. (2004). Energy and nutrient intake of young-old, old-old and very-old elderly in Germany. *European journal of clinical nutrition*, *58*(8), 1190-1200. doi: 10.1038/sj.ejcn.1601950

Ungar, M., Ghazinour, M., & Richter, J. (2013). Annual research review: What is resilience within the social ecology of human development? *Journal of Child Psychology and Psychiatry*, *54*(4), 348-366. doi:10.1111/jcpp.12025

Wells, M. (2012). Resilience in older adults living in rural, suburban, and urban areas. *Online Journal of Rural Nursing and Health Care*, *10*(2), 45-54.

Wahl, H. W., & Oswald, F. (2010). Environmental perspectives on ageing. In D. Dannefer & C. Phillipson (Eds.), *The SAGE handbook of social gerontology* (pp. 111 - 124). Thousand Oaks, CA: Sage Publications.

3.

Cultures of Medical Disabilities

**Rachel Rugh Fraser, MA, MAEd, Pavel Litvin, MA,
Scott Curry, MA, and Samantha F. Hill, MSW**

"About a year ago, I had a grand mal seizure while at my best friend's daughter's graduation ceremony. The woman who was sitting to my left looked at me and would not help my mother put me into a recovery position. She got up and walked away. I see her occasionally, from time to time, and, to this day, she will not make eye contact with me and tries to steer clear of me." – Rebekka, 45-year-old woman with epilepsy

"As soon as I heard the diagnosis, I immediately thought of being in a wheelchair—my life is over." – Alyssa, 28-year-old woman with multiple sclerosis

"We all know that MS is not pleasant; however, you can find the positive in it and it will change your life—in some ways I view my MS as a blessing because I realized working all day and night took me away from my family and friends, and it took a significant toll on my health and overall life. Now I am aware of what truly matters and I live in appreciation for each moment." – Sam, 53-year-old woman with multiple sclerosis

"I really don't go out in public. It's like my social life got robbed from me. While part of me is like, 'Screw it, I can do what I want,' the truth is—I don't want to upset or hurt anyone." – John, 19-year-old man with Tourette's syndrome

"As an individual who has had Tourette's since childhood, I can tell you every day is a struggle; however, if I had a choice to be someone else I wouldn't change who I am or what I am." – Michael, 38-year-old man with Tourette's syndrome

Introduction

As seen in the excerpts above, impairment due to disease, whether it be physical or neurological, impacts individuals significantly, yet *differently* (i.e., experiences differ not only from disease to disease but also among those diagnosed with the same disease). Despite the fact that there were 56.7 million people (a whopping 19% of the U.S. population) who reported having a disability in 2010, the experiences and culture of those with a disability in general are often misunderstood and underrepresented (US Census, 2010). While the media has attempted to better represent those with certain types of disability, oftentimes their representations are inaccurate and even offensive (e.g., think, the television show *Hoarders,* where the most dramatic and sensationalized aspects of the disorder are illuminated, and the movie *Me Before You,* which presents an immensely limiting view of disabled existence). Instead of spreading awareness and understanding, such media-based representations stigmatize various disorders and impairments. Similarly, even examining related literature and research can be limiting, in that oftentimes only isolated or specific aspects of a group's experience may be elucidated. Such work generally presents commonalities and correlations found within groups, not necessarily differences. Unfortunately, such misunderstanding of the experience of having a particular disability is not just found in limited research or media—sometimes it is found closer than we think. Take, for example, Mr. Smith, a 19-year-old male who disclosed his anger about his little sister's disability (cerebral palsy) in a therapy session:

> I feel so angry that she has this disease. She doesn't deserve this! It breaks my heart that she can't dance with her friends, has to find a ramp, or occasionally needs to be carried. She has such a positive attitude, and is such a sweet and smart kid. She loves life. Why couldn't it have been me and not her?

73

While the quote above demonstrates the care and concern of a loving sibling, it also illustrates the misunderstanding of another's life experience. Even though Mr. Smith indicates that his sister loves life and has a positive attitude, he cannot see beyond her difficulties and makes the assumption that she cannot see beyond them either. This scenario elucidates the importance of stepping beyond what we think we know about clients based upon what the limited research, media, and even personal experience have led us to believe about individuals with disability due to disease.

Although disease and disability are typically inclusive of thousands of both physical and neurological-based disorders that typically cause a significant impact on functioning, for the purpose of this chapter, we will be examining the experiences of individuals diagnosed with a neurological disease (i.e., disorders of the nervous system where abnormalities are found in the brain, spinal cord, or other aspects of the nervous system that can cause an array of symptoms such as seizures, pain, weakness of the muscles, paralysis, gait instability, loss of sensation, and reduced state of consciousness), particularly epilepsy, multiple sclerosis, and Tourette's syndrome, as these disorders provide an important glimpse into the impact of disease on functioning, living, and overall quality of life.

This chapter will attempt to deconstruct assumptions, stereotypes, and the perceived universality of experience of those with a disability. For the purpose of this work, "disability" will refer to an impairment in activities of daily living (ADLs), limitations in other activities, and constraints in participation due to neurological disorders that may involve adversities related to symptoms (e.g., reductions in cognitive or mobility abilities, pain), difficulties acclimating to reduced functionality, changes within social and familial roles and relationships, changes in ability to work and provide income, as well as comorbidities, such as depression. Several case studies will be examined to provide the reader with a better understanding of the diversity of experience between and within disabled groups.

Models of Disability

Once upon a time in the ancient world, there were two men who both had the identical behavioral indicators of what we now call "epilepsy." One of the men walked into a village in Mesopotamia, and had a violent seizure in the middle of a crowd. Everyone around him stopped what they were doing and immediately sent for someone to evaluate the behavioral abnormality. Within hours the man was diagnosed as being under the control of a celestial god, and an exorcism was performed—he was deemed unworthy to live and work in the village, even as a slave. The other man walked into a village in Greece, and the same thing occurred—he had a violent seizure in the midst of a crowd. While these particular Greeks also believed his behavior to be a result of celestial and godly possession, the members of this village called upon a spiritual leader to confirm the man's likely divinity and brilliance from being blessed by the gods. Two men—same disability, very different experiences based upon the society's model of disability. Which man likely had a more positive integration into society, more positive sense of self, and better quality of life?

As the above story demonstrates, exactly how disease and disability are conceptualized and treated can differ greatly, and can have immense implications for how an individual with a disability integrates into their particular society and, ultimately, the quality of their life. While the sophistication in disability conceptualization has a long and unfinished history, in modern times disability is often conceptualized through the lens of one of several models of disability. For the purposes of our work, we will examine two prominent models: the biomedical model and the environmental and functional models.

Biomedical Model

While the ancient Greeks were somewhat conflicted about

75

conceptualizing such behavioral manifestations of the functional impact of disease—some believing it was a negative possession, others affirming its divine and sacred nature—it was not until Hippocrates rejected the notion that the disease was a result of spiritual possession. Instead, he postulated that diseases such as epilepsy could be much more accurately conceptualized as a medical-based and possibly treatable condition of the brain, which set the foundation of the medical model of disability (Magiorkinis, Kalliopi, & Diamantis, 2010). With firm foundations in the scientific method, the biomedical model has been salient in forming our modern understanding of disability. What typically draws physicians and clinicians to this model is its strong explanatory prowess, which surpasses the explicatory power of other modern models. Because this model defines disability in medical terms, it tends to lend itself to more scientific credibility. However, a result of this conceptualization is the propagation of the idea that disabilities are an entirely individual experience, causing it, unfortunately, to be criticized for being socially unjust (Smart & Smart, 2006). To explain, the biomedical model holds that pathology is present and that disabilities are conditions that are measurable and exist separate from any social constructs or other factors. Criticisms relating to social unjustness stem from the potential for this model to dehumanize the individual with a disability due to a sole emphasis on pathology.

The current biomedical model conceptualizes disability as a problem of the individual that is caused by trauma, disease, or other illnesses that necessitate continued medical-based management of symptoms. In this model, the goal is treating the disability in hopes of finding a cure or reasonable facsimile, or aiming to assist the individual in medically relevant adjustment (Donovan, 2012). A benefit of this model is that, because the main concern is access to and use of continuous medical treatment, this model has historically served to be the catalyst for improving healthcare policy. A more clinically relevant aspect of this model is that it is not an interactional model, which means that collaboration between professionals is not as commonplace as one would expect (Smart & Smart, 2006). The implications for this are profound for aspiring clinicians who want to treat non-medical aspects of an individual, working to treat the whole individual as they interact and exist in their environment. The aforementioned advantages and criticisms of the biomedical model are critical for future clinicians to keep in mind when working with those with disabilities.

Environmental and Functional Models

As criticisms and limitations of the biomedical model became more salient, the need for a more interactive model arose, thus leading to the development of environmental and functional models of disability. These two models are considered to be interactive due to the belief that an individual's disability interacts directly with that person's environment and level of functioning (Smart & Smart, 2006). Thus, in this model, the conceptualization of disability is not solely attributed to the mere biology of the individual, but instead recognizes that, while biology is undeniably important, the environment has the power to effect, exacerbate, and even *cause* disability (think back to the example of the two men in ancient times) (Smart & Smart, 2006).

The clinical implications for this ideology are profound—if the source of the disability changes from an individually derived phenomenon to an environmentally implicated phenomenon, the responsibility then changes from solely individual responsibility for change to a cumulative responsibility of those that exist in the environment, which lends itself more to an interactional model involving collaboration between medical professionals, social workers, and psychologists. Thus, individuals in the helping professions can tailor interventions to improve an individual's ability to adapt to their environment and help meet functional demands that meet the individual where they are and where they want to be (i.e., rehabilitation) (Smart

& Smart, 2006).

The environmental and functional models facilitate an environment where the conceptualization and understanding of disability is more immune to the dehumanizing qualities found in the biomedical model for several key reasons, with the most salient reason being that, when an individual with a disability is seen as a complete person, separate from their medical categorization and functional ability, the power differential is diminished because some of the responsibility for reactions to disability are delegated to society in a push to provide an environment that is non-prejudiced (Smart & Smart, 2006).

Regardless of which model is adhered to, the fact remains that individuals with disabilities are among the most vulnerable in any society, particularly in light of the implications of both medical and environmental contributions. An important aspect to consider is that such vulnerability may be equally, if not more, profound among those with disabilities that are not as obvious as some physical disabilities (i.e., neurologically based disorders such as epilepsy or multiple sclerosis), where the weight of the disability may lie within more internally than externally obvious mechanisms.

Carlos Mencia is a stand-up comedian who warns his audiences that at any time during his show 90% of them will be laughing while the other 10% will be highly offended. The barbs of his humor strike at all groups, including the disabled. As part of his show, Mr. Mencia talks about waiting in line for four hours for a roller coaster ride at a well-known amusement park. In his story, after the long wait he was about the get on the ride when he was stopped, and park staff brought a man in a wheelchair to the ride in front of him.

At this point, Mr. Mencia talks a little bit about what equality might mean, and how he would have liked to have seen this individual in line just like everyone else. He also acknowledges being frustrated that what he perceived as his seat being given to someone else. He describes a confrontation with the disabled man and the park staff about whether or not this individual should be allowed to go to the front of the line or not. As the story develops, Mr. Mencia relates telling the man in the wheelchair that if he wants to be treated as an equal he will treat him as an equal, and that if he wants to be treated as disabled, which includes being allowed to the front of the line because of this status, he will do the same. However, Mr. Mencia relates that if the man wanted to be treated as disabled, he would need to acknowledge that Mr. Mencia is "faster, stronger, and more intelligent" than he. Now the man did not wish to do so, and would not say Mr. Mencia was "superior," which elicited a response from Mr. Mencia that this man should then go to the back of the line.

This did not occur, the man was allowed in front of Mr. Mencia, and Mr. Mencia relates that he had to "pull the beaner card" in order to not be thrown out of the line (and possibly the amusement park). It is here that the story takes an interesting twist. As Mr. Mencia got on the ride, he was placed right next to this same individual. In a subsequent conversation with the man, Mr. Mencia relates that the man told him that others do not see him; they only see a wheelchair. He went on to state that Mr. Mencia saw him as a person who was trying to take advantage and get to the front of the line, and that in so doing, Mr. Mencia had made him feel like "a regular person." Mr. Mencia ends the story by telling that he and this man then went on numerous other rides that day, with Mr. Mencia pushing the wheelchair to the front of all the lines, and that the two developed a friendship from this encounter.

Mr. Mencia makes an important point in this story. It is very easy for any one of us to just see the wheelchair, or the disability, when confronted with a disabled person. Unfortunately, how we see this individual is in part a social construct that is intertwined with racism and privilege.

The Disabled in History

Attitudes about the disabled and impaired are neither homogeneous nor static across societies. The ancient Greeks and Romans regarded the "feeble" as inferior. Early Christian thinking proposed that disease and disability were ways to purification and grace. However, with Martin Luther's revolution, attitudes toward the mentally retarded and disabled changed to consider them to be possessed by evil spirits, and thus this population was exposed to torture and other mistreatment that attempted to drive the spirits out (Munyi, 2012). During the 14th through the 16th centuries, infants were killed at birth if they were deformed, as they were associated with sin and unholy activities (Cherney, 2011).

In the 17th century, it was common practice for countries in Europe to deport the disabled, which is the source of the phrase "ship of fools" (Johnstone, 2004). In the mid-19th century, at approximately the same time that the concept of race was first being forwarded, individuals with disabilities were regarded as mad, deviant, medical maladies, and as objects of charity. Europeans were associating non-whites with disabled people, and classifying both groups as delayed in evolution or "throwbacks" (Johnstone, 2004; Baynton, 2008).

Part of this phenomenon was due to Charles Darwin. When Darwin first proposed his theory of evolution, he was faced with the challenge of explaining the fossil gap between apes and human beings. Skeptics of his theory challenged him to produce proof of "a talking race of monkeys, or a mute race of men" (Taylor, 1841, as cited in Gelb, 2008, p. 2). One strategy Darwin used to support his theory was to claim there was no need to provide fossilized proof of "the missing link" as they were living among men at the current time in the form of the "savages" and the "idiots," who were intermediate beings between the apes and civilized men. He supported this contention by describing the disabled as being dirty, having animalistic (i.e., unlearned and uncivilized)

80

behavior, and even the fact that some of this population were more hirsute than others. Darwin used intellectual disability as a way to provide support for his theory by attempting to link the disabled with a less than human animal quality. He presented "idiots" as being between the primates and humans, examples of waste that is characteristic of natural selection, where low intelligence provided one possibility of the "lowest" of the species, and was thereby characteristic of earlier stages of human evolution. The intellectually disabled provided Darwin with exemplars of the weakest to be culled from a population in order to strengthen the strong, and described the mind of the utter idiot as being lower than the lowest of animals, and the most unfit members of the human "race." One of the outcomes of Darwin's positions was the reinforcement of prejudice against indigenous peoples and individuals with disabilities (Gelb, 2008).

There has been an assumption in the West since the 19th century that the white race was the "normal race" and other races were defective and deviants from this norm. For example, the reason Down syndrome was initially called Mongolism was because the physician who first identified the condition perceived it to be a reversion from the Caucasian to the Mongol racial type. Additionally, American Blacks were presented has having any number of physical deformities (varying from the Caucasian "norm"), which provided a rationale for the defenders of slavery to indicate that they were unfit to live in freedom (Smith, 2004; Baynton, 2008).

The Constructs of Disability

The World Health Organization distinguishes between impairment, which is due to an organic condition; disability, which is the restriction of activity considered for a "normal" human being; and handicap, which is the consequences one might experience socially as a result of the disability (Crisp, 2000). There is an understandable and even useful taxonomy of disability that includes cognitive, sensory, physical, psychiatric, intellectual, developmental, and environmental impairments that manifest through appearance and functioning (Garland-Thomson, 2014). The medical model perspective of disability pertains to impairment, while the social model of disability pertains to society's attitudes toward people with a disability that tends to marginalize them. Just as with racism, "ableism" as an ideology claims there is a biological inferiority and stratification where people without disability are considered "normal" or even superior, while those with disability are seen as being not equal, or inferior (Smith, 2004). There is a perspective in our society, which has its roots in ancient Greece, that proposes deviance in any form, including disease and physical features not considered the norm, is a sign of evil. An example of this is found in the 19th century belief that the "club foot" was thought to be a sign of the Christian devil. Disability is a complex social and cultural construct that serves to classify individuals as abnormal. The concept cannot be defined without the definition of being "able," and is better understood in the context of where the individual fits in within the community (Crisp, 2000; Smith, 2004; Garland-Thomson, 2014).

The disabled are often categorized as a single group (i.e., "the disabled") rather than a more specific classification (Smith, 2004). However, those with a disability or impairment are not a homogenous group. For example, individuals who suffered the physical consequences of contracting polio might describe themselves as "polios" (Garland-Thomson, 2014), and the concerns for this population will be much different than that for the deaf, the blind, or individuals with different physical limitations. Functional limitations of disability can be exacerbated by how society regards the disabled, which often view them as "freaks" and less than human, and this stigma can have a direct effect on what individuals can and cannot do. Stigma restricts access, which leads to isolation and other negative ramifications (Smith, 2004; Bourke & Waite, 2013).

People with disabilities are seen as individuals to whom something has happened, where something has gone wrong, and as such they face the challenges of managing their bodies and their interaction with society. The disability identity is one most individuals are reluctant to accept, given the stigma and discrediting that can accompany it. Disability shapes the way individuals go about day-to-day living as well as how they relate to others. Culture, discourse, and social relations, in the context of the physical body, makes all individuals who they are and who they are understood to be (Garland-Thomson, 2014).

Marginalization of the Disabled

There is a wide range of attitudes toward the disabled in Occidental and non-Occidental societies. In some African cultures, being disabled is seen as being less than human and a curse, which results in infanticide, and infants being left along river banks and in the sea in order to "return to their own kind." Other cultures revere the mentally disabled as manifestations of gods, and these disabled receive great care. Some societies treat the disabled with respect, and allow them to participate to the fullest extent of their capability, though this does not always correlate with a society's resources or knowhow. Attitudes toward the disabled range from tolerance to love to fear and revulsion, but most societies regard the disabled as "deviants" in some fashion. In most societies, the disableds' opportunities are limited due to rejection, discrimination, barriers, and inaccessibility, and thus the way a society views the disabled is a factor in the success (or lack thereof) they may experience (Munyi, 2012).

In the U.S. there is a deep-rooted perspective toward disability that centers on a medical model involving limited functioning that prevents individuals from fulfilling normal societal roles; this results in marginalization, stigmatization, and isolation. The social model further exacerbates this by denying the disabled access to the rights and resources of the mainstream. Individuals with disabilities are treated differently than their "abled" peers, and the disabled can have a negative self-image that affects their long-term health and quality of life (Bourke & Waite, 2013).

"Ableism" is an attitude that permeates U.S. culture much in the same way that racism and chauvinism have, and is so ingrained in our cultural assumptions that the assumptions are considered truth. Take the example of stairs. These are obviously pervasive in our society, and those who are not disabled hardly give them a second thought. If a person without disability considers stairs, it is typically in an architectural context. However, for the disabled person who is incapable of climbing them, stairs give a message about who is desired in that particular place (Cherney, 2011). Individuals with disabilities move between fitting in and not fitting in to society, and any discomfort they may experience has more to do with lack of access to resources rather than as a consequence of the disability itself (Garland-Thomson, 2014). Disability is seen as an unclean status, and society reacts to disability by eliminating it, segregating it, and labeling it dangerous (Johnstone, 2004; Smith, 2004).

There are urban legends in the U.S. about a "Hook Man" that serve the latter purpose. One such story is about a young couple on a date who have gone to a local "lover's lane" to engage in sexual activity on a foggy night. While they are there, there is a news bulletin about a man with a hook for a hand in the vicinity who is wanted for rape and murder. The young woman in the story becomes frightened, and insists she be taken home. The young man who is driving reluctantly agrees, and either in fear or frustration "peels out" as they drive away. When they arrive at the young woman's home, the young man gets out, and goes to open the car door for the, and finds the hook hanging from the door handle.

There is an intersection between race and disability that goes back to the eugenics movement. Eugenics created the concept of the normal and, through the use of statistics, the abnormal, which in turn created a different classification from the ideal human being. Eugenic "science" can still be found in special education, psychology, and the institutions that serve the disabled (Smith, 2004). Intelligence, and some statistics as they are currently utilized in psychology and education, are the result of the work initially done by Francis Galton, who among all of his accomplishments established the concept of eugenics. Essentially, any characteristic that is different than Eurocentric Caucasian defines "others" as not white, not able, and inferior. The remnants of eugenics can be found in the disproportionate number of minority students labeled as disabled and accordingly classified into special education classes (Beratan, 2006).

Despite the apparent good intent that the Individuals with Disabilities Education Act (IDEA) may have had, it actually serves to continue to put children of varying abilities into a hierarchical structure that continues to favor the "normal" student for whom it was designed. The entire system is based on a deficit-based perspective where impairment and disability are conflated, and which perpetuates the concept that the disabled are considered "less than" the able (Beratan, 2006).

The concept of learning disability (LD) originated in the 1950s and 1960s ostensibly in reaction to Sputnik to insure America's superiority. However, it also emerged during the time that segregation was being challenged in court, and schools were being forced to integrate. African American and Hispanic children were initially identified as mildly mentally retarded, which allowed schools to place them in segregated classrooms. However, as LD began being applied to white students, the minority students received different classifications or, if not reclassified, experienced a much different educational experience than their white counterparts. Generally, white LD students receive more accommodation within mainstream classrooms, while minority LD students were more prone to be placed in self-contained classrooms (i.e., be segregated from the general student body). The term LD is used to deem white students as more intellectually superior than minority students, and they experience more school success (i.e., lower dropout rates), success after school, and acceptance by society (Smith, 2004; Blanchett, 2010).

Society is much more willing to accept individuals with a disability who do not look all that much different from the "norm." Race and class continues to have a significant role in who is identified as LD, and the concept of LD in the educational system serves to prevent the integration of white children with children of color, and to insure the successful completion of school for white males. It is very much a concept of privilege, and the categories of abled and disabled are assumed to be separate, distinct, binary, and phenotypic, where society focuses on the differences the disabled have from the abled rather than to focus on the commonalities (Blanchett, 2010; Gelb, 2008; Smith, 2004). In addition to society's general attitude toward the disabled, there can be negative attitudes among the disabled and impaired themselves (Johnstone, 2004; Bourke & Waite, 2013).

In general, the disabled, regardless of disability, are regarded as "unfit," and are treated with disdain, indifference, and fear by greater society. As a result, the disabled are often only seen as their disability (as Mr. Mencia related in his story), which can result in individuals taking steps to hide their disability or join those who have the same condition. As a result, in the more recent past, the idea of disability as an identity has led to individuals with disabilities identifying as such, and becoming empowered and assertive in society (Johnstone, 2004). Racial groups and the disabled have been subject to discomfort, fear, discrimination, persecution, and segregation, and both groups have developed their own cultures that have their own distinct beliefs and value systems (Smith, 2004).

Disability Culture

Individuals with disabilities produce and maintain their own culture, which provides both a sense of belonging within shared experience and a common voice that allows for navigation in greater society (Johnstone, 2004). The range of differences among the disabled is immense, making the disabled community the most diverse there is. At the same time, being a member of the disabled culture is but one identity among many, such as race, ethnicity, national origin, sexual preference, etc. (Johnstone, 2004; Brown, 2010).

A disability culture acknowledges disability as a way of life, and this does not mean the existence is tragic or devalued, though society may attempt to place limitations on the disabled. Disability is not viewed as a disaster, and any discomfort disabled individuals might experience is likely to have more to do the obstacles and assumptions society makes or puts in place. Disability culture is made up of the artifacts, beliefs, and expressions created by the disabled to describe their life experience. For example, some might regard the Deaf (capitalized purposefully) as being communication disordered, yet American Sign Language (ASL) is considered a language in and of itself. While it is true ASL developed out of a need for those with hearing problems to communicate, and while it is true there may be other neurological deficits brought about by the lack of hearing, the Deaf are not necessarily disordered. Rather, they have their own language, and are capable of making contributions to society as a whole. The Deaf do not view their lack of hearing as an impairment, but rather consider themselves a linguistic minority (Johnstone, 2004; Brown, 2010).

Identity can be externally ascribed, which is a disempowering phenomenon. Down syndrome is an example of such an external classification, and these are typically created by the medical field and society as a whole. Identity can be overcompensated, which is what

87

occurs when individuals feel it necessary to overcompensate for their disabilities, such as needing to be the valedictorian because of a hearing impairment. There are identities that shift attention away from the disability, which can result in denial. This leads to the final perspective of accepting the disability as a matter of pride in an empowered identity equivalent to the concept of "Black is beautiful." In this context, the disabled become a minority group just as all the other minority groups do, and are asserting themselves to receive equal recognition, access, etc. Often, all of these identities can run together in a complex identity that is a source of both pride and scorn. In the end, disability identity must be regarded in the individual context. Disability means different things to different people (Johnstone, 2004; Michalko, 2010)

The Disabled Client

It is a great disservice to categorize the disabled as a single universal group, and there are significant bodies of knowledge that have been created among the disabled that have been ignored by the able. Individuals with disabilities have to navigate tensions between the self and socially constructed identities of everyday life on a daily basis, and therapists must be attuned to how clients perceive the disability, the extent to which these perceptions are reflected by others, clients' sense of human agency, and the support they perceive they have. Individuals with disabilities have to deal with others who may perceive the disability as a pathology and those who perceive the disability in the context of how society perceives the particular disability. There is a broad range of social and biological categories and social experiences that influences individuals' self and social perception. The therapist should learn to listen to what the disabled person says and means about the disability rather than accepting the common perceptions or misperceptions society has about the particular disability, or adhering to any particular agenda they may think is appropriate for the patient (Crisp, 2000; Shuttleworth, 2001).

In the therapeutic setting, patients should be encouraged to see themselves in relation to a problem, rather than having or being a problem, as patients have varying degrees of ability and disability within themselves. The patient will need to manage the self-perception of the disability as well as the social and biomedical perceptions of the condition, and there are multiple versions of reality. Disability should not be characterized as a pathology, a personal tragedy, or something that exists solely within the individual. At the same time, the condition should also not be regarded as existing solely outside the individual. Rather, the meaning of disability derives from shared interactions. Individuals with disabilities may not seek to assimilate into mainstream society, or accept society's norms for them, and there are many standpoints the disabled may have that differ from what the non-disabled may think (Crisp, 2000).

My Own Experience With Disability

Disability is always a potential status for every human being (Smith, 2004), and just about everyone will become disabled at some point in their lives (Garland-Thomson, 2014). All it takes is time, or being in the wrong place at the wrong time with the right circumstance. For me, it turned out this was a congenital condition. Sometime around 2003 or 2004, I was visiting relatives in Seattle, Washington during the fall. I am a Utah native, and am used to desert (i.e., arid) weather. Thus, being exposed to a more humid cold climate brought on some different body sensations, and I was suddenly bothered by a deep ache in my right hip that would not go away. One of my relatives is a retired orthopedic surgeon, and he did some manipulations of my legs, and told me, bluntly and kindly, that I would need a hip replacement. My initial reaction was one of incredulity, but I did not dismiss what he told me. Rather, when I got home, I made an appointment at a sports medicine clinic, and had an x-ray done. I remember being amazed when I saw the picture. The ball joint of my right hip looked like a melted ice cream cone, and the doctors examining me confirmed that I would need the surgery. Everyone, including me, was surprised by my condition, as I was in my early 40s at the time. The typical hip replacement patient is in their later 60s or even 70s.

This is where the story gets a bit interesting. I have trained in the martial arts since I was 16 years old, have served in the military, and have always been active. When I consulted with surgeons about the surgery, and what I would be able to do physically afterwards, the first doctors I spoke with told me I would not be able to train or run again. This was information I was unwilling to accept, and I sought a second opinion. The second doctor I spoke with told me I should be able to continue to train, which gave me some solace, as I had experienced several weeks of thinking that the life I was accustomed to living would be at an end, and I was not sure what my subsequent life might look like.

In the end, I decided I would delay the surgery as long as I could, and essentially run my joint "into the ground." The next summer I was at an international karate camp, where I was training nine hours a day with some of the best practitioners in the world. I was sitting in my dorm room kitchen after a training day was done, and realized my knee had swollen to the point where I could not see the joint. In a flash I realized my knee was compensating for the limited range of motion in my hip, and was suffering damage. I knew it was time for the surgery.

Six months later I had the surgery, and I was determined to live as much of my life as I had been used to, including training. Somewhere in this decision was something I had learned during my later teens. During that time in my life, I would work on my brother's ranch during the summers, and I recalled something that a farmer friend of my brother's had talked about. This man had lost an index finger, and was talking about being able to do about 90% of what he had been able to do with the index finger on that hand. He stated that he used the hand normally, and had not "babied it." There were some things that were not possible, such as tightening nuts in closed spaces, but otherwise he talked about "normal" use of the hand. I was similarly determined not to "baby" the joint.

This led to a few painful experiences, and to make a long story short, I had to allow my body time to heal, and either relearn how to do things, or learn new ways of doing things. I am still not "whole" or, more accurately, the way I was. I still have difficulty standing up from a kneeling position. Running remains difficult. At the same time, I can kick much better with the leg than I ever was able to do before. I always have a fun time going through metal detectors now, which was a more interesting experience in international airports.

Do I consider myself disabled? Not at all. However, in a strict sense of the definition I am, as I have a physical impairment, abilities that may lie outside of the "norm," and a prosthetic in the form of a $40,000 titanium shank in my leg. Not only that, but I had to adjust to the changes brought on by my condition.

I never sought assistance from a therapist at any time during the process. Rather, I relied on introspection and talking with friends, and prior to writing this chapter I never gave any thought to what I might have needed to hear from a therapist during the transition. In retrospect, I think what would have been the most helpful would have been assistance in finding the strength to create my life as I wanted it. I think that had anyone suggested that I accept a diminished capacity in my life it would have been the last time that person and I would have a conversation. I realize what I did was focus on my ability, even if this was redefined or remade, and even if reality dictated that the ability was not what it once was.

Disabilities

As with any disease or disorder, those who are unaffected have a dearth of understanding of what it is like to live with a particular chronic disease or disability. In the following discussions on disability due to disorders including epilepsy, multiple sclerosis, and Tourette's syndrome, information about the particular disorders will be discussed, in addition to clinical cases that illuminate first-hand accounts of the experience of living with a neurological-based disability. Such cases will not only serve to uncover aspects of individual experience that are not typically covered in the literature, but will also serve to illuminate the variability between individual experiences.

Epilepsy

Individuals with epilepsy are usually treated more like children than adults. They are not permitted to drive or live on their own, and there is pressure not to stay out late. They are viewed as different by a lot of our society and are frequently embarrassed by their seizures. Can you imagine yourself at age 15 at a party having a seizure and becoming incontinent? To this day one of our major religions will not ordain people with a history of epilepsy because of supposed possession by the devil.

Epilepsy is a chronic disorder marked by seizures; however, seizures and epilepsy are not the same thing. An epileptic seizure is a transient occurrence of symptoms due to abnormal neuronal activity. For many individuals with epilepsy, seizures vary and can co-occur with other neurological disorders as well. For individuals with epilepsy, EEG testing, medical history, and family history are all items they have to be memorized for frequent visits to the individual's neurologist. Though a seizure often affects multiple parts of the human body, it is the electrical events that occur in the brain that produce the seizure. The location of the electrical event determines the length of the seizure as well as the parts of the body involved. Having epilepsy can affect all aspects of a person's life from safety, relationships, work, and driving to much more. In this chapter, we hear the stories of individuals that have been diagnosed with epilepsy and how their situations vary. The stories from these individuals shed light on some of the difficulties within this disease and the diversity within experiences of this disease.

First look: a college student. I was first diagnosed with epilepsy when I was 14 years old. At the time, I was in the military ROTC program at my high school. We were having a military inspection and I was standing in formation when I had my first seizure. They rushed me to the hospital for my first ambulance ride. At the hospital, they asked me a lot of questions I did not know the answers to as I'm adopted. After months of testing, I learned that my biological mother used drugs while I was in the womb. As a result, I have epilepsy activated in the left occipital lobe from a blood clot in my brain at birth.

Now, more than a decade later, my seizures are well controlled, but it has not been an easy road to get here. I have had seizures in the shower that have led to concussions and a seizure in my bedroom where I hit my head on the bedframe. When I have a seizure, I feel paralyzed; I can't breathe or move my muscles. Oftentimes I have amnesia and cannot remember what happens after the seizure for at least two hours. I know now that just before I get a seizure I have an aura in my right eye. I will see flashing colors continually increasing in size and color and I know I need to find a safe place. I have a therapist that has taught me grounding techniques, such as deep breathing, that allow me to calm down, and I have had success in calming myself down enough to stop a seizure. I also know that my triggers are loud music, lasers, or television.

I have been fortunate enough in college to be accepted to study abroad in Japan, a dream come true for me. Until I got there I had a hard time filling my prescriptions. I currently take two medications to control my epilepsy and I am grateful that I have not run out of options yet. When I was in Japan, my medications were not at the pharmacy and had to be shipped to my location. Medications are expensive and insurance is very hard to get. I have a 30% copay for my medications

93

and I have to fill them every 30 days.

I'm in a relationship with epilepsy. Employers ask about it and it determines my mode of transportation. In Arizona, if I am seizure-free for one year, I can apply to have a driver's license. However, I stick with public transportation and I'm grateful that my city has a reliable public transit system. Before I found my current job, I would be asked in interviews how often I have seizures and whether I was taking medications for them. People have a fear of epileptics, as they do not know what to do when someone is having a seizure. Really, just make sure I'm lying on my side, and cushion my head. Don't try to stop my body, just let it move on its own. Track how long the seizure is and check for consciousness. As far as I know, I won't swallow my tongue—that's just a myth.

My biggest battle with epilepsy is my own self-perception based on how everyone else responds when they find out I have epilepsy. I already have challenges with my own thoughts, as I feel below everyone else because I cannot do the same activities as others. For me, I wanted to be in the military, but that's not an option anymore because of my diagnosis. Now, I'm close to graduating in May with a degree in kinesiology and I'm excited for what the future holds.

Second look: a mother. Regardless of how old someone is, I believe everyone should know more about epilepsy. For some, epilepsy is developed in childhood and can be outgrown, whereas for others, like me, it's something I'm going to deal with for the rest of my life. I live in California, by all means an "accepting" state, though I am still viewed as having a low status because I have a disability. I do not have just epilepsy either; I also have bipolar disorder. I was first diagnosed with epilepsy at age 12 and since then I have taken more than 10 different medications to manage the illness.

My first seizure was the scariest moment of my life and an event that I will never forget. My mother kept telling me "stop throwing a fit" but my body was tingling and I was forgetting what was going on around me. I was at the doctor getting my regular exam when the tingling happened again. I ended up going to the hospital and all these people kept coming and going from my room, sticking electrodes on me. Eventually the doctor came in and told my mother that I had epilepsy and would have to take medications for the rest of my life. I remember my mother sobbing as the doctor handed her a prescription for phenobarbital.

My epilepsy was well managed on this medication for years until I graduated from high school and got my first job as a front-desk assistant. I did not tell my employer that I had epilepsy, as I had faced stigma in school for my seizures. Then the day came that I had my first seizure while at work. I was called into the supervisor's office and asked why I had not told them before. I was met afterword with welcoming arms from coworkers that just wanted to understand my struggles and be supportive. I left that job to start a family with my at-the-time husband. Through weekly visits to the doctor, I was able to mother two healthy children while also having to greatly reduce my epilepsy medications during the pregnancies to limit possible birth defects from the medications. After the birth of my children, my seizures got much worse and my husband became my ex-husband.

I became a single mother and experienced 10 years of trial and error managing my seizures. My medications stopped being effective and I ended up losing my job, missing my mortgage payments, and also my drive to live. I was hospitalized in a psychiatric institution in my early 30s after my first suicide attempt. My beautiful children went to live with my mother at the request of Child Protective Services, and I never felt lower in my life. Being hospitalized, was perhaps the best thing that could have happened for me though, as I found a therapist and was able to start new medications under supervision for side effects (the most common reason I would stop taking my medications).

Today, I currently take three medications to manage my seizures: levetiracetam; lamotrigine; and valproate, as well as other medications for bipolar disorder. I work for a fast-food company, with limited hours because of my seizures. I see my therapist every two weeks, my neurologist every month, and a psychiatrist once a month. Epilepsy has been an almost three-decade learning experience for me, and just when I think I have it figured out, there's a surprise waiting for me. I'm currently battling a memory loss side effect and am in discussions with my family about whether or not moving into a group home would be the best for me. I'm scared of moving to a home with strangers and not being allowed to take my beloved pets but, for me, staying well and managing my illness is worth it.

Third look: a father's view. I think first and foremost I want people to know that there is nothing positive about epilepsy. There's nothing about epilepsy that I enjoy watching: the falls, the stitches, the ambulance, my wife screaming. Every time my cell phone rings, my heart almost stops along with it, afraid of what I will hear on the other end. Whether it's my wife, or the ambulance company saying they are on their way, or even my neighbor saying they heard sirens and asking if it's my son again.

My son had his first seizure when he was three; he's now almost 10. I remember his first fall as if it was yesterday. His beautiful blue eyes seemed to fade to grey while he was looking at me, and then he fell and started to shake. He wet himself and my wife came around the corner screaming. I remember yelling "call 9-1-1!" We went for our first ambulance ride as my son lost consciousness. We spent three days in the hospital for monitoring and got the diagnosis. Endless drug trials all ended with the seizures getting worse. My son started to ask me "Daddy, did I do something wrong to have these?" We still do not have answers for why my son has epilepsy and I'm not sure we ever will. He has frequent blood draws as his current medication is Depakote, a drug that has been most effective for him, but does have serious side effects to watch for.

In the future, I hope epilepsy research gets more funding to provide more answers and, I hope, a brighter future for my son. He is currently homeschooled, as his seizures limit his ability to attend regular school. My darkest hours are marked by thoughts of what the future holds for my son and the lack of answers we have.

Epilepsy is a common and serious neurological disorder that affects nearly 50 million individuals across the globe (Jacoby, Snape, & Baker, 2005). Epilepsy is characterized by recurrent seizures that are typically unprovoked. Generally, epileptic seizures can be classified into two main categories: those with partial onset in which the epileptic event starts in one area of the brain, and those where initial involvement is implicated in many areas (Jacoby et al., 2005). Because the types of seizures differ depending on the location of the initial activity and how it spreads, seizures can manifest as transitory breaks of attention or severe convulsions that can last for long periods of time. Even though there are significant differences between the types of epilepsy that individuals may have, perceptions about epilepsy typically implicate the classic and dramatic (i.e., grand mal) form of seizures. Of note, seizures can be effectively treated with antiepileptic drugs in the vast majority of those affected (Jacoby et al., 2005). Furthermore, after seizures have subsided for a period of time (i.e., remission), medication treatment can often be stopped. Therefore, for a significant number of individuals diagnosed with epilepsy, there is generally a positive clinical prognosis (Jacoby et al., 2005).

Conversely, for approximately 20% to 30% of individuals, seizures are impervious to treatment and these individuals are thus at higher risk for psychiatric comorbidity and reduced quality of life (Jacoby et al., 2005). Impacts on quality of life have been investigated in recent years, with results indicating that individuals with epilepsy can experience functional impact in several domains, including loss of independence (driving restrictions), changes in employment status, and social functioning, to name a few. Although most individuals who have epilepsy have a benign form, the associated stigma is prevalent across geographic locations and can have a significant negative impact on the social identity of individuals with the disorder (Jacoby et al., 2005).

In the following case, a personal account of struggling with epilepsy is presented by JB, a 50-year-old Caucasian male who was diagnosed with epilepsy when he was 49.

Mr. B grew up in a small Midwestern town and continues to reside in the same area. He has been married once; that marriage lasted for approximately 12 years. He has two children, a daughter (age 24) and a son (age 21). He reported that he does not have a relationship with his ex-wife, and did not see the need to communicate with her once their children became adults. He endorsed having a "good relationship" with his two adult children, though he expressed a desire to see them more often. He reported that his social life diminished after he stopped working. Mr. B is currently retired, but held a job as a truck driver, traveling across the U.S. He expressed that although the job was not always easy, particularly driving for several hours without a break, he very much enjoyed it. He endorsed enjoying "getting paid to explore the country." For recreation, Mr. B enjoyed flying small planes out of the local airport. However, due to his diagnosis, he is no longer able to drive or fly. In addition to reporting feelings of sadness and loss due to his inability to drive or fly, Mr. B indicated that he has experienced several instances of other people treating him differently due to his diagnosis:

> I have epilepsy and am now 50 years old. Yes, many
> days I feel like I don't like my life, but I came to the

realization that just because I have big seizures and sometimes they happen in front of people, it does not make me stupid, even though I have had a few people calling me such names or insinuating as much.

The experience of Mr. B likely illustrates the misunderstanding of his disease by others, and the resultant effect on his sense of confidence and self-efficacy, which in turn affects his socialization. Not only is Mr. B acclimating to life with more restrictions and less independence, he is immersed in an environment that is stigmatizing. Clinical implications for his experience and experiences like his are immense, as environmental contributors exacerbate his disability.

The following case is a personal account of living with epilepsy by JR, a 34-year-old Hispanic female who has lived with epilepsy since she was a child.

Ms. R currently lives in a suburban town in California with her husband and daughter. After completing high school with excellent grades, she attended a local four-year university where she obtained her bachelor's degree in sociology. Ms. R reported that she works part-time in a clothing store when her daughter is in school. She reported enjoying being a wife and mother and values the traditions of her family. She reported excellent social support from her friends and family, and indicated that though she has been medically cleared to drive since she has not experienced a seizure for about a year, her husband and friends offer to drive her anywhere she needs to go, including to work. For recreation, Ms. R expressed enjoyment from dancing, singing, and reading.

Although having seizures kind of puts a target on my back for my friends and family. . . like, if I am just listening to music or just thinking and I zone out, everyone kind of freaks out and thinks I'm going to have a seizure, so it's kind of hard to be normal in that way, but, overall, everyone has been so concerned about me and offered to do anything I need. I miss driving myself at times, but it's nice to know people will be there for you when you need them. I don't know what I would do without that support.

Several themes can be found in Ms. R's discussion about living with epilepsy. Namely, her references to social support seem to emphasize the importance of feeling supported within familial and social relationships. She described an instance of not feeling "normal" when her family reacts to the possibility of her having a seizure. Although this is indicative that her family does care about her, it may be perceived as stigmatizing and may illuminate how others with epilepsy are made to feel different, even by those they love.

Multiple Sclerosis

Multiple sclerosis is a chronic neurological disease with an array of symptoms that differ in severity from individual to individual. Particularly, while the disease can be strikingly progressive and result in severe disability in some, it can manifest more benignly in others, with fewer instances of relapses (Wenneberg & Isaksson, 2014). The onset of the disease is typically between the ages of 20-40 years, with symptoms including deficits in vision, pain, fatigue, and impaired coordination. Multiple sclerosis (MS) is generally characterized by an unpredictable prognosis, which amounts to a significant amount of stress and emotional duress. Recent literature has found that such uncertainty and emotional trauma can negatively impact the individual's self-perception and overall well-being (Wenneberg & Isaksson, 2014). Research has also demonstrated that reductions in quality of life in those with MS are not solely impacted by higher levels of disability and reduced functioning; associated cognitive difficulties and limitations in roles significantly impact satisfaction (Wenneberg & Isaksson, 2014). However, while the literature generally examines factors that contribute to quality of life, recent studies have aimed to illuminate not only the negative experiences associated with a diagnosis of MS, but positive experiences and functional adaptation as well (Wenneberg & Isaksson, 2014).

In the following case, a personal account of struggling with multiple sclerosis is presented by MT, a 31-year-old Caucasian female who was diagnosed with multiple sclerosis when she was 19:

> Having MS means that on some days I have trouble walking and I almost always feel tired even if I do nothing at all. What this means is that I can't work a typical-length work day, but, I do work part-time. You would not believe how hard it is to find good jobs where they let you work less than eight hours in sequence. I take a medication called Fingolimod, which helps me a lot, although I have to buy it, since I do not have health insurance at the moment. But it is worth it. I also have to do other things, like take rests or small naps each day. I try to get physical exercise in, like walking, but it is difficult. Obviously MS impacts me a lot. I do have a family. . . I have a husband and son, and even though my husband helps with household chores it is sometimes too much for him. I feel bad about that. We had to hire someone to come clean. . . I try to do what I used to be able to, but it's just not possible now. Still, sometimes I believe that my family does not really understand how I feel. I keep trying to do what I was able to do before MS, but it's not possible.

Ms. T's statement illuminates several salient themes, including feeling misunderstood by family, a reduced sense of self-efficacy and access to proper healthcare services, as well as guilt about not being able to contribute to her family the way she used to (i.e., shift in roles).

In the following case, a personal account of living with multiple sclerosis is discussed by RH, a 29-year-old Hispanic female who was diagnosed with multiple sclerosis when she was 20:

> One night I got very drunk and just divulged out to my brand-new boyfriend that I had MS, which was very recently diagnosed at that time. I am not sure why it came out, but all I knew when it happened was that I really couldn't lie about it or pretend that I didn't have it to someone I liked and cared about. But you know what, three years later we got married! Well, then things went bad and about one year after we got married, my symptoms turned and became very severe, and I could no longer walk. After that we went through a really rough time as my husband struggled to acknowledge I was not exactly the same girl he married. But he really loves me and so he came to the realization that beyond my symptoms and hard days and disability, I remained the same girl he loved for so long. We've stuck together and are closer than I could ever imagine.

Ms. H's account of pursuing love after an MS diagnosis revealed several important themes, particularly that it is important to consider how MS changes romantic life for those who desire to be in or already are in romantic relationships. Furthermore, gaining a better understanding of how MS symptoms might affect intimacy and sexuality is critical. Notably, individuals, regardless of MS diagnosis, maintain the need and desire to give and receive love and intimacy. Clinically, this is a critical aspect of living with MS that must be considered when working with an individual with this disease.

Tourette Syndrome

Tourette syndrome is a neuropsychiatric disorder characterized by multiple motor tics and one or more vocal tics, which may include blinking of the eyes, sniffing, clearing of the throat, and other unwanted facial movements (Ben-Ezra et al., 2017). Such tics tend to ebb and flow, depending on factors that can include stress and anxiety, and they can be temporarily suppressed. Furthermore, the tics generally follow an unwanted sensation and desire to move the particular muscles. Tourette's has a prevalence of 0.3% to 0.9% for children and 0.3% to 0.8% for adults. This is relatively low when compared to mood and psychotic disorders (Ben-Ezra et al., 2017), though there are no specific tests to diagnose Tourette's; therefore it is not always identified. Furthermore, many cases are mild, often diminishing in severity as the individual reaches adulthood. Unfortunately, like many disorders, Tourette's is highly stigmatized, in large part due to misrepresentation in the media.

In the following case, a personal account of living with Tourette syndrome is presented by MB a 34-year-old Caucasian male who has Tourette's:

> As an individual who has had Tourette's since childhood, I can tell you every day is a struggle; however, if I had a choice to be someone else I wouldn't change who I am or what I am. Hollywood is something else. They depict people with Tourette syndrome as basically retarded in the movies, which is simply not true. Tourette's doesn't impact intelligence! Something that always pisses me off is that they choose to show the worst symptoms people can have with this

103

disease. . . it's not always loud and offensive outbursts
or barking. People need to understand that oftentimes
someone can have Tourette's and you would never
know it even if they were standing next to you; we're
everyday people just like everyone else.

In Mr. B's excerpt, the impact of misrepresentation and
stigmatization is discussed, as is a desire to be treated equally with
individuals who do not have Tourette's. The clinical implications of
Mr. B's case are profound; a clinician should keep such themes in mind
when working with an individual with Tourette's, as what we think we
know about the disorder has been misrepresented in the media.

In the following case, a personal account of living with Tourette
syndrome is presented by AD, a 29-year-old Caucasian male who has
Tourette's.

I have coprolalia, which means I basically have verbal
outbursts from my Tourette's, which unfortunately
can include a variety of colorful curse words. Right
now my life is very stable, thanks to my long-standing
girlfriend, Eliza. I basically have an ideal home
situation, which helps a lot. It wasn't like that in
high school and college, though. There was so much
anxiety that I would encounter each day. I would think
to myself: If I go into this room, are there going to be
a lot of people in there? If I went into the room and
there were a lot of people, I would immediately start
having symptoms. As soon as the stress and nerves go
up, that impacts the rest of my day. When the stress
builds up, it makes the symptoms a lot worse. I would
think: Okay, you have a choice; you can try to fight
this suppress the symptom, which may help for a little

while but will actually increase stress over time or I'll just have the symptoms. But is it worth it because I'm at my cousin's first communion? Is it worth it because I'm interviewing for a job? I think that's important for other people to know, because all you see is the symptoms we either have or do not have; you have no clue about the internal struggle and battle that is always raging. Sometimes if people know you have Tourette's and you happen to not be showing any symptoms in front of them they're like, "he must be doing great." In reality, there can be this horrible internal war that is going on within. I remember this one time in my Spanish class I was trying to suppress my verbal outbursts while sitting in the back of the room. I felt like a volcano ready to erupt, and it did come out. I had no idea I could make that noise with my throat. I must have made that noise periodically for over 10 minutes, despite my teacher threatening that I better stop. After that, my parents took me to the doctor and, strangely enough, being diagnosed with Tourette's was one of the best things that has ever happened to me, because it meant that there was an actual reason for how I was feeling and my odd behaviors that I had demonstrated for the majority of my life. It gave me something to tell people when my symptoms happened in public and they just thought I was weird. Nowadays, people don't really even know I have Tourette's, so they think I'm normal. They have no idea of the debilitating fear I have of embarrassing myself every time I am around others. The anxiety is like nothing else.

Mr. D's first-hand account demonstrates several clinically relevant themes, namely the importance of social support and feeling validated. Also, feeling misunderstood by others, both when he has symptoms and when he does not, surfaced during his account. Further, it is noteworthy to examine the differences between Mr. D's and Mr. B's experiences with living with Tourette's, as it demonstrates that there is variability between individuals' experiences of living with this disorder.

Conclusions

As discussed before, exactly how disease and disability are conceptualized and treated can differ greatly, and can have immense implications for how an individual with a disability integrates into society and their quality of life. The goal of this chapter was to deconstruct assumptions, stereotypes, and a perceived universality of experience of those with a disability, particularly epilepsy, multiple sclerosis, and Tourette's syndrome, as these disorders provide insight into the impact of disease on functioning, living, and overall quality of life.

The selected disorders and cases capture some of the frequently occurring themes that individuals living with a disability experience. Individuals with a disability are a very heterogeneous group. Thus, it is critical to ensure that clinical assumptions are not made based upon what we think we know about individuals with any particular disorder, as there is significant variability between individual experiences. We encourage clinicians to keep in mind some of the themes illuminated through the cases provided, including individuals' desire for validation, relationships, and feeling understood by those around them. Further, environmental factors such as social support were found to have an immense impact on how individuals assimilate their lives with disability, as well as their overall quality of life. Another critical aspect to consider is the stigmatization of this population and the effect on their sense of self-efficacy. Lastly, this population may be susceptible to comorbidities such as depression and anxiety, which can also exacerbate symptoms and diminish quality of life.

References

Baynton, D. (2008). Disability in history. *Disability Studies Quarterly, 28*(3).

Ben-Ezra, M., Anavi-Goffer, S., Arditi, E., Ron, P., Atia, R. P., Rate, Y., & Kaniasty, K. (2017). Revisiting stigma: Exposure to Tourette in an ordinary setting increases stigmatization. *Psychiatry Research, 248*, 95-97.

Beratan, G. (2006). Institutionalizing inequity: Ableism, racism and IDEA 2004. *Disability Studies Quarterly, 26*(2).

Blanchett, W. (2010). Telling it like it is: The role of race, class, & culture in the perpetuation of learning disability as a privileged category for the white middle class. *Disability Studies Quarterly, 30*(2).

Bourke, L., & Waite, C. (2013). "It's not like I have a disability or anything!" Perceptions of disability and impairment among young, rural people. *Disability Studies Quarterly, 33*(3).

Broe, G. A., Jorm, A. F., Creasey, H., Grayson, D., Edelbrock, D., Waite, L. M., & Casey, B. (1998). Impact of chronic systemic and neurological disorders on disability, depression and life satisfaction. *International Journal of Geriatric Psychiatry, 13*(10), 667-673.

Brown, S. (2002). What is disability culture? *Disability Studies Quarterly, 22*(2).

Burchardt, T. (2004). Capabilities and disability: the capabilities framework and the social model of disability. *Disability & Society, 19*(7), 735-751.

Cherney, J. (2011). The rhetoric of ableism. *Disability Studies*

Quarterly, 31(3).

Crisp, R. (2002). A counselling framework for understanding individual experiences of socially constructed disability. *Disability Studies Quarterly, 22*(3).

Donovan, R. (2012). The global economics of disability. Return on Disability.

Garland-Thomson, R. (2014). The story of my work: How I became disabled. *Disability Studies Quarterly, 34*(2).

Gelb, S. ((2008). Darwin's use of intellectual disability in The Descent of Man. *Disability Studies Quarterly, 28*(2).

Jacoby, A., Snape, D., & Baker, G. A. (2005). Epilepsy and social identity: the stigma of a chronic neurological disorder. *The Lancet Neurology, 4*(3), 171-178.

Johnstone, C. (2004). Disability and identity: Personal constructions and formalized supports. *Disability Studies Quarterly, 24*(4).

Magiorkinis E., Kalliopi S., Diamantis, A. (2010). Hallmarks in the history of epilepsy: epilepsy in antiquity. *Epilepsy & Behavior, 17*(1), 103–108.

Mailhan, L., Azouvi, P., & Dazord, A. (2005). Life satisfaction and disability after severe traumatic brain injury. *Brain Injury, 19*(4), 227-238.

Michalko, R. (2010). What's Cool about Blindness? *Disability Studies Quarterly, 30*(3/4).

Munyi, C. (2012). Past and present perceptions toward disability: A historical perspective. *Disability Studies Quarterly, 32*(2).

Oliver, M. (2013). The social model of disability: Thirty years on. *Disability & Society, 28*(7), 1024-1026.

Shuttleworth, R. (2001). Exploring multiple roles and allegiances in ethnographic process in disability culture. *Disability Studies Quarterly, 21*(3).

Smart, J. F., & Smart, D. W. (2006). Models of disability: Implications for the counseling profession. *Journal of Counseling & Development, 84*(1), 29-40.

Smith, P. (2004). Whiteness, normal theory, and disability studies. *Disability Studies Quarterly, 24*(2).

Wenneberg, S., & Isaksson, A. K. (2014). Living with multiple sclerosis: The impact of chronic illness. *Nordic Journal of Nursing Research, 34*(3), 23-27.

4.

TRANSGENDER POPULATION

Margaret Loo, PhD

The increasing visibility of transgender people, highly publicized incidences of violence toward transgender individuals such as Brandon Teena, Gwen Araujo, and Lawrence King; the recent deaths of 49 lesbian, gay, bisexual, and transgender (LGBT) people who were killed in a Florida night club (Ring, 2017); and the fact that 29 homicides of transgender persons occurred in 2017 and 21 as of November, 2018 (Human Rights Campaign, 2018), stresses the urgency to better understand factors of prejudicial attitudes and behaviors toward transgender people. Underscoring this need is the tragic fact that 22 transgender individuals were murdered in 2016 (Ring, 2017) compared to 21 transgender and gender nonconforming people who were murdered in 2015 and 20 in 2014 (Steinmetz, 2015). One theory of the increased number of murders of transgender people is that because there is more exposure of transgender people in the media, people who have transprejudice are triggered to react.

Like other minorities, transgender individuals face stigma, prejudice, and discrimination when they come out to family, work, and the general public. The experiences of prejudice, discrimination, and microaggressions are strongly adversely associated with quality of life and mental health for transgender individuals (Institute of Medicine, 2011; Cramer, McNeil, Holley, Shumway, & Boccellari,

2012. Specifically, transgender, lesbian, and gay individuals who do not adhere to traditional gender norms can experience greater levels of discrimination and prejudice. Among sexual minorities, biological males who have not transitioned yet but display feminine characteristics in both appearance and behavior can experience an even greater amount of prejudice, discrimination, and violence due to the stigma of not conforming to traditional masculine gender roles (Nagoshi et al., 2008; Levahot & Lambert, 2007).

Additionally, it has been found that heterosexual persons who believe that gay men and lesbians have voluntarily chosen to deviate from heterosexuality are more homoprejudiced than those who believe there is a biological reason for a homosexual lifestyle (Wood & Bartkowski, 2004). The latter believe that a biological reason for being homosexual is not by choice and is something that the individual cannot change. Therefore, attribution to life-choice or biology is strongly correlated with negative or positive attitudes respectively toward political policies concerning gay rights (Wood & Bartkowski). Because transgender individuals are seen as outwardly dressing and behaving against the traditional typology of their assigned gender at birth, it may be construed as their lifestyle choice to do so, thus the potential for greater prejudicial attitudes.

It is important to understand the factors that contribute to prejudice against transgender people in order to better develop outreach programs to educate the public about transprejudice and the harm it can produce, and to train counselors, educators, employers, and social service workers to be more knowledgeable about the people they serve or hire. It would also be useful for psychotherapists not only in treating victims of transprejudice but also in understanding perpetrators of violence against transgender people. It can also aid in developing more effective programs and interventions to decrease transprejudice. Many people have limited exposure to transgender individuals, which may contribute to maintaining transgender stereotypes and stigma. Triangle Coalition President Erin Horth, stated, "Misinformation leads to discrimination," stressing awareness of transgender issues (Case, 2013).

Although there is a plethora of LGBT research that has focused on gay men and, to a lesser degree, lesbians (Meezan & Martin, 2003), there is a need for research that focuses on transgender people (Nadal, 2013). Articles often use the acronym LGBT; however transgender identity is not usually tracked or measured in the research (Nadal, 2013). It should be noted that lesbian, gay, bisexual, and transgender groups are distinct, each with their own experiences, concerns, and needs. Combining these groups under one acronym can obscure their uniqueness even though what they share is nonconformity in gender roles and sexual orientation.

There is some research that addresses transprejudice as a different construct from homoprejudice; however, despite the omission of specific measurements of transsexual issues from research on homoprejudice, it is often assumed that the findings on LGB issues will be equally informative toward the transgender population based on their shared adversarial relationship with traditional sex and gender norms (Testa et al., 2012), despite being different constructs with their own issues.

Although same-sex relationships and non-dimorphic gender orientations have existed and were accepted, even celebrated, in some parts of ancient Greece (Pickett, 2011), recent history has not been so kind. This is evidenced from recent stories of gay bashing, gay bullying, and LGBT violence, particularly the murders of transgender women, which have strongly affected LGBT people (US Department of Health and Human Services Centers for Disease Control, 2012). In the 2011 Centers for Disease Control Youth Risk Survey, it was found that LGBT youths in grades 7-12 were more than twice as likely as heterosexual youths to have attempted suicide (Centers for Disease Control and Prevention, 2011). In a pool of more than 7,500 transgender and gender nonconforming participants who responded to online and paper surveys, 41% reported attempting suicide compared to 1.6% of the general population (Grant et al., 2011). In addition, the LGBT youths who came out at a younger age, were rejected by their families, and were thrown out of the home were more likely to attempt suicide than individuals who came out as adults (Ryan & Futterman, 1998).

Although there has been a shift toward greater acceptance of lesbian, gay, bisexual, and transgender (LGBT) people in the United States (Herek & McLemore, 2013), approximately 50% of transgender adults are victims of verbal insult or abuse because of their sexual orientation or gender identity (Herek, 2009). The Federal Bureau of Investigation (2006) reported that 60% to 70% of reported abuse was directed toward gay or transgender men. In addition, LGBT people of color experience homoprejudice from their respective ethnic communities, racism from the predominantly white LGBT community, and racism and homoprejudice from society at large (National Gay and Lesbian Task Force, 2003). This magnitude of intolerance begs the question as to what factors or personality traits influence people to continue to express prejudice despite the trend toward politically correct expression concerning minority groups.

According to the 2013 FBI's Hate Crime Statistics report, there were 1,402 hate crime offenses motivated by sexual orientation bias, of which 60.6% were motivated by bias against anti-gay men; 13.2% by anti-lesbian bias; 1.9% were classified as anti-bisexual bias; 22.6% were prompted by anti-LGBT (mixed group) bias; and 1.7% as a result of anti-heterosexual bias (Federal Bureau of Investigation, 2014), insult, or abuse because of their sexual orientation or gender identity (Herek, 2009).

The impact on those who experienced transgender discrimination, according to a national survey, further demonstrates the devastating effects of receiving this form of prejudice.

A staggering 41% of respondents reported attempting suicide compared to 1.6% of the general population, with rates rising for those who lost a job due to bias (55%), were harassed/bullied in school (51%), had low household income (transgender individuals are approximately four times more likely to have a household income of less than $10,000 per year), were the victim of physical assault (61%) or sexual assault (64%) (Grant et al., 2011, p. 2).

Despite the pervasiveness of aggressive and microaggressive acts against transgender people, only 17 states and Washington DC currently have prohibitions against transgender discrimination (National Gay and Lesbian Task Force, 2013). This emphasizes the limited public awareness of how societal stigma and discrimination against transgender people affect both their physical and emotional health throughout their lives (Harper & Schneider, 2003).

It is important to understand the dynamics of prejudice against transgender individuals and whether the same variables that have been found to influence homoprejudicial attitudes can also be employed to examine transprejudice. If so, the added knowledge will facilitate developing programs and policies that help to decrease prejudice and discrimination against transgender individuals as it commensurately increases the quality of their lives.

The phenomenon of prejudice has likely existed for as long as any group of humanity has recognized that a difference existed between their neighbors and themselves; however, the term *prejudice* was first used in the 15th century (Merriam-Webster, 2014). The *Merriam Webster Dictionary* (2014) defines prejudice as a preconceived judgment and an adverse opinion formed without just grounds or before sufficient knowledge, and an irrational attitude of hostility directed against an individual, a group, a race, or their supposed characteristics. Crandall and Eshlemen (2004) defined prejudice as "a negative evaluation of a social group, or a negative evaluation of an individual that is significantly based on the individual's group membership" (p. 237). Zick, Küpper, and Höverman (2011) explained that it is irrelevant whether or not out-group members see themselves as out-group members, but that prejudice originates with the person holding or expressing negative attitudes toward out-group members. Zanna and Rempel (1988) described prejudice as an attitude consisting of a feeling of overall superiority to all out-groups and is based on three sources of information: (1) cognitive information (beliefs and values); (2) affective information (emotions associated with the object); and (3) information concerning behavior toward the object.

In his seminal book *The Nature of Prejudice,* Allport (1954) defined prejudice as "an aversive or hostile attitude toward a person who belongs to a group, simply because he belongs to that group, and is therefore presumed to have the objectionable qualities ascribed to the group" (p. 7). According to Allport (1954), the word *prejudice* underwent three stages of transformation. First derived from the Latin noun *praejudicium*, which meant "precedent," a judgment derived from previous experiences (Allport, 1954), later the English term took on the meaning to include a hasty judgment without examination of the facts. Now, the term adds the emotional aspects of favorableness or unfavorableness.

Allport (1954) describes prejudice as "an antipathy based upon a faulty and inflexible generalization. It may be felt or expressed. It may be directed toward a group as a whole, or toward an individual because he is a member of that group" (p. 9). He describes five levels of prejudicial behavior: (1) Antilocution – expressing antagonism freely with like-minded friends or strangers; (2) Avoidance – avoiding members of the out-group; (3) Discrimination – actively excluding members of the outgroup from things such as housing, employment, churches, medical attention, and other social privileges; (4) Physical attack – acts of violence toward individuals and property of the outgroup; (5) Extermination – Acts of the ultimate degree of violence such as genocide.

There is extensive research on racial prejudice. There is also an extensive literature that attempts to define racial prejudice and to categorize or describe different forms of racial prejudice. One common typology defines three types of prejudice traditionally described in the literature: aversive; ambivalent; and genuine. Kovel (1970) coined the term "aversive racism," which refers to people's support of egalitarian racial principles, thus believing they are nonprejudiced but unconsciously harboring aversive negative attitudes toward minority groups (Dovidio & Gaertner , 2000). Son Hing, Chung-yan, Hamilton, and Zanna (2008) explain that aversive racists will believe that they hold nonprejudiced beliefs and would deny having discriminatory attitudes, and yet will unconsciously hold negative attitudes and stereotypes toward out-group members. Aversive racists feel a discomfort or fear of minority groups and show avoidant and prejudicial behavior in subtle and indirect ways (Pearson, Dovidio, & Gaertner, 2009). For example, a White woman believes she is not prejudiced, yet when she sees a Black man walking toward her in daylight on a populated street, she consequently holds her purse tighter.

Katz, Whackenhut, and Hass (1986) describe "ambivalent racism," specifically toward Blacks, as American values of humanitarianism and egalitarianism influencing attitudes of sympathy toward societally disadvantaged Black people, conflicting with the values of the Protestant work ethic and individualism, and how these influence attitudes of an anti-Black effect. People with high levels of ambivalent racism exhibit high levels of both pro-Black and anti-Black attitudes. Concerning transprejudice, there may be more tolerance toward transgender males (female-to-male) because females who look and behave in a masculine manner are often considered "tomboys" and more readily accepted. However, a male who has feminine characteristics is more stigmatized and less accepted, often being called "a sissy."

The final form of racism in the popular three-part typology is "genuine racism." Genuine racism refers to an ingrained, illogical persistent belief that Blacks are inferior, with feelings of disgust and animosity toward Blacks (Sniderman & Tetlock, 1986). The expression of genuine prejudice is usually modified to meet social norms (Prentice-Dunn & Rogers, 1980). Prentice-Dunn and Rogers (1980) suggest that people often seek justifications for the expression of their prejudice to give grounds for their behavior. Therefore, if genuine prejudice is high and justification is high, then expression of prejudice will be high.

Beyond the three traditional forms of racism, genuine prejudice has morphed into subtler forms referred to as symbolic racism (Sears, 1988), also known as modern racism (McConahay, 1986). The main feature of symbolic or modern racism is rejection of blatant racism; it emphasizes a façade of egalitarian ideals due to socially acceptable attitudes (Sears & Henry, 2003). Symbolic racism consists of beliefs about Blacks, some of which are that Blacks no longer face discrimination, that they should work harder to overcome their negative situation, are too demanding, and have gotten more than they deserve (Sears & Henry, 2003). Some beliefs are stereotypical concepts, such as the idea that Black people are morally inferior to Whites and violate traditional White values such as hard work and self-reliance. The belief is that racial minorities receive an excess of resources and make demands that are unfair (McConahay, 1986). These beliefs are expressed behaviorally by covert acts such as voting against a Black candidate, or opposing affirmative action.

Because symbolic racism is not overtly linked to acts of racism directed at specific individuals but through political and social acts, the symbolic racist does not see him or herself as prejudiced; however they act in ways that are (Whitley & Kite, 2009). Sears and Henry (2003) looked at racial attitudes, political conservatism, and symbolic racism and found that the theory of symbolic racism blended racial prejudice with conservative values. Symbolic racists, in the politically correct environment of the United States, do not perceive themselves as being racist, and try to avoid the appearance of being racist. However, if they believe there is a plausible reason or rationalization, they often will discriminate (Schnake, Beal, & Ruscher, 2006).

Merton's (1948) typology on racial prejudice and discrimination describes four categories of prejudice and discrimination. Two categories describe different degrees of unprejudiced: (1) the unprejudiced non-discriminator or the "all-weather liberal"; and (2) the unprejudiced discriminator or the "fair-weather liberal." The first category, unprejudiced non-discriminator or all-weather liberal, refers to activists who work to reduce prejudice and discrimination, and the second category, unprejudiced discriminator or fair-weather liberal, refers to those who may support discriminatory efforts but feel guilt from acting against their egalitarian beliefs. The other two categories describe different degrees of prejudice: (3) the prejudiced non-discriminator or the "timid bigot"; and (4) the prejudiced discriminator or the "all-weather bigot." The prejudiced non-discriminator or timid bigot refers to those who believe in stereotypes and feel hostility toward out-groups but remain silent in the presence of unprejudiced people, and the prejudiced discriminator or "all-weather bigot" refers to those who experience no guilt or shame for their prejudiced attitudes and behavior and will discriminate and openly express their prejudiced beliefs.

Uhlmann and Nosek (2012) investigated motivational influences on cultural attributions for racial bias. They found that many people believed that spontaneous experiences of negative cognitions and emotions toward minorities are socially conditioned, providing an easy explanation for their prejudice and thus obscuring the discrepancy between their behavior toward minorities and how they "should" behave. The authors' results suggested that one of the motives for attributing racial biases to culture is ego-protection. In the face of an ego-threatening experience, participants were more likely to make cultural attributions for their racial biases. Additionally, personality traits affect willingness to accept more positive attributes that disconfirm the stereotype. Openness to experience has been found to particularly determine this attribute (Flynn, 2005).

As complex as this can be, prejudicial attitudes may not be fixed and immutable. Flynn (2005) studied how openness to experience alleviates negative stereotyping of Blacks by Whites and found that those who were more open tended to have more tolerant racial attitudes toward Blacks. He also found that three of the Big Five personality factors—extraversion, agreeableness, and conscientiousness—were not correlated with any of the measures of prejudice that he used, which were the Modern Racism Scale, the Pro-Black Scale, and the Discrimination and Diversity Scale. However, surprisingly, he found that Neuroticism was negatively correlated with the Modern Racism Scale, which suggested lower levels of prejudice for high levels of neuroticism. However, the correlation was weak and possibly merits further investigation.

Judd et al. (1995) investigated out-group homogeneity effects (stereotyping) and ethnocentrism effects among Black and White American college students. They found that Black college student participants had more negative judgments and stronger stereotypes of the Black out-group than the in-group, whereas White college student participants often showed less stereotyping of Blacks than did the Black participants.

In addition, White college participants did not show ethnocentrism.

They explained that the Black college subset might be seen as very different from the stereotypical Black; thus the unique nature of Black college students may affect White college student participants' judgment of this target group. Researchers initially suggested that the results from the White participants may be due to concerns about social desirability on their part. However, they assessed the White participants for social desirability effect and the results cast doubt on this explanation. With regard to stereotyping, they suggested that the Black students had been socialized to value their ethnic heritage and maintain cultural differences. On the other hand, the White students had been socialized to believe in equality and that it was wrong to make distinctions based on skin color. They explained that the White students had been socialized in a relatively segregated environment with limited contact with Blacks and these beliefs were easy to maintain.

When using a more diverse pool of participants from a large metropolitan area, as opposed to limiting the participants to college students, Judd et al. (1995) found that the younger Black participants demonstrated greater out-group stereotyping and ethnocentrism than the older Black participants. Conversely, the younger White participants showed less ethnic stereotyping and less ethnocentrism than their older cohorts. They suggested that White American youths were being educated to deemphasize ethnic differences and stereotyping, thus being taught to suppress ethnic stereotyping and animosity based on ethnic differences. On the contrary, the Black youths were socialized to take pride in and value their ethnicity and ethnic differences. The two groups were being socialized in opposite directions.

In addition, certain personality traits are associated with prejudice, such as agreeableness and openness, which have been found to have a negative effect on prejudice (Graziano & Tobin, 2009). In regard to one of the Big Five personality traits, openness to experience, Flynn (2005) assessed White undergraduate college student participants for their level of openness to experience and racial prejudice. He found that those who scored relatively high on openness to experience formed more favorable impressions of Black interviewees, particularly concerning Black racial stereotypes. Furthermore, White individuals who score high on openness to experience may be more receptive to stereotype-disconfirming information. People with higher levels of openness to experience are more open to seeking opportunities to learn new ideas that oppose conventionalism (McCrae, 1987). However, White individuals who score higher on openness to experience may also want to portray themselves as having a fair-minded self-image (Flynn) and succumb to social desirability when answering self-report measures for prejudice.

Transprejudice

The definition of the term "transgender" is complicated and quite broad, because it is commonly a collective term for several categories of individuals including those of mixed or blended gender identity such as crossdressers, people who live crossgender, drag kings and queens, and androgynies. Transsexual individuals usually seek social, legal, and/or medical measures to change their gender identity (Dickey, Burnes, & Singh, 2012).

Often people confuse homosexuality and transgenderism as being similar, without the knowledge that sexual orientation and gender identity are different constructs. Sexual orientation refers to the romantic or sexual attraction toward individuals of the opposite sex (heterosexual), same sex (gay or lesbian) or either sex (bisexual) (American Psychological Association, 2011a). Individuals who are transgender can be heterosexual, gay, lesbian, bisexual, or asexual. For example, if a pre-surgery transgender male (female-to-male, FTM) whose biological sex is female but who identifies as male, and is sexually or romantically attracted to a person whose biological sex is female and/or is female identified, he would consider himself to be heterosexual despite having female genitalia.

Garnets and Peplau (2002) describe three dimensions of sexual orientation: the affective dimension, the behavioral dimension, and sexual identity. The affective dimension refers to the desire and love for another person regardless of gender. The behavioral dimension refers to sexual behavior as well as forming an intimate relationship with someone. The third dimension, sexual identity, refers to an individual's self-concept of being lesbian, gay, bisexual, or heterosexual. However, the authors propose that attraction and behavior are continua from exclusively same-gender to exclusively other-gender.

On the other hand, gender identity refers to one's self-concept of being male or female or any degree in between, influenced by norms of appearance and behavior currently dominant in the person's culture. Transsexual individuals have a self-concept of being male or female that is incongruent with their biological sex. Although the way transgenderism is viewed in academia and popular culture is constantly changing, when one's gender assigned at birth is not congruent with his or her own gender self-concept, that person would be considered transgender in American society (American Psychological Association, 2011b).

Heterosexual issues are the most debated issue for heterosexual transgender people (i.e., male-to-female transsexual people attracted to males and female-to-male transsexual people attracted to females) (American Psychological Association Task Force on Gender Identity and Gender Variance, 2009). Further, lesbians have different issues than gays have due specifically to differences in gender. The problem of lumping all transgender-identified people into one group is that it obscures differences between gender nonconformity and transsexual changes due to hormone therapy and sex reassignment surgery. There are also significant issues of gender bias in this society that result in significant differences in the issues for male-to-female transsexuals and female-to-male transsexuals transitioning, and differences in the treatment of gender nonconforming women and gender nonconforming men.

The difference between biological sex and gender identity should also be explained. Biological sex refers to chromosomal identification, which is expressed, usually, through the external genitalia and internal reproductive systems. Gender identity refers to the self-concept of being male, female, or other gender. There are minimal data on the proportion of transgender people in the United States. Conway (2002) estimated that the prevalence of sex reassignment surgeries are 1:2,500 for individuals who were assigned male gender at birth and 1:7,500 who were assigned female gender at birth. Conway also estimated the intrinsic prevalence of MTF transsexualism to be approximately 1:500. However, the adults who sought treatment for gender dysphoria at specialty clinics in the United States has been quoted as 1:100,000 for transsexual women (male-to-female, MTF) and 1:400,000 for transsexual men (female-to-male, FTM) and that number is increasing (National Research Council, 2011) due to the prohibitively high cost of treatment.

These prevalence estimations have major implications for the problem of transprejudice and discrimination, as it becomes a greater problem with a larger transgender population. These estimates are based on data from medical professionals and focus on transsexual individuals who have had or are seeking gender confirmation surgery (Ettner, 1999). A 1960 survey done by a gender identity clinic in the Netherlands found the prevalence to be 1:11,900 for MTF transsexuals and 1:30,400 for FTM transsexuals by counting patients who were diagnosed as transsexual and sought sex reassignment surgery (Bakker, van Kesteren, Gooren, & Bezemer, 1993). The County of Los Angeles' Public Health Division HIV and STD programs (2012) estimated that the prevalence of transgender people is 0.1% to 0.5% of the general

United States population.

Despite the fact that transgender individuals have been portrayed in movies, television shows, and the news, rates of prejudice and discrimination against transgender people are quite high (Federal Bureau of Investigation, 2006). Aggressive and violent acts toward those who cross the sexual and rigid gender role dichotomy have become more public. The threat of violence is a common experience for transgender individuals; just being themselves is enough to provoke transphobic behavior. As a result, a transgender person is always vigilant to possible problematic situations (Betron & Gonzalez-Figueroa, 2009). Transgender women (MTF) and transgender people of color have a higher rate of experiencing discrimination and homicide than LGBT individuals generally (National Coalition of Anti-Violence Programs, 2013). This is likely due to the combination of sexism and racism with hostility toward transgender people. In fact, in 2012, lesbian, gay, bisexual, transgender, questioning (LGBTQ), and HIV-positive people of color comprised 73.1% of LGBT homicides (National Coalition of Anti-Violence Programs, 2013).

Ninety percent of transgender people reported they had experienced harassment in the workplace and, as a consequence, have economic and personal hardships (Weiss, 2011). According to the National Gay and Lesbian Task Force (2013), 78% of transgender people reported experiencing harassment or mistreatment on the job, 28% lost a job, 25% were denied a promotion, and 50% were not hired. Due to employment discrimination, transgender people are likely to experience poverty at a higher rate than the general public with 6% to 60% of the transgender population reported being unemployed and 22% to 64% of employed transgender people earning less than $25,000 per year (Badgett, Lau, Sears, & Ho, 2007). Fifty-six percent were verbally harassed in a place of public accommodation or service and 15% reported being refused medical care due to their gender identity.

Stephanie, a 40-year-old who transitioned from male to female "on the job," stated to me:

> It was difficult to transition at my workplace. In meetings where before I transitioned, I was respected and my ideas were listened to, now I am disrespected and treated as unimportant. I feel I have lost male privilege and I am discriminated against. I don't know whether it is due to being transgender or being female.

Heterosexual people may react negatively toward transgender men or women whose physical appearance does not "pass" as their self-identified gender identity. Societal stigma can manifest in different forms from overt personal and psychological behavior to derogatory and microaggressive remarks that are not in the perpetrator's awareness, such as using the incorrect pronouns (Herek, Gillis, & Cogan, 2009).

In addition, transprejudice that exists in the gay community can affect transgender individuals who identify as gay. Female-to-male transsexuals who are gay often experience oppression and discrimination by the gay community (Dickey, Burnes, & Singh, 2012). Often transgender individuals who are exploring their sexuality find themselves hindered by the transprejudice in gay communities (Dickey, Burnes, & Singh). Homoprejudice has been found to be more prevalent among heterosexual men. Bernat, Calhoun, Adams, and Zeichner (2001) suggested that these findings are due to elevated anxiety among heterosexual men toward gay men because of discomfort with gay men who express feminine characteristics as a possible threat to their masculinity.

There has been some research on factors that affect attitudes toward transprejudice such as traditional gender role attitudes (Tebbe & Moradi, 2012), cognitive rigidity (Johnson, Rowatt, Barnard-Brak, Patock-Peckham, LaBouff, & Carlisle, 2011), and socially conservative attitudes (Nagoshi et al., 2008) in relation to negative attitudes toward

LGBT individuals. Other issues of negative attitudes toward LGBT individuals that have been explored include religiosity (Herek, 1988; Hansen, 1982), intergroup contact (Pettigrew & Tropp, 2006), and negative reactions about sexuality (Black & Stevenson, 1984; Ficarotto, 1990). Furthermore, when attribution of a person's sexual orientation is to external factors (uncontrollable) it is less negatively perceived than when it is attributed to internal factors (controllable) (Tygart, 2000), which suggests that this would include attributions to being transgender. It has been found that there is a strong correlation between authoritarian attitudes and homoprejudice (Wilkinson, 2004). In addition, religious fundamentalism plays a role in homophobic attitudes (Duck & Hunsberger, 1999). However, there are few articles on how these factors affect transprejudice.

On a more general note, but applicable to LGBTs as a minority group, Altemeyer and Dion (1990) found that right-wing authoritarianism and social dominance orientation are strongly related to prejudice toward minority populations. In addition, low social dominant-oriented individuals were found to have a lower level of prejudice than those high in social dominance (Hodson, 2008). Hodson (2008) proposed that those low in social dominance have a general belief in intergroup equality and therefore are less likely to be prejudiced than those who have the view that the world is a "competitive jungle characterized by a ruthless, amoral struggle for resources and power in which might is right and winning is everything" (Duckitt, 2001, p. 69).

In reading about violent hate crimes and observing microaggressive behavior against LGBT individuals, it becomes apparent that homoprejudice and transprejudice are still an issue in our society. In 1991, 72% of public opinion on homosexual behavior considered same-sex sexual relations "always wrong" whereas in 2010, 44% considered it "always wrong" (Smith, 2011). In 2008, California briefly allowed same-sex marriages only to have them voted against (Proposition 8)

126

and made not legally recognized. In 2013, the Supreme Court ruled the Defense of Marriage Act as unconstitutional because it violated the Fifth Amendment (Peralta, 2013). Finally, in June 2015, the Supreme Court ruling invalidated Proposition 8, which allowed same-sex marriage to become federally recognized.

Concerning transprejudice, on June 9, 2010, the US Department of State approved a new policy that removed the requirement that transgender individuals were required to have had sex reassignment surgery before they could change their gender on their passports. On June 13, 2014, the Office of Personnel Management sent a letter allowing insurance companies to cover sex reassignment surgery in 2015, which is significant because, according to the Transgender Law Center (2014), sex reassignment surgery costs range from $7,000 to $50,000. However, the Office of Personnel Management stated that federal employers would be able to choose whether or not to provide such coverage and must issue a letter in writing of their decision by June 30, 2014 (Associated Press, 2014). On October 28, 2009, President Obama signed the Trans-Inclusive Hate Crimes Law, which became the first federal law providing civil rights protection for transgender people (Massachusetts Transgender Political Coalition, 2009). So, on a positive note, a sitting President has extended advocacy to the least-researched group out of the acronym LGBT, the transgender group.

Homoprejudice

Psychologist George Weinberg introduced the term "homophobia" in 1972 and it surfaces frequently in the literature in reference to an irrational condemnation of homosexual individuals resulting in discrimination and violence (Weinberg, 1972). Weinberg believed that homophobia was a fear of homosexuals and the belief that homosexuality may be contagious. In addition, he stated it is associated with the fear of the disintegration of home, family, and is a religious fear, which leads to brutality. However, the *Diagnostic Manual of*

Mental Disorders, Fifth Edition describes Specific Phobia as:

Marked fear or anxiety about a specific object or situation. The phobic object or situation almost always provokes an immediate fear or anxiety. The phobic object or situation is actively avoided or endured with intense fear or anxiety. The fear or anxiety is out of proportion to the actual danger posed by the specific object or situation and to the sociocultural context (American Psychiatric Association, 2013, p. 197).

This then begs the question, Is homophobia based on fear or prejudice?

To resolve this confusion of whether anti-homosexual responses were phobic or prejudicial, Logan (1996) suggests that the term does not refer to a phobia but rather to prejudicial attitudes. Because homophobic individuals are not diagnosed as phobic, but have attitudes of prejudice against LGB people, "homoprejudice" is a more appropriate term (Logan, 1996). Likewise, transprejudice is the term that will be used instead of transphobia to refer to anti-transgender attitudes. The high rate of violence, microaggressions, and discrimination against those communities (Nadal, 2013) underscores the importance of determining ways to decrease transprejudice. In this regard, the studies on homoprejudice can shed light on understanding transprejudice and how to address it.

Approximately 2.8% of the men and 1.4% of the women in the United States identify as homosexual or bisexual and 11% of the population report a "same sex" attraction (National Research Council, 2011). Despite the trend toward more tolerant attitudes, beliefs about homosexuality as being "wrong" still remain below 50% (National Research Council). The 2010 Gallup annual Values and Beliefs survey indicated that 43% of public opinion view same-sex relations as "always" or "almost always" wrong (Saad, 2010). However, in 1987,

82% of the public felt this way (Craig, Martinez, Kane, & Gainous, 2005). Gallup's annual Values and Beliefs survey conducted each year has documented increasing public acceptance of gay and lesbian relations since 2006 (Saad, 2010).

There have been significant gains for the LGBT community in legal rights and protections, such as the Mathew Shepard and James Byrd, Jr. Hate Crimes Prevention Act of 2009, which added sexual orientation and gender identity to federal hate crimes and made them punishable by federal law. The Don't Ask Don't Tell Repeal Act of 2010 allowed homosexual men and women to serve openly in the military. In June 2016, the ban on transgender people serving in the armed forces was lifted; and in June 2015, the Supreme Court ruling on the Defense of Marriage Act made same-sex marriage legal in the United States; and on June 26, 2015, adoption by same-sex couples was legalized. Also, in July 2014, President Obama added federal protection from discrimination in hiring and employment for LGBT people. Despite these gains, there are still only 27 states that specifically include transgender people in their anti-discrimination laws (American Civil Liberties Union, 2016).

In 2012, 7,164 hate crimes were reported by law enforcement agencies, including offenses of vandalism, intimidation, assault, rape, and murder, of which 3,467 were racially motivated and 1,376 were due to sexual orientation bias (Federal Bureau of Investigation, 2013). Gay people of color are particularly impacted by prejudice because they face multiple forms of discrimination based upon their race, sexual orientation, gender identity, and gender expression (Harper, Jernewall, & Zea, 2004). In addition to overt prejudicial acts, people often exhibit microaggressive behaviors. Sue et al. (2007) describe microaggression as "brief and commonplace daily verbal, behavioral, or environmental indignities, whether intentional or unintentional, that communicate hostile, derogatory, or negative slights and insults toward members of oppressed groups" (p. 273), such as a stranger asking a third-generation Japanese American woman how she likes it here in the United States compared to her country, negating her American heritage. The main difference between a microaggression and an overt racist action is the intent and consciousness of the person that is committing the act (Nadal, 2013). The person committing the overt racist action is purposefully attacking the target person, whereas the person committing a verbal or behavioral microaggressive act may not even be cognizant of the derogatory action committed automatically or unconsciously.

For instance, if a teenager criticizes his friend and tells him "that's gay," the teenager may not intentionally mean it to be derogatory toward gay males per se, despite the fact that when confronted by a teacher and reprimanded, he may realize he should not have said it. However, this would be a microaggression if a homosexual male overhears the remark and would understand it as derogatory toward gay people—this despite the fact that the teenager may not be aware that he has done anything wrong.

According to the Institute of Medicine's 2011 literature review report on the health status of LGB people, due to homoprejudice and stigma, LGB people experience more mood and anxiety disorders, and increased risk for suicidal ideation and suicide attempts compared to heterosexual people. Little research has examined the prevalence of mood and anxiety disorders among transgender people. However, Clements-Nolle, Mars, Guzman, and Katz (2001) interviewed 392 male-to-female and 123 female-to-male transgender individuals and found an increased rate of suicidal ideation and suicide attempts among transgender people compared to the heterosexual population.

In addition, several studies have found that heterosexual males tend to be more homoprejudicial than heterosexual women, especially toward gay males (Herek, 1988; Kite, 1984). Herek (1988) found that people viewed gay males more negatively compared to lesbians due to anti-effeminate male bias. If these factors of homoprejudice relate to gender norm violations, then it can be inferred that people would have similar views about MTF transsexuals.

People who tend to be dogmatic possess a closed mindset that blocks acceptance of people or ideas that stray from their norms (Maykovich, 1975). Cullen, Wright, and Alessandri (2002) investigated attitudes and behaviors that differentiate those who are homoprejudicial from those who are more accepting of alternative lifestyles. They found that the personality factor of openness to experience and previous contact with homosexual people are critical factors in identifying those likely to express homoprejudice. They explained that having an open cognitive structure may allow for more contact with gay men or lesbian women, thus eliminating the mystery and fears that they may have. On the other hand, they found that participants who had less contact with homosexual people were more likely to be homoprejudiced.

Research has also shown that, among heterosexual people, right-wing authoritarianism is strongly correlated with homoprejudice. High authoritarians have self-righteous attitudes, maintain traditional Judeo-Christian values, and have aggressive tendencies toward those who threaten those traditional values (Altemeyer, 1981). Franssen, Dhont, and Van Hiel (2012) found that older people tend toward authoritarianism and traditional values, and that age is positively correlated with racial prejudice and is mediated by right-wing attitudes.

Personality Traits Related to Prejudice

Whitley and Kite (2009) propose a cognitive theory of prejudice in which people develop an "us versus them" attitude. In line with this notion of prejudice as a learned response, prejudice has roots in early childhood when children form a sense of group membership, for instance, around race, religion, neighborhood, socioeconomic status, and culture. Prentice-Dunn and Rogers (1980) suggest that deindividuation by group membership lowers self-awareness and weakens suppression of prejudiced behavior. True to the malleable nature of their youth, children are also expected to acquire their parents' loyalties and prejudices. Allport (1954) theorized that people usually identify with their parents, and with their own race, religion, neighborhood, and cultural traditions. There is a sense of ego-protection and belonging in identifying with their in-group; as such it is beneficial for people to evaluate their in-group more positively than the out-group. There is a generalized tendency for people who express prejudice toward one group to also express prejudicial behavior toward other groups, suggesting that people who are racially prejudiced or homoprejudiced can also be transprejudiced (Akrami, Ekehammer, & Bergh, 2010).

Two general hypotheses concerning the relationship between childhood attachment and religiosity are (a) the Compensation Hypothesis and (b) the Correspondence Hypothesis, both derived from attachment theory (Kirkpatrick, 1992). The Compensation Hypothesis posits that individuals who have experienced insecure attachment in childhood with their primary caretaker have a greater need to compensate for an attachment relationship in order to gain a sense of security and to regulate distress. On the other hand, the Correspondence Hypothesis refers to a secure attachment experienced in childhood that has established the foundation upon which a corresponding relationship with a religious figure could be built (Granqvist, 2002).

A study by Kirkpatrick and Shaver (1990) found that people who reported having insecure attachment histories were found to be more religious if their parents displayed low levels of religiosity, whereas those who reported having secure histories were found to be more religious when their parents had high levels of religiosity (Kirkpatrick & Shaver, 1990). They explained, "Much like an infant's primary caregiver, God may serve as a secure base and as a safe haven of safety and comfort for believers" (Kirkpatrick & Shaver, 1992, p. 267).

Streyffeler and McNally (1998) investigated the difference between the personality characteristics of liberal versus fundamentalist Protestant Christians. Participants recruited from a liberal church and a fundamentalist church completed the NEO-FFI. The authors found little difference between the two groups in terms of personality characteristics of neuroticism, agreeableness, conscientiousness, and extraversion. However, they found significant differences in openness to experience. The fundamentalists scored significantly lower than the liberals on openness to experience.

In addition, individuals high in religious fundamentalism were found to have higher levels of prejudice and were reported to have strong childhood training in their religion (Altemeyer, 2003). This suggests that the emphasis on family religion may be related to "us-them" discriminations (Altemeyer, 2003, p. 17). The characterizations of being closed-minded and unwilling to question beliefs or consider other points of view are linked to religious fundamentalists (English, 1996).

Funder (2001) describes personality as a people's patterns of thought, emotion, and behavior and the psychological mechanism behind them. The Big Five personality traits consist of extraversion, agreeableness, conscientiousness, neuroticism, and openness to experience. Extraversion refers to people who have good social skills, are friendly, and whose behavior draws attention to themselves (Ashton, Lee, & Paunonen, 2002). Agreeableness refers to people who are cooperative, empathic, and enjoy being with others (Dupue & Morrone-Strupinsky, 2005). Perry and Sibley (2012) studied whether personality traits predicted social dominance orientation and right-wing authoritarianism and found that low Agreeableness predicted group dominance and superiority, otherwise known as social dominance orientation (SDO). Conscientiousness refers to people

133

who are goal-directed, persistent, and are attentive to details (Jensen-Campbell, Iyer-Eimerbrink, & Knack, 2015). Jensen-Campbell, Knack, Waldrip, and Ramirez (2009) found that people who have a low level of conscientiousness tend to express anger aggressively and have poor self-control, which predicts victimization. Neuroticism refers to emotional instability and people with a high level of neuroticism tend to be anxious, moody, and depressed. They also tend to have negative perceptions of others and thus have negative interpersonal relationships. Heritability of these traits, from twin studies research, is estimated to be 50% (Bouchard, 2004).

According to the Big Five Model of Personality, Openness to Experience refers to adjusting to new ideas and situations from the attitudinal and behavioral norms of society (Digman, 1990). People who are high in Openness to Experience prefer novelty, variety, and more intense experiences (McCrae & Costa, 1997). Perry and Sibley (2012) found that a high level of Openness to Experience negatively predicted right-wing authoritarianism. Recent studies have found an inverse relationship between openness to experience and homoprejudice (Miller, Wagner, & Hunt, 2012; Cramer, Miller, Amacker, & Burks, 2013). In addition, those who have low levels of openness tend to adhere to rigid and conventional beliefs as well as cognitive closure, suggesting a right-wing authoritarianism and prejudice pathway.

Influences of Right-wing Authoritarianism and Social Dominance Orientation on Prejudice

Research has provided support for SDO and RWA personality types that explain prejudice (Altemeyer, 1998; Whitley, 1999). Authoritarian personality and social dominance orientation have been major factors in predicting prejudice toward ethnic and sexual minority groups (Altemeyer, 1998). Individuals high in right-wing authoritarianism (RWA) tend to adhere to traditional values and submit to authority. They also tend to view the world as a dangerous place and harbor negative attitudes toward people who violate conventional norms (Altemeyer, 1998). People who are high in RWA have an intense yet insecure attachment to their group that demands strict and rigid group cohesion. Those who have a higher sense of subordination to the group tends to have a stronger perception that the group is an extension of themselves and are more likely to discriminate (Parkins, Fishbein, & Ritchey, 2006).

Social dominance orientation refers to a preference for group hierarchies with in-group domination over out-groups (Jackson & Poulsen, 2005) and a belief that in-groups deserve superior treatment, which increases aggression toward out-groups (Parkins, Fishbein, & Ritchey, 2006). People that belong to social groups that are higher in the hierarchy display a higher level of in-group bias than those that belong to lower level groups (Sidanius & Pratto, 1999).

Cramer, Miller, Amacker, and Burks (2013) found a linkage between rigid thinking, low degree of openness to experience, and strong right-wing authoritarianism to homoprejudice. In fact, not only is right-wing authoritarianism positively correlated with antigay prejudice, it may be the strongest predictor of homoprejudice (Whitley & Lee, 2000). Right-wing authoritarianism involves an individual's level of conventionalism, authoritarian aggression, and authoritarian submission (Heaven & Quintin, 2003). Indeed, those with high right-wing authoritarianism are rigid on several issues, such as viewing unfamiliar and marginal out-groups as immoral or unworthy of equal treatment (Altemeyer, 1988). In addition, RWA has been associated with aggressive behavior toward out-groups (Whitley, 1999), and studies have also revealed that people with high RWA tend to endorse traditional sex roles (Altemeyer, 1996).

Heaven and Quintin (2001) studied the extent of prejudice toward Asians and Australian Aborigines determined by right-wing authoritarianism, social dominance orientation, and factors of either personal or national group identity salience using 174 volunteer Australian psychology student participants. They found that right-wing authoritarianism and social dominance were significant predictors of racial prejudice in different ways. Social dominance orientation was a greater predictor than right-wing authoritarianism when the participants self-identified as Australians rather than as individuals. According to the principles of social dominance theory, people with a high level of social dominance orientation are more supportive of inequitable social hierarchies and are more likely to apply discriminatory ideologies (Sidanius & Pratto, 1999).

Based on measures of SDO, people who have higher levels of SDO tend to be more conservative, more patriotic and more prejudiced and show a strong relationship between SDO and homoprejudice (Whitley & Lee, 2000), whereas those who score low on SDO are more favorable to gay and women's rights and other equitable social programs. Guimond, Dambrun, Michinov, and Duarte (2003) found that SDO is relative to people's location in the social hierarchy, and the more dominant the position, the more prejudiced people are. It has been debated that prejudiced attitudes toward different groups influence levels of SDO; however, after conducting a longitudinal study, Kteily, Sidanius, and Levin (2011) found that SDO is indeed influenced by different social contexts. SDO chronically predicts prejudicial attitudes and behaviors that perpetuate hierarchy among those groups.

Religious Fundamentalism in Relation to Prejudice

Although it has long been known that religious people tend to be prejudiced against homosexual people (Allport & Ross, 1967), investigators are looking at what subset of religious people are distinctly prejudiced. In this regard, religious fundamentalism is another factor that may affect attitudes toward transsexual people. Religious fundamentalism refers to absolute and unquestionable religious beliefs (Altemeyer & Hunsberger, 1992).

Altemeyer (1996) described religious fundamentalism as an attitude toward religious beliefs as opposed to the set of beliefs themselves. Altemeyer and Hunsberger (2004) suggested that religious fundamentalism is a religious form of authoritarianism and right-wing authoritarianism that mediates the relationship between religious fundamentalism and various forms of prejudicial attitudes. Similar to the right-wing authoritarian embrace of traditional values, the beliefs of religious fundamentalists provide consistency and closure, and in order to protect this certainty, out-groups that challenge this consistency are rejected. Fundamentalist groups' need for closure partially mediated their derogation of gays and lesbians (Brand & Reyna, 2010). Altemeyer (2003) found that religious fundamentalism highly correlated with religious ethnocentrism, hostility toward homosexuals, and racial prejudice.

Religious views on homosexuality are partly based on the scriptures in the Old Testament: Genesis 19:5-8; Leviticus 18:22 and 20:13; and the New Testament: Romans 1.26-27; and 1Corinthians 6.9, and it is important to be knowledgeable about the different interpretations of these scriptures. When taken in context, references in the scriptures to same-sex sexual behavior address the issue of gender role distinction (Sayler, 2005). These scriptures are referred to as "proof" of condemnation of homosexuality by many religious fundamentalists, and the debate as to what these verses mean has come to an impasse (Sayler, 2005).

Johnson, Rowatt, and LaBouff (2010) examined the direct effect of religion on racial attitudes and hypothesized that participants primed with Christian words such as heaven, salvation, and God would self-report more racial prejudice than participants primed with neutral words, even when controlling for the effects of preexisting levels of religiousness and spirituality. The authors completed a lexical decision task designed to subliminally prime Christian or neutral concepts.

Immediately after being primed, the participants were administered a series of items that assessed feelings toward Blacks using the Racial Argument Scale. They found that activation of Christian religious concepts increased subtle and overt prejudice toward Blacks.

Jonathan (2008) examined the influence of religious fundamentalism, right-wing authoritarianism, and Christian orthodoxy on measures of attitudes toward homosexuals. He defined religious fundamentalism as "restrictive religious ideologies" (p. 318) and Christian orthodoxy as "the internalization of Christian beliefs" (p. 318). He found that religious fundamentalism was a strong predictor of explicit negative attitudes toward homosexuals in a pool of University of Davis students. In addition, he found that religious fundamentalism and right-wing authoritarianism predicted higher levels of homoprejudice, whereas Christian orthodoxy predicted lower levels.

Kite and Whitley (2008) also identified religious fundamentalism as a factor that is correlated with homoprejudice. They found that people who believe that homosexuality is a lifestyle choice are more likely to have a higher level of homoprejudice than people who believe biology is a factor that determines homosexuality. In general, those who are true believers in their religion tended to be authoritarians. Altemeyer (1988) suggests that this is an extension of people's submitting to the established authorities in their lives. Religious fundamentalists were found to reject gays and lesbians even if they were celibate, and they rejected homosexuals who are not celibate more than heterosexuals who had sex outside of marriage (Fulton, Gorsuch, & Maynard, 1999).

Although religious fundamentalism and right-wing authoritarianism have been widely researched as predictors of prejudice against racial minorities and homosexuals, Laythe, Finkel, and Kirkpatrick (2002) found that while authoritarianism was a strong positive predictor of both forms of prejudice, religious fundamentalism was found to be a negative predictor of racial prejudice and a positive predictor of homoprejudice.

They suggested that Christian fundamentalism consists of authoritarian beliefs and also a component related to Christian beliefs that discourages some forms of prejudice including racial prejudice but not other forms such as homoprejudice, which in part may be because of evangelical pursuits. Rowatt and Franklin (2009) found that general religiousness strongly correlated with homoprejudice and negligibly toward racial prejudice among a national random sample of American adults. This remained true when right-wing authoritarianism and demographics such as age, income, education, and gender were controlled.

Stefurak, Taylor, and Mehta (2010) found that religious fundamentalism as a correlate to homoprejudice is more common in females, and discrepancy from masculine gender roles as a correlate to homoprejudice is specific to males. Right-wing authoritarianism is a universal correlate of homoprejudice. Right-wing authoritarianism and religious fundamentalism have been found to have a strong correlation with one another (Altemeyer, 1996). In a meta-analysis, Whitley (2008) found that individuals who have high levels of religious fundamentalism report a higher level of anti-homosexual attitudes. As such, since some boundaries of transgender and homosexual issues are blurred, religious fundamentalism was found to also relate positively with transprejudice.

Age Relative to Prejudice

Race, gender identity, and sexual orientation are categorizations that define who we are, yet age is something all of us experience. There is limited research on how age affects prejudicial attitudes, but previous studies have shown that older people tend toward right-wing authoritarianism and prejudicial attitudes (Henry & Sears, 2002). In addition, earlier generations tend to have more traditional attitudes compared to younger generations that have more accepting attitudes toward LGBT individuals (NORC, 2011).

Concerning homoprejudice, the zeitgeist of when people were

developing values and beliefs affects their current attitudes toward LGBT people (Institute of Medicine, 2011). During the 1940s, sodomy laws criminalized same-sex behavior and, by 1960, sodomy was outlawed in every state (Loftus, 2001). In 1953, President Eisenhower declared homosexuality was grounds for dismissal from federal employment, and this status lasted until 1993 (The Williams Institute, 2001). In 1952, the first *Diagnostic Statistical Manual of Mental Disorders* was published, listing homosexuality as a serious mental disorder (American Psychiatric Association, 1952). Therefore, people currently over 60 years of age grew up in an atmosphere in which homosexuals were viewed as criminals who were seriously mentally ill.

Subsequent to that period, on June 28, 1969, police raided the Stonewall Inn, a gay bar in Greenwich Village, New York. The patrons there rioted in protest and, in the aftermath, gay and lesbian groups throughout the country began to organize (Dunlap, 1999). In 1986, homosexuality as a diagnosis of a mental disorder was completely removed from the American Psychiatric Association's *Diagnostic and Statistical Manual of Mental Disorders, Third Edition* (Herek, 2012). After 1991, public attitudes toward homosexuality began to change toward greater acceptance (Loftus, 2001; Smith, 2011). It is hypothesized that because of the greater degree of homoprejudice and discrimination in American society in previous decades, older individuals who lived through that period have a higher level of homoprejudice than younger individuals.

Cohort effects also influence changes in Big Five personality factors. There has been an increase in extraversion through the years (Twenge, 2001). There has also been an increase in neuroticism (Goodwin, 2003), but no difference in openness to experience (Smits et al., 2011). However, there is the problem of the social desirability effect, which refers to answering questions in a favorable way as to not appear prejudiced. The aging process often involves deterioration of the frontal neural substrates, which control executive functioning. Executive functioning in this instance refers to the ability to inhibit impulsive behavior as a reaction to thought processes that clash with goals. Loss of executive control can lead to socially inappropriate behavior and responses (Henry, von Hippel, & Baynes, 2009). It can also lead to increased stereotyping and prejudice (von Hippel, Silver, & Lynch, 2000).

Cunningham et al. (2004) found that when Black and White faces were flashed in front of participants, the Black faces evoked a stronger activation in the prefrontal cortex and anterior cingulate cortex areas, which are associated with executive functions such as inhibition (Beauregard, Lévesque, & Bourgouin, 2001). Richeson and Shelton (2003) found that, after an interaction with a Black partner, White participants who had strong racial bias on implicit measures of race attitudes showed more impaired performance on executive control measures than those who showed less bias. The authors suggest that this was due to a depletion of executive control capacity from the demands of interacting with a Black partner. Von Hippel, Silver, and Lynch (2000) found that elderly people were more prejudiced and tend to rely on stereotyping more than young people, and these differences were mediated by age differences in inhibitory ability. They suggested that because elderly people expressed a stronger desire to control their prejudiced reactions than young people, age-related inhibitory failure can cause the elderly to have more prejudicial reactions than desired.

Older adults are often stereotyped as "speaking their mind" in a socially inappropriate fashion (von Hippel & Dunlop, 2005). Von Hippel and Dunlop (2005) studied diminished ability for inhibitory functioning associated with socially appropriate behavior. They found that the ability to differentiate between public and private settings was less likely in older participants compared to younger participants. This was associated with decreased closeness with their peers because of social inappropriateness, which may cause others to avoid interaction with them. The authors suggest that decreased inhibitory ability in older adults may lead to unintentional social inappropriateness. This suggests that less inhibitory control may lead to inappropriate utterances including those that reveal genuine prejudice.

Hasher and Zacks (1988) found that cognitive deficits due to aging create the loss of ability to inhibit inappropriate information. This can lead to uninhibited expression of stereotypes and prejudice due to older adults' decreased ability for restraint in expressing politically incorrect beliefs. On the same note, Gonsalkorale, Sherman, and Klauer (2009) found that older adults showed greater implicit bias due to decreased ability to regulate automatic associations as opposed to holding greater associations.

Impact of Exposure to Other Groups on Prejudice

In 1954, Allport introduced the intergroup contact theory. The concept that exposure to transgender people can influence people's attitudes about transgenderism is congruent with the contact hypothesis, which postulates that prejudicial attitudes and stereotypes against members of a minority group is decreased by equivalent-status contact between majority and minority groups in the pursuit of a common goal (Allport, 1954). Contact with a diverse population also produces the effect of self-expansion.

In a meta-analysis of intergroup contact theory in 2006, Pettigrew and Tropp found that intergroup contact reduces prejudice (Pettigrew & Tropp, 2006). In addition, the quality of contact rather than the quantity significantly reduced the level of SDO and prejudice (Dhont, Van Hiel & Hewstone, 2014).

Similarly, Lowery, Hardin, and Sinclair (2001) investigated the "social tuning effect" of interracial contact by measuring the automatic prejudice and stereotyping tendencies of European Americans in the

142

presence of a Black experimenter compared to a White experimenter. They tested the hypothesis that social influence affects automatic prejudice. They found that European American participants exhibited less automatic prejudice (unintentional and unconscious negative feelings and stereotyping of minorities) in the presence of a Black experimenter than a White experimenter, as measured by the Implicit Association Test (Greenwald, McGhee, & Schwartz, 1998). They suggest the possibility of influencing societal change not by focusing on changing people's attitudes but rather on the situations that create these attitudes. Relating to homoprejudice, Wood and Bartkowski (2004) found that the only form of exposure that influences increased support is having a close gay or lesbian friend.

Summary

Despite extensive research regarding the factors that influence racial prejudice and homoprejudice, comparatively less research has focused on its relevance to transprejudice. Although studies in racial prejudice have served as a guide to prejudice in general, we have seen in the case of religious fundamentalism where its correlation to racial prejudice was small compare to homoprejudice, because although there is the expectation of doing good and to assuage their prejudice, religious fundamentalists view homosexuality as a threat to their religious beliefs (Hunsberger & Jackson, 2005). This underscores the need for studies such as this one with a sharp focus on transprejudice in order to better understand it in relation to, and apart from, general LGB issues. Focused studies also give voice to issues that the transgender community may not otherwise be inclined to pursue owing to their general desire to "pass" and live "under the radar" in their post-operation gender status rather than calling attention to themselves as "transsexual." In this aspect they differ from the gay-lesbian community, generally preferring anonymity to activism, but this may also contribute to their problems when they are "outed" by hostile transprejudiced acquaintances.

There is a higher percentage of suicidal ideation and attempts among LGBT people that is influenced by social stigma, prejudice, and discrimination. It is therefore important to understand these factors in an effort to improve education programs for the public, perhaps by encouraging inclusion and discouraging microaggression. Mental health professionals might also better serve transgender clients by understanding the perpetrators of transprejudice, actual or potential, who would cause them grief and perhaps suggest alternatives. Determining correlations between the variables of some of the factors that have been found to predict racial prejudice with regard to individuals who are transgender may increase understanding and can begin to improve quality of life for transgender people.

References

Adams, H., Wright, L.W. Jr., Lohr, B. A. (1996). Is homophobia associated with homosexual arousal? *Journal of Abnormal Psychology, 105*, 440-445.

Akrami, N., Ekhammer, B., & Bergh, R. (2010). Generalized prejudice: Common and specific components. *Psychological Science, 22*, 57-59.

Allport, G. (1954). *The nature of prejudice.* New York: Perseus Books.

Altemeyer, B. (1981). *Right-wing authoritarianism.* Winnipeg, Ontario, Canada: University of   Manitoba Press.

Altemeyer, B. (1988). *Enemies of freedom.* San Francisco, CA: Jossey-Bass.

Altemeyer, B. (1996). *The authoritarian specter.* Cambridge, MA: Harvard University Press.

Altemeyer, B. (1998). The other "authoritarian personality." In M. Zanna (Ed.), *Advances in experimental social psychology* (Vol.

30, pp. 47-92). San Diego, CA: Academic Press.

Altemeyer, B. (2003). What Happens When Authoritarians Inherit the Earth? A simulation. *Analyses of Social Issues and Public Policy.* Retrieved September 6, 2013 from http://www.overcominghateportal.org/uploads/5/4/1/5/5415260/when_rwa_inherit_the_earth.pdf

Altemeyer, B. (2003). Why do religious fundamentalists tend to be prejudiced? *International Journal for the Psychology of Religion, 13,* 17-28.

Altemeyer, B., & Dion, K. (1990). Enemies of freedom: Understanding right-wing authoritarianism//review. *Canadian Psychology, 31,* 374-377.

Altemeyer, B., & Hunsberger, B. (1992). Authoritarianism, religious fundamentalism, quest, and prejudice. *International Journal for the Psychology of Religion, 2,* 113-133.

Altemeyer, B., & Hunsberger, B. (2004). A revised religious fundamentalism scale: The short and sweet of it. *The International Journal for the Psychology of Religion, 14,* 47-54.

American Civil Liberties Union. (2016). *Know your rights: Transgender people and the law.* Retrieved September 23, 2016 from https://www.aclu.org/know-your-rights/transgender-people-and-law

American Psychiatric Association (2013). *Diagnostic and statistical manual of mental disorders, fifth edition.* Arlington, VA: American Psychiatric Association.

American Psychological Association (2011a). Definition of terms: Sex, gender, gender identity, sexual orientation. Retrieved November 29, 2013 from www.apa.org/pi/lgbt/resources/sexuality-definitions.pdf

American Psychological Association (2011b). Guidelines for Psychotherapy with lesbian, gay, and bisexual clients. Retrieved

December 9, 2013 from www.apa.org/practice/guidelines/
glbt.pdf

American Psychological Association Task Force on Gender Identity
and Gender Variance. (2009). *Report of the task force on gender
identity and gender variance.* Washington, DC: Author.

Ashton, M., Lee, K., & Paunonen, S. (2002). What is the central feature
of extraversion? Social attention versus reward sensitivity.
Journal of Personality   and Social Psychology, 83, 245- 252.

Associated Press (2014). Without fanfare, Obama advances transgender
rights. Retrieved June 24, 2014 from http://nj1015.com/
without-fanfare-obama-advances-transgenderrights/

Badgett, M.V., Lau, H., Sears, B., & Ho, D. (2007). Bias in the workplace:
Consistent evidence of sexual orientation and gender identity
discrimination. Retrieved November 13, 2013 from https://
williamsinstitute.law.ucla.edu/wp-content/uploads/Badgett-
Sears-Lau-Ho-Bias-in-the-Workplace-Jun-2007.pdf

Bakker, A., van Kesteren, P., Gooren, L, & Bezemer, P. (1993).
The prevalence of transsexualism in the Netherlands. *Acta
Psychiatrica Scandinavica, 87*, 217-238.

Beauregard, M., Lévesque, J., & Bourgouin, P. (2001). Neural
correlates of conscious self-regulation of emotion. Retrieved
March 7, 2014 from http://www.jneurosci.org/content/21/18/
RC165.full.pdf+html?sid=f3a396f2-5d31-49bc- b 8 7 c -
7f6ffd0cee54

Bernat, J., Calhoun, K, Adams, H., & Zeichner, A. (2001). Homophobia
and physical aggression toward homosexual and heterosexual
individuals. *Journal of Abnormal Psychology, 110*, 179-187.

Betron, M., & Gonzalez-Figueroa, E. (2009). Gender Identity, violence,
and HIV among MSM and TG: A literature review and a call
for screening. Washington, DC: Futures Group International.

Black, K., & Stevenson, M. (1984). The relationship of self-reported sex role characteristics and attitudes toward homosexuality. In J. De Cecco (Ed.), *Homophobia: An overview* (pp. 83-93). Philadelphia, PA: Hawthorne Press.

Bouchard, T. J., Jr. (2004). Genetic influence on human psychological traits: A survey. *Current Directions in Psychological Science, 13*, 148-151.

Case, A. (2013). Transgender awareness week promotes education, remembrance. *The Maneater*. Retrieved April 28, 2013 from http://www.themaneater.com/stories/2009/11/17/transgender-awareness-week-promotes-education-reme/

Centers for Disease Control and Prevention (2011). Lesbian, gay, bisexual, and transgender health. Retrieved February 22, 2013 from http://www.cdc.gov/lgbthealth/youth.htm

Clements-Nolle, K., Mars, R., Guzman, R., & Katz, M. (2001). HIV prevalence, risk behaviors, health care use, and mental health status of transgender persons: Implications for public health intervention. *American Journal of Public Health, 91*, 915-921.

Conway, L. (2002). How frequently does transsexualism occur? Retrieved September 15, 2014 from http://ai.eecs.umich.edu/people/conway/TS/TSprevalence.html

Craig, S., Martinez, M., Kane, J., & Gainous, J. (2005). Core values, value conflict, and citizens' ambivalence about gay rights. *Political Research Quarterly, 58*, 5-17.

Cramer, J., McNiel, D., Holley S., Shumway, M., & Boccellari, A. (2012). Violent crime victims: Does sexual orientation matter? *Law and Human Behavior, 36*, 87-95.

Cramer, R., Miller, A., Amacker, A., & Burks, A. (2013). Openness, right-wing authoritarianism, and antigay prejudice in college students: A meditational model. *Journal of Counseling Psychology, 60*(1), 64-71.

Crandall, C., & Eshleman, A. (2004). The justification-suppression model of prejudice: The history of prejudice research. In C. Crandall & M. Schaller (Eds.), *Social psychology of prejudice: Historical and contemporary issues.* Lawrence, Kansas: Lewinian Press.

Cullen, J., Wright Jr., L., & Alessandri, M. (2002). The personality variable openness to experience as it relates to homophobia. *Journal of Homosexuality, 42,* 119-134.

Cunningham, W. A., Johnson, M. K., Raye, C. L., Gatenby, J. C., Gore, J. C., & Banaji, M. R. (2004). Separable neural components in the processing of Black and White faces. *Psychological Science, 15,* 806-813.

Dhont, K., Van Hiel, A., & Hewstone, M. (2014). Changing the ideological roots of prejudice: Longitudinal effects of intergroup contact on social dominance orientation. *Group Processes Intergroup Relations, 17,* 27-44.

Dickey, L., Burnes, T., & Singh, A. (2012). Sexual identity development of female-to-male transgender individuals: A grounded theory inquiry. *Journal of LGBT Issues in Counseling, 6,* 118-138.

Digman, J. M. (1990). Personality structure: Emergence of the Five-Factor Model. *Annual Review of Psychology, 41,* 417-440.

Dovidio, J., & Gaertner, S. (2000). Aversive racism and selection decisions: 1989 and 1999. *Psychological Science, 2,* 315-319.

Duck, R. J., & Hunsberger, B. (1999). Religious orientation and prejudice: The role of religious proscription, right-wing authoritarianism, and social desirability. *The International Journal for the Psychology of Religion, 9,* 157-179.

Duckitt, J. (2001). A dual-process cognitive-motivational theory of ideology and prejudice. *Advances in Experimental Social Psychology, 33,* 41-113.

Dunlap, D. (1999). Stonewall, gay bar that made history, is made a landmark. *New York Times*, June 26.

Ettner, R. (1999). *Gender loving care: A guide to counseling gender variant clients*. New York, NY: W.W. Norton.

Federal Bureau of Investigation. (2006). Uniform crime reports: Hate crime statistics, 2005. Retrieved September 6, 2013 from http://www.fbi.gov/about-us/cjis/ucr/hate-crime/2005

Federal Bureau of Investigation (2014). Hate crime statistics 2013. Retrieved December 11, 2014, from https://www.fbi.gov/news/pressrel/press-releases/fbi-releases-2013-hate-crime-statistics.

Ficarotto, T. (1990). Racism, sexism, and erotophobia: Attitudes of heterosexuals toward homosexuals. *Journal of Homosexuality, 19*, 111-116.

Flynn, F. (2005). Having an open mind: The impact of openness to experience on interracial attitudes and impression formation. *Journal of Personality and Social Psychology, 88*, 816-826.

The williams Institute (2001). Chapter 5: The Legacy of Discriminatory State Laws, Policies, and Practices, 1945- Present. Retrieved on August 22nd, 2019 from: https://williamsinstitute.law.ucla.edu/wp-content/uploads/5_History.pdf

Franssen, V., Dhont, K., & Van Hiel, A. (2012). Age-related differences in ethnic prejudice: Evidence of the mediating effect of right-wing attitudes. *Journal of Community and Applied Social Psychology,* retrieved October 14, 2012 from https://onlinelibrary.wiley.com/doi/abs/10.1002/casp.2109.

Fulton, A., Gorsuch, R., & Maynard, E. (1999). Religious orientation, antihomosexual sentiment, and fundamentalism among Christians. *Journal for the Scientific Study of Religion, 38*, 14-22.

Funder, D. (2001). On the accuracy of personality judgment: a realistic approach. *Psychological Review, 102*, 652-670.

Garnets, L., & Peplau, L. (2002) A new paradigm for women's sexual orientation: Implications for therapy. *Women and Therapy, 24,* 111-121.

Gonsalkorale K., Sherman J. W., Klauer K. C. (2009). Aging and prejudice: Diminished regulation of automatic race bias among older adults. *Journal of Experimental Social Psychology, 45,* 410-414.

Goodwin, R. (2003). The prevalence of panic attacks in the United States: 1980 to 1995. *Journal of Clinical Epidemiology, 56,* 914-916.

Graziano, W., & Tobin, R. (2009). Agreeableness. In M. R. Leary & R. H. Hoyle (Eds.) *Handbook of individual differences in social behavior* (pp. 46-61). New York, NY: Guilford.

Greenwald, A., McGhee, D., & Schwartz, J. (1998). Measuring individual differences in implicit cognition: The Implicit Association Test. *Journal of Personality and Social Psychology, 74,* 1464-1480.

Guimond, S., Dambrun, M., Michinov, N., & Duarte, S. (2003). Does social dominance generate prejudice? Integrating individual and contextual determinants of intergroup cognitions. *Journal of Personality and Social Psychology, 84,* 697-721.

Hansen, G. (1982). Measuring prejudice against homosexuality (homosexism) among college students: A new scale. *The Journal of Social Psychology, 117,* 233-236.

Harper, G. W., Jernewall, N., & Zea, M. C. (2004). Giving voice to emerging science and theory for lesbian, gay, and bisexual people of color. *Cultural Diversity and Ethnic Minority Psychology, 10,* 187-199.

Harper, G. W., & Schneider, M. (2003). Oppression and discrimination among lesbian, gay, bisexual, and transgender people and communities: A challenge for community psychology. *American Journal of Community Psychology, 31,* 243-252.

Hasher, L., & Zacks, R. T. (1988). Working memory, comprehension, and aging: A review and a new view. In G. H. Bower (Ed.), *The psychology of learning and motivation: Advances in research and theory* (Vol. 22, pp. 193-225). San Diego, CA: Academic Press.

Heaven, P., & Quinten, D. (2003). Personality factors predict racial prejudice. *Personality and Individual Differences, 34,* 625-634.

Henry, J., von Hippel, W., & Baynes, K. (2009). Social inappropriateness, executive control, and aging. *Psychology and Aging, 24,* 239-244.

Herek, G. M. (1988). Heterosexuals' attitudes toward lesbians and gay men: Correlates and gender differences. *The Journal of Sex Research, 25,* 451-477.

Herek, G. M. (2009). Sexual stigma and sexual prejudice in the United States: A conceptual framework. In D. A. Hope (Ed.), *Contemporary perspectives on lesbian, gay, and bisexual identities* (pp. 65-111). New York: Springer Science + Business Media .

Herek, G. M. (2012). Facts about homosexuality and mental health. Retrieved March 7, 2012 from: https://psychology.ucdavis.edu/rainbow/html/facts_mental_health.html

Herek, G., Gillis, J., & Cogan, J. (2009). Internalized stigma among sexual minority adults: Insights from a social psychological perspective. *Journal of Counseling Psychology, 56,* 32-43.

Herek, G., & McClemore, K. (2013). Sexual prejudice. *Annual Review of Psychology, 64,* 309-333.

Hing, L., Chung-yan, G., Hamilton, L., & Zanna, M. (2008). A two-dimensional model that employs explicit and implicit attitudes to characterize prejudice. *Journal of Personality and Social Psychology, 94,* 971-987.

Hodson, G. (2008). Interracial prison contact: The pros for social dominant cons. *British Journal of Social Psychology, 47*, 325-351.

Human Rights Campaign. (2018). Violence against the transgender community in 2017. Retrieved November 30, 2018 from https://www.hrc.org/resources/violence-against-the-transgender-community-in-2018

Hunsberger, B., & Jackson, L. (2005). Religion, meaning, and prejudice. *Journal of Social Issues, 61*, 807-825.

Institute of Medicine. (2011). The health of lesbian, gay, bisexual, and transgender people: Building a foundation for better understanding. Washington DC: The National Academies Press.

Jackson, J., & Poulsen, J. (2005). Contact Experiences Mediate the Relationship Between Five-Factor Model Personality Traits and Ethnic Prejudice. *Journal of Applied Social Psychology, 35*, 667-685.

Jensen-Campbell, L., Knack, J., Waldrip, A., & Ramirez, M. (2007). The importance of personality and effortful control processes in victimization. In M. Harris (Ed.), *Bullying, rejection, and peer victimization: A social cognitive neuroscience perspective* (pp. 113-115). New York: Springer Publishing Co.

Jensen-Campbell, L., Iyer-Eimerbrink, P, & Knack, J. (2015). Interpersonal Traits. Chapter 16, pages 351-368 at: *APA Handbook of Personality and Social Psychology: Vol. 4. Personality Processes and Individual Differences, American Psychological Association.*

Johnson, M., Rowatt, W., Barnard-Brak, L., Patock-Peckham, J., & Carlisle, R. (2011). A meditational analysis of the role of right-wing authoritarianism and religious fundamentalism in the religiosity-prejudice link. *Personality and Individual*

Differences, 50, 851-858.

Johnson, M., Rowatt, W., & LaBouff, J. (2010). Priming Christian religious concepts increases racial prejudice. *Social Psychology and Personality Science, 1*, 119-126.

Judd, C., Park, B., Ryan, C., Brauer, M., & Kraus, S. (1995). Stereotypes and ethnocentrism: Diverging interethnic perceptions of African Americans and White American youth. *Journal of Personality and Social Psychology, 69*, 460-481.

Katz, I., Whackenhut, J., & Hass, R. (1986). Racial ambivalence, value duality, and behavior. In J. Dovidio & S. Gaertner (Eds.), *Prejudice, discrimination, and racism* (pp. 35-59). New York: Academic Press.

Kirkpatrick, L. A. (1992). An attachment-theoretical approach to the psychology of religion. *International Journal for the Psychology of Religion, 2*, 3-28.

Kirkpatrick, L. A., & Shaver, P. R. (1990). Attachment theory and religion: Childhood attachments, religious beliefs, and conversion. *Journal for the Scientific Study of Religion,29*, 315-334.

Kirkpatrick, L. A., & Shaver, P. R. (1992). An attachment-theoretical approach to romantic love and religious belief. *Personality and Social Psychology Bulletin, 18*, 266-275.

Kite, M. E. (1984). Sex differences in attitudes toward homosexuals: A meta-analytic review. *Journal of Homosexuality, 10*, 69-81.

Kite, M. E., & Whitley, B. E., Jr. (2008). Stereotyping and prejudice. In S. F. Davis & W. Buskist (Eds.), *21st century psychology* (pp. 100-119). Thousand Oaks, CA: SAGE.

Kovel, J. (1970). *White racism: A psychohistory.* New York: Pantheon.

Laythe, B., Finkel, D., & Kirkpatrick, L. (2002). Predicting prejudice from religious fundamentalism and right-wing authoritarianism: A multiple-regression approach. *Journal for the Scientific Study of Religion, 40,* 1-10.

Levahot, K., & Lambert, A. (2007). Toward a greater understanding of anti-gay prejudice: On the role of sexual orientation and gender role violation. *Basic and Applied Social Psychology, 29,* 279-292.

Loftus, J. (2001). America's liberalization in attitudes toward homosexuality, 1973 to 1998. *American Sociological Review, 66,* 762-782.

Logan, C. (1996): Homophobia? *Journal of Homosexuality, 31,* 31-53.

Lowery, B., Hardin, C., & Sinclair, S. (2001). Social influence effects on automatic racial prejudice. *Journal of Personality and Social Psychology, 81,* 842-855.

Massachusetts Transgender Political Coalition. (2009). Obama signs Trans-Inclusive Hate Crimes Law. Retrieved March 14, 2014 from http://www.masstpc.org/massachusetts-transgender-political-coalition-praises-federal-hate-crimes-law-signing/

McConahay, J. (1986). Modern racism, ambivalence, and the Modern Racism Scale. In J. F. Davidio & S. L. Gaertner (Eds.), *Prejudice, discrimination, and Racism* (pp. 91-125). Orlando, Florida: Academic Press.

McCrae, R. (1987). Creativity, divergent thinking, and openness to experience. *Journal of Personality and Social Psychology, 52,* 1258-1265.

McCrae, R., & Costa, P., Jr. (1997). Conceptions and correlates of openness to experience. In R. Hogan & J. Johnson (Eds.), *Handbook of personality psychology* (pp. 825-847). San Diego, CA: Academic Press.

Meezan, W., & Martin, J. (Eds.). (2003). *Research methods with gay, lesbian, bisexual, and transgender populations.* Binghamton, NY: Haworth Press.

Merriam-Webster Unabridged. (2014). Retrieved March 15, 2014 from http://www.merriam-webster.com/dictionary/prejudice

Merton, R. (1948). Discrimination and the American creed. In R.M. MacIver (Ed.), *Discrimination and national welfare,* (pp. 99-126). New York: Harper & Brothers

Miller, A. K., Wagner, M. M., & Hunt, A. N. (2012). Parsimony in personality: Predicting sexual prejudice. *Journal of Homosexuality, 59*, 201-214.

Nadal, K. (2013). *That's so gay: Microaggressions and the lesbian, gay, bisexual, and transgender community.* Washington DC: American Psychological Association.

Nagoshi, J., Adams, K., Terrell, H., Hill, E., Brzuzy, S., & Nagoshi, C. (2008). Gender differences in correlates of homophobia and transphobia. *Sex Roles, 59*, 521-531.

National Coalition of Anti-Violence Programs. (2013). Lesbian, gay bisexual, transgender, and HIV-affected hate violence in 2012. Retrieved March 10, 2014 from: http://avp.org/wp-content/uploads/2017/04/ncavp_2012_hvreport_final.pdf

A report from Funders for Lesbian and Gay Issues (2005). Racial and Economic Justice Issues in Lesbian, Gay, Bisexual and Transgender Communities. Retrieved August 23, 2019 from: https://www.lgbtagingcenter.org/resources/pdfs/LGBT-REJ.pdf

American Civil Liberties Union. (2019). Non-Discrimination Laws: State by State Information. Retrieved August 23, 2019 from: https://www.aclu.org/other/non-discrimination-laws-state-state-information

National Research Council. (2011). *The Health of Lesbian, Gay, Bisexual, and Transgender People: Building a Foundation for Better Understanding.* Washington, DC: The National Academies Press.

NORC at Chicago University. (2011). Americans move dramatically toward acceptance of homosexuality finds GSS Report. Retrieved October 25, 2017 from http://www.norc.org/ NewsEventsPublications/PressReleases/Pages/american-acceptance-of-homosexuality-gss-report.aspx

Parkins, I., Fishbein, H., & Ritchey P. (2006). The influence of personality on workplace bullying and discrimination. *Journal of Applied Social Psychology, 36*, 2554-2577.

Pearson, A., Dovidio, J., & Gaertner, S. (2009). The nature of contemporary prejudice: Insights from aversive racism. Retrieved May 3, 2013 from research.pomona.edu/sci/ files/2011/09/PDF1.pdf

Peralta, E. (2013). Court overturns DOMA, sidesteps broad gay marriage ruling. Retrieved March12, 2014 from http://www. npr.org/blogs/thetwoway/2013/06/26/195857796/supreme-court-strikes-down-defense-of-marriage-act

Perry, R., & Sibley, C. (2012). Big-five personality prospectively predicts social dominance orientation and right-wing authoritarianism. *Personality an Individual Differences, 52*, 3-8.

Pettigrew, T. F., & Tropp, L.R. (2006). A meta-analytic test of intergroup contact theory. Journal of Personality and Social Psychology, 90, 751-783.

Pickett, B. (2011). Homosexuality. E.N. Zalta (Ed.), *The Stanford encyclopedia of philosophy*. Retrieved February 19, 2014 from http://plato.stanford.edu/archives/spr2011/entries/ homosexuality/

Prentice-Dunn, S., & Rogers, R. (1980). Effects of deindividuating situational cues and aggressive models on subjective deindividuation and aggression. *Journal of Personality and Social Psychology, 39*,104-113.

Richeson, J. A., & Shelton, J. N. (2003). When prejudice does not pay: Effects of interracial contact on executive function. *Psychological Science, 14*, 287-290.

Ring, T. (2017). Trans woman murdered in Mississippi: First of 2017. *The Advocate.* Retrieved January 31, 2017 from http://www. advocate.com/transgender/2017/1/06/trans-woman-murdered-mississippi-first-2017

Ryan, C., & Futterman, D. (1998). *Lesbian and gay youth: Care and counseling.* New York: Columbia University Press.

Saad, L. (2010). Americans' acceptance of gay relations crosses 50% threshold. Retrieved March 29, 2014 from http://www. gallup.com/poll/135764/americans-acceptance-gay-relations-crosses-threshold.aspx

Sayler, G. (2005). Beyond the biblical impasse: Homosexuality through the lens of theological anthropology. *Dialog: A Journal of Theology, 44*, 81-89.

Schnake, S., Beal, D., & Ruscher, J. (2006). Modern racism and intergroup bias in causal explanation. *Race, Gender, and Class, 13*, 133-138, 140-143.

Sears, D. (1988). Symbolic racism. In P. Katz & D. Taylor (Eds.). *Eliminating racism: Profiles in controversy.* (pp. 53-84). New York, NY: Plenum Press.

Sears, D., & Henry, P. (2003). The origins of symbolic racism. *Journal of Personality and Social Psychology, 85*, 259-275.

Sidanius, J., & Pratto, F. (1999). *Social dominance: An intergroup theory of social hierarchy and oppression.* Cambridge: UK: Cambridge University Press

Smith, T. (2011). Public attitudes toward homosexuality. Retrieved March 7, 2014 fromhttp://www.norc.org/PDFs/2011%20 GSS%20Reports/GSS_Public%20Attitudes%20Toward%20 Homosexuality_Sept2011.pdf

Smits, I., Dolan, C., Vorst, H., Wicherts. J., & Timmerman, M. (2011).

Cohort differences in Big Five personality factors over a period of 25 years. *Journal of Personality and Social Psychology, 100*, 1124-1138.

Sniderman, P. M., & Tetlock, P. E. (1986). Symbolic racism: Problems of motive attribution in political debate. *Journal of Social Issues, 42*, 129-150.

Stefurak, T., Taylor, C., & Mehta, S. (2010). Gender-specific models of homosexual prejudice: Religiosity, authoritarianism, and gender roles. *Psychology of Religion and Spirituality, 2*, 247-261.

Steinmetz, K. (2015). Why transgender people are being murdered at a historic rate. *Time*, June 26. Retrieved November 10, 2016 from http://time.com/3999348/transgender-murders-2015/

Stones, C. (2006). Antigay prejudice among heterosexual males: Right-wing authoritarianism as a stronger predictor than social-dominance orientation and heterosexual identity. *Social Behavior and Personality, 34*, 1137-1149.

Streyffeler, L., & McNally, R. (1998). Fundamentalists and liberals: Personality characteristics of Protestant Christians. *Personality and Individual Differences, 24*, 579-580.

Tebbe, E., & Morandi, B. (2012). Anti-transgender prejudice: A structural equation model of associated constructs. *Journal of Counseling Psychology, 59*, 251-261.

Transgender Law Center. (2014). Recommendations for transgender health care. Retrieved June 30,2014 from http://www.transgenderlaw.org/resources/tlhealth.htm

Twenge, J. (2001). Birth cohort changes in extraversion: A cross-temporal meta-analysis, 1966-1993. *Personality and Individual Differences, 30*, 735-748.

Tygart, C. (2000). Genetic causation attribution and public support of gay rights. *International Journal of Public Opinion Research,*

12, 259-275.

Uhlmann, E. L. & Nosek, B. A. (2012). My culture made me do it: Lay theories of responsibility for automatic prejudice. *Social Psychology, 43*, 108-113.

US Department of Health and Human Services: Centers for Disease Control (2012). Youth risk behavior surveillance—United States, 2011. *Surveillance Summaries*, 1-162.

von Hippel, W., & Dunlop, S. (2005) Aging, inhibition, and social inappropriateness. *Psychology and Aging, 20*, 519-523.

von Hippel, W., Silver, L. A., & Lynch, M. E. (2000). Stereotyping against your will: The role of inhibitory ability in stereotyping and prejudice among the elderly. *Personality and Social Psychology Bulletin, 26*, 523-532.

Weinberg, G. (1972). *Society and the healthy homosexual*. London: St. Martin's Griffin.

Weiss, D. (2011). "Staggering" rate of attempted suicides by transgenders highlights injustices.
Retrieved July 1, 2013 from https://groups.google.com/forum/#!msg/transgender-news/KNt_sENF14Q/NPIYOcBD3J4J

Whitley, B. (1999). Authoritarianism, social dominance orientation, and prejudice. *Journal of Personality and Social psychology, 77*, 126-134.

Whitley Jr., B. (2008). Religiosity and attitudes toward lesbians and gay men: A meta-analysis. *International Journal for the Psychology of Religion, 19*, 21-38.

Whitley, B., & Kite, M. (2009). *The psychology of prejudice and discrimination*. Belmont, CA: Wadsworth.

Whitley, R. E., Jr., & Lee, S. E. (2000). The relationship of authoritarianism and related constructs to attitudes toward homosexuality. *Journal of Applied Social Psychology, 30*, 144-

170.

Wilkinson, W. W. (2004). Religiosity, authoritarianism, and homophobia: A multidimensional approach. *International Journal for the Psychology of Religion, 14*, 55-67.

Zanna, M., & Rempel, J. (1988). Attitudes: A new look at an old concept. In D. Bar-Tai & A. Kruglanski (Eds.), *The social psychology of knowledge* (pp. 315-334). Cambridge, England: Cambridge University Press

Zick, A., Küpper, B., & Höverman, A. (2011). Intolerance, prejudice, and discrimination. Retrieved March 7, 2014 from http:// library.fes.de/pdf-files/do/07908-20110311.pdf

5.

AFRICAN AMERICANS

Angelina J. Prince-Jeffers, MA

African American is a term often used interchangeably with Black American. The identity and meaning that encompass the term "African American" is becoming increasing difficult to define. Whether one checks a box identifying as African American or attempts to explain to another individual what it means to be "Black" in America, there is great variability in the meaning. Berlin (2010) released a special report in *The Smithsonian*'s online journal attempting to highlight the factors that contribute to the evolving concept of being African American. One factor discussed was the rapid influx of Black people from Africa and the Caribbean. Berlin (2010) states that, prior to 1965, the percentage of Blacks who foreign born was nearly nonexistent, but at the turn of the 21st century nearly 10% of all Black people were immigrants or children of immigrants. As these demographics change, does the definition of African American shift? The term African American can be defined as an individual living in America who has family lineage of African descent. For the purposes of this chapter, the term Black will be used interchangeably.

We have already established that race is predominantly a social construct, so being Black is not necessarily defined by genetics. Even though there is sufficient evidence to support the notion that race is a social construct, it does not make it any less real. What does it truly mean to be Black? There are several aspects of experience that can be considered in answering this question. Perhaps it is defined by shared history, commonality in cultural practices, meaning derived from experiences, geographic and anthropological origin, or simply appearance. In this chapter, we will explore these and other factors as we delve deep into the meaning of being African American.

Hardship and History

Unlike many other racial/ethnic groups, most African Americans do not have the ability to trace their family lineage past a few generations. This is largely because of slavery. Without citing specific dates that mark the beginning and end of slavery, it is essential to note that Blacks in America were enslaved approximately 100 years longer than they have been free. Most history documentation suggests that the enslavement of the Africans in the Americas began 1619 and ended with the 13th Amendment to the Constitution was ratified in December of 1865.

It is impossible to understand the experience of African Americans without drawing attention to the long-lasting impact of slavery. The notion that personal experience or familial experience with slavery is necessary to be impactful in this present day and time is asinine and reflects a limited understanding of cultural transmission. Masses of Blacks were forcibly shipped across the Atlantic to the Americas and the Caribbean against their will, and forced to work in inhumane conditions against their will. Cultural traditions were lost; families were separated; and entire lineages died off. Hardship marked the beginning of the history of most Blacks in America and this is unlike any other racial/ethnic group in American history.

How is this relevant to Black people living in America today? The cultural transmission theory can assist in exploring the pertinence. Language, food preferences, customs, and even trauma can be passed down from generation to generation. This cultural transmission of information plays an integral role in a group's experience. The cultural transmission theory is often applied to linguistics in attempts to understand how human language develops and passes on. It can be transmitted horizontally among individuals of the same generation; vertically, in which an older generation passes language to a biological family member of another generation; or obliquely from individuals of one generation to another who are not related biologically. These elements of transmission can be applied to the African American experience dating back to slavery. First, the notion of cultural trauma must be explored in order to understand the cultural transmission of trauma.

Alexander, Eyeran, Giesen, Smelser, and Sztompka (2004) define cultural trauma: "Cultural trauma occurs when members of a collectivity feel they have been subjected to a horrendous event that leaves indelible marks upon their group consciousness, marking their memories forever and changing their future identity in fundamental and irrevocable ways" (p. 1). Alexander et al. state that cultural trauma is not naturally occurring; instead it is created by societies. The advent of enslavement of Blacks can certainly fit within the above definition of cultural trauma.

The cultural view of trauma starkly differs from the Lay Trauma Theory, which deems traumas as naturally occurring events that have the propensity to alter the well-being of an individual or collectivity (Alexander et al., 2004). The ensuing reaction to the traumatic event is the trauma experience that occurs in a natural, unreflexive manner. This view insinuates that interaction with the event and the individual must occur for traumatization to take place.

In order to understand how trauma can be culturally transmitted, trauma must first be acknowledged as a social process. Alexander et al. (2004) do not equate trauma with the experience of pain; instead it relates to the collective discomfort that impacts the very identity of a group of

163

people. During slavery, the identity of generations of individuals was shattered in multiple ways. This 264-year multigenerational trauma became a part of the cultural identity of everyone who experienced it; it was a culturally traumatic event. The advent and continuation of slavery was a societal process that can be easily identified and is readily acknowledged as a significant occurrence across history. In this regard, trauma is not conceptualized as simply being impactful at the individual level; it transcends to the collective. Furthermore, we must also acknowledge how the actual event contributes to the creation of trauma in one generation that transcends future generations.

We have established that cultural trauma is painful and alters the identity of a group of people. In part, this occurs when the defining stories of a group of people become connected to that cultural trauma. In the case of slavery, slavery created a new master narrative that became a defining aspect of the African American experience. Alexander et al. (2004) identify four dimensions that are central to the creation of a new master narrative. They can be applied to slavery as follows:

The nature of the pain. This speaks to the events that transpired to the group. Slavery involved the coercive domination of millions of people. Maltreatment ranged from forced labor to rape and murder.

The nature of the victim. This component identifies the group of individuals who experience the traumatizing pain. In the case of slavery, the victims can be clearly identified as Africans who were forcibly removed from their homelands and forced into the slave trade, and their offspring who were also enslaved. Secondary victims are not as readily identified or acknowledged. Secondary victims in the case of slavery did not directly experience slavery, but their lives were negatively impacted due to the lasting setback slavery had on African American people.

Relation of the trauma victim to the wider audience. This aspect examines the extent to which witnesses or audiences to the trauma identify with the traumatized group. In the case of slavery, this may apply to individuals who were not enslaved or enslavers. It may be particularly relevant to individuals who actively protested slavery and their offspring. It raises questions about the potential traumatization of individuals who witnessed slavery and its aftermath.

Attribution of responsibility. This component, as outlined by Alexander et al. (2004), denotes the importance of identifying a perpetrator in order to fully grasp the trauma narrative. In the case of slavery, we ask, who actually injured the victims? In examining who carried out the enslavement, it is immediately clear that there are a multitude of perpetrators.

We can utilize the above model to understand more about how slavery rewrote the narrative of African Americans and resulted in cultural trauma. Eyerman (2004) identifies cultural trauma as occurring when there is a dramatic loss of identity and meaning and that impacts a group of people who are connected in some way. Eyerman further notes that the trauma does not have to be directly felt by everyone in the group or directly experienced by all members. This standpoint gives support to the notion that the cultural trauma of slavery has the ability to transcend to Blacks who, in generations following slavery, and even descendants of Blacks who were not enslaved in the Americas. The trauma has been transmitted vertically, horizontally, and obliquely in a manner that still impacts the experience of modern-day African Americans. The content of this chapter hinges on the underlying belief that modern-day African Americans still carry the repercussions of the impact of slavery generations after its abolition. It has altered the subjective experience of what it means to be African American and defined components of "blackness" today.

Being Black in America

Victimization. While it is essential to highlight the role that this plays in the African American experience, it is equally as important to highlight another central defining feature such as resilience. Thus far, the discussion of the African American experience has been one of endured slavery, the inequality of the Jim Crow laws, generational trauma, and discrimination that persists to this very day. However, there is a long-lasting theme of persistent fighting to overcome the struggles of inequality that has tremendously contributed to the advancement of Black people in America.

The year 2018 marked 55 years since Dr. Martin Luther King, Jr. marched on the Capitol and gave his "I Have a Dream" speech in an attempt to advocate for equality for Blacks on several levels. Widespread discrimination, poverty, lack of jobs, and racial inequality were at the core of King's drive for the overall better treatment of Black people in America. Since then, there has been great progress in improving the treatment and livelihood of Blacks in America. There are no longer laws that dictate the ill treatment of Black Americans, nor are basic rights denied. However, even after a Black man served two terms in office as President of the United States there is still strong evidence of discrimination that negatively impacts the experiences of African Americans. These issues are often ignored or explained away when they are not overt and come in forms such as microaggressions, but issues with acknowledgement are also present even when the racial discrimination is more explicit.

Let us begin with a discussion of racial microaggressions. The term was initially coined by Chester Pierce to describe the subtle and typically spontaneous putdowns that Blacks in America face on a near daily basis (Pierce, Carew, Pierce-Gonzalez, & Willis, 1978). While microaggressions can certainly impact other marginalized groups, the term was initially coined in recognition of the daily issues many African Americans face. Sue and Sue (2008) provide an updated version of microaggressions to be defined as brief, daily exchanges that send

166

denigrating messages to a particular target group. Microaggressions are perpetuated in a subtle manner, and oftentimes they are enacted involuntarily. They can be enacted in an intentional or unintentional manner. Many individuals are not aware they are committing them. Consider the example below:

> Niqua, a 25-year-old African American woman, went shopping for new work clothes at an upscale department store. She was not assisted by store associates, even though people who came in after her were assisted. None of them were Black. Within 10 minutes of her browsing, two other women who were not Black came up to her asking for assistance regarding the stock of sizes. She calmly explained that she was not an employee and resumed her browsing. Several minutes later she approached a sales associate and requested assistance in finding a few blazers. The sales associate pointed Niqua to the sale rack without looking up at her. When Niqua went to check out her purchases of six items totaling $950.00, the associate requested two forms of ID and also asked another associate to inspect the IDs. When Niqua asked why they were inspecting her IDs and requesting multiple forms, she was told it was "policy." There were no sign indicating this and Niqua had never witnessed this when she accompanied her white friends to shop at the same location. When she attempted to speak to these same friends later that day, they were confused as to what occurred and had a difficult time understanding what was wrong.

There were several microaggressions present in the above example. An inherent assumption was made that Niqua could not afford the clothing in the store and she was largely ignored and pointed to the sale rack. Another microaggression was present when other customers assumed that she was working and not a customer. Lastly, Niqua was treated with suspicion and indirectly accused of theft when she attempted to check out.

Racial microaggressions are damaging, and one way to address the transgressions is to heighten awareness and command change. The first step in eliminating microaggressions is to make the "invisible" visible. This speaks to the need to get the masses to acknowledge the presence and impact of microaggressions. By bringing the presence and impact of microaggressions to light, we can increase visibility and promote change. Sue and Sue (2008) state that this is a necessary occurrence to improve the livelihoods of marginalized groups such as African Americans.

It is unfortunate that being Black in America often means being treated differently simply because you identify as Black or share features that individuals associate with being Black. On one end of the spectrum is the negative perpetuation of Black individuals in the media that contributes to negative views of Blacks and on the opposite end is unequal treatment. Sometimes this treatment can be deadly.

The 2013 shooting death of Trayvon Martin and the acquittal of his killer George Zimmerman sparked fires in the Black community. The calls for justice and outright protests pointed to one ultimate factor that was underlying this tragic loss of life—racism. The Black Lives Matter (BLM) movement emerged following the death of Trayvon Martin and has been active in organizing protests and marches to facilitate change in the treatment of Blacks. The organization's official website states that BLM seeks to achieve justice for individuals who have been impacted by state-sanctioned violence and anti-Black racism. BLM was also active in the 2014 deaths of Eric Garner and Michael Brown, two separate incidents involving shooting deaths of young Black males by law enforcement. This new movement can be classified as a new civil rights movement, and the various chapters have also been instrumental in protesting White supremacist rallies and other occurrences that are believed to be oppressive to Black people in America. Many still deny the presence of subtle and overt racism and unequal treatment of Black Americans in present times, but the experiences of many indicate that racism is ever-present.

The experiences of being Black in America vary widely. Some individuals are plagued by inequality and racism on a frequent basis and others do not face as many encounters. Nonetheless, these occurrences warrant attention and are noteworthy in a discussion of what it means to be Black in America.

Ask any Black person in America what it actually means to be Black in America, and you are likely to get as many differing responses as you do people. Here are several responses that were gathered:

Being Black means being misunderstood and judged without being known. It means being underestimated and described in a negative way. In college and at work it means having to work twice as hard to get what others are readily handed. Being Black is hard because we are still viewed as less. But, being Black also means being powerful and feared, strong and unique, and deeply misunderstood. As Black people, we are united by the struggle but there's still so much division. – *J.P, 56-year-old black male*

As a black woman, I think that being Black means always having to be strong. At least that's what it's been like for me and what it seems other people expect from you. When my mother died suddenly, I was really messed up and depressed, but everyone around me just kept saying to "hold it together" and "be strong." I was reminded of all my obligations to my household, family, and myself. I get it, though. Our ancestors were slaves and they didn't have the option of being weak or down. Black women have been forced to endure so much across the centuries and now we are expected to continue to do so without breaking down.

– A.J, 29-year-old black female

For me to be Black is to embody the potential to reorder the world. That is, Blackness provides glimpses into human freedom capable of undoing the erasure of humanness caused by Euromerican culture. In America, however, my Black skin makes me a problem instead of a person. It feels like my life—every detail of my personal story that makes me unique—is either treated as a fetishized accessory for the White world or a threat to it. I could tell you several stories of microaggressions and racist hostility, but within and beyond those are two things that keep me going: (1) the knowledge that the sad state of the world is the result of old lies and false loves and; (2) the determination to fix it. *– A.B, 26-year-old black male*

Am I Black?

Identifying as Black may come with a set of expectations that may be based in stereotypes or perceptions of what experiences are closely associated with being Black. When there is ambiguity in identifying as African American due to expectations being violated, then it may lead to questions being raised about your racial identity.

Abeo is the 16-year-old son of Nigerian-born parents. He has resided in the United States since he was an infant. His parents moved to the U.S. in hopes of securing better opportunities and new experiences

170

for their children. Abeo's mother earned a master's degree in education and became a school principal; his father works as an engineer. English is the primary language spoken at home and Abeo and his six siblings consider academic success to be of the utmost importance. While his family lives in a predominantly upper middle-class neighborhood with few people of color, his family identifies strongly with their Nigerian background and often dresses in Nigerian attire. Abeo and many of his siblings have recently been engaging in more activities with their American counterparts and have shifted the way that they eat, dress, and interact with others. Abeo has become aware of some major differences in his upbringing when compared to his counterparts with American-born parents. For example, his friends often spend long periods of time watching TV or playing outside, while Abeo works a part-time job to save for college. His friends often call adults by their first name, but Abeo was raised referring to familiar adults as Aunty or Uncle. Abeo did not grow up observing any traditional Western holidays such as Christmas or Thanksgiving; instead his family observed Id el Kabir and Id el Fitr. When Abeo was recently filling out paperwork for college applications, he was unsure of what to select for race. He was certain that he was Black but not sure if he identified as being African American.

Lena was born in rural Mississippi to a first-generation Cuban father and a Black mother who was a native of Mississippi. Within her household, she was able to identify as Black and Latina, but family members on either side did not embrace her multiethnic identity. Lena often struggled with not feeling "Black enough" and not looking like her other Latina relatives. She often felt forced to choose and experienced a great deal of confusion with her racial identity. Her mother's side of the family was close-knit, placed emphasis on Christianity and going to church, and spoke with a great deal of pride that came with being Black. In discussions with friends about racism, she was often told that she would not understand because she was "light-skinned" and not really "Black." In time, Lena began to identify as Afro-Latina and embraced her multiethnic identity.

Jamari was born and raised in inner-city Chicago. He lived in the projects for most of his childhood and in a small apartment in an impoverished neighborhood until he graduated from high school and left for college. Jamari always did well in school and was often made fun of by others in his neighborhood for his academic achievement. He attended a university with a predominantly White student body and felt out of place most of the time. In time, Jamari changed the way he talked and dressed to be more similar to his peers. He even began dating the sister of one of his fraternity brothers. When Jamari returned home during the summer of his junior year, his old friends referred to him as an "Oreo" and a "sellout." His sisters did not approve of his dating a White woman and his mother said that she was disappointed in his choice, because he knows how hard "good Black men" are to come by. Jamari went on to become a doctor and he married his college girlfriend. He often felt guilty for his success and did not return to his old neighborhood anymore because he felt out of place. Most of his new friends were White, and Jamari's children had very limited contact with other African Americans.

Each of the above scenarios reflects actual experiences of individuals who identify as being Black in America, but each situation varies widely from the others. Several common issues were highlighted that resulted in racial identity being called into question. Interracial interactions and marriage, multiethnic background, financial success, and even having parents who were not born in America all resulted in a degree of uncertainty in fully identifying as being African American. This raises the opportunity for more overt discussion of what constitutes "being Black." As we were gathering quotes from individuals about what it means to be Black, many individuals indicated that they were not sure or that they had never thought about what it means. A level of ambiguity surrounding racial identity was apparent.

African American Culture and Psychotherapy: The Gap

There has been a recent trend that emphasizes multicultural training for clinicians who provide mental healthcare services, with a goal of providing society with culturally competent professionals. The American Psychological Association (2012) has even established guidelines for multicultural education, training, research, and practice. The American population is becoming more and more diverse, and this increases the likelihood that clinicians will interact with individuals of diverse ethnic, cultural, sexual, and socioeconomic backgrounds. Is the mental healthcare system equipped to address the needs of such a diverse nation? Furthermore, are mental healthcare services, such as psychotherapy, sufficient to assist diverse groups? This section seeks to explore a number of barriers that contribute to a lack of mental

173

health care and psychological services being provided to African Americans or Blacks. There will also be discussion on factors that have contributed to these barriers and the implications for the future direction of mental health care.

Ethnic minorities are disproportionately represented in the psychiatric population, but they are far less likely to receive mental healthcare services. Lo, Cheng, and Howell (2014) note that African Americans are more likely to experience chronic mental illness than their Caucasian counterparts but less likely to receive mental healthcare services. This study utilized a nationally representative sample and the results suggested that financial difficulties posed a barrier to care for both African Americans and Caucasians (Lo, et al.). Researchers note that even when socioeconomic status was controlled for, affordability of care posed a bigger barrier for Blacks than for Whites in America (Lo, et al.). However, financial difficulties cannot account for the significant disparity in the delivery of mental healthcare services when comparing racial groups. This disparity is undeniable and other factors that can be attributed to the lack of care being provided to African Americans must be explored.

It is critical to briefly discuss the implications of this disparity prior to further discussion on possible barriers. Mental health services are necessary components for reducing the occurrence and severity of mental illness in Americans. Lo et al. (2014) note that there is a strong relationship between the duration of mental illness and the use of mental healthcare services, in that Blacks tend to seek services less often than Whites and typically present with more pronounced symptomology than their White counterparts. Lo et al. (2014) also suggest that a lack of access to proper services is a contributing factor because not receiving appropriate care in a timely manner can exacerbate symptoms of mental illness. Lo et al. also point to the serious repercussions of not receiving care including prolonged illness, legal issues, injury, and even death. In addition, untreated mental illness contributes to an overall lower quality of life.

Mental Illness Stigma and Other Barriers to Care

Briggs, Banks, and Briggs (2014) utilized the results from Lo et al. (2014) as a rationale for further exploration of the underutilization of care by African Americans. Researchers insist that finding solutions to this underutilization issue first requires an examination of the history of the issue. This discussion is critical because it cannot be assumed that the current underutilization of mental healthcare services by African Americans is directly related to the current state of affairs. The participation of African Americans in mental healthcare services has traditionally been nonexistent. During the slave trade, there was a common misconception that Blacks were not likely to become mentally ill (Briggs et al., 2014). When Blacks became mentally ill, how were they then treated? It is hypothesized by the author that the misconception that Blacks could not become mentally ill, coupled with a lack of access to care dating back to the post-Abolition era, have contributed to Blacks having negative attitudes toward traditional treatment and seeking alternative methods of treatment.

Briggs et al. (2014) also make note of the surge in the number of African Americans who were institutionalized and treated inhumanely following the abolition of slavery. Many of the African Americans who were institutionalized did not actually suffer from mental illness, but they were placed in asylums because many of the "protective factors" that slavery "offered" were no longer present (Briggs et al., 2014). It is logical to hypothesize that this ill treatment continued to contribute to the development of negative attitudes toward seeking mental health care. The period of deinstitutionalization, from 1955-1980, left hundreds of thousands of mentally ill patients on the streets. This in itself was an issue for individuals of all races, but legislation in the 1970s that provided public mental healthcare systems did not include care for African Americans (Briggs et al., 2014). While many mentally ill Caucasians were transferred to nursing homes or received treatment in public facilities, many African Americans were left on the streets or incarcerated. It is clear that Blacks have been historically denied proper access to mental health care and commonly mistreated when care was provided. Modern-day clinicians and researchers must take this unique history into consideration when examining the attitudes of African Americans toward the mental healthcare system and the subsequent underutilization of services.

Many of the theories that relate to the underutilization of care in African American populations are multifaceted and attribute this occurrence to a variety of factors. Briggs (2011) proposed a logic model that purports to explain the underutilization of mental healthcare services by African Americans and the overrepresentation of African Americans in incarcerated populations. This model points to factors that are internal to the mental health system, such as cost and professional bias; factors that are external to the mental healthcare system, such as education and socioeconomic status; and other related individual factors, such as distrust of the system and stigma.

It can be argued that the distrust and stigma against the mental healthcare system are simply logical reactions to years of mistreatment. There was earlier discussion of the ill treatment of African Americans during slavery and soon after abolition. In addition, African Americans were subject to experiments and other unethical medical treatment during the 20th century. Briggs et al. (2014) explain that African Americans were used as unwilling test subjects in the Tuskegee experiment. The ill treatment may also have contributed to an overall distrust for modern Western medicine. These and other events have collectively contributed to the formation of an atmosphere of fear surrounding treatment.

Stigma undoubtedly poses a barrier to seeking current help in

African American populations. Murry, Heflinger, Suiter, and Brody (2014) conducted research examining mental healthcare help-seeking among rural African American families. This study involved over 180 individuals and results suggested that participants preferred family, churches, and school as sources of support instead of traditional mental healthcare providers. Stigma in the community against children and families seeking mental healthcare services was frequently endorsed as a perceived barrier (Murry et al., 2014).

Many African Americans who seek mental healthcare services are also impacted by barriers to treatment in the therapeutic process. Cruz et al. (2008) conducted qualitative research on depressed African Americans in treatment, and participants reported a number of barriers that prevent or impede effective treatment. Some of the barriers reported included racism, financial issues, mistrust of clinicians, negative familial attitudes toward seeking services, community-based stigma, dysfunctional or alternative coping behaviors, limited information about treatment services, and religious beliefs (Cruz et al., 2008). These barriers may be significant in terms of seeking mental healthcare services and they are also barriers to therapy adherence and progress.

Perhaps there is a cultural disconnect between the mental healthcare system and the African American community. Franklin (1999) suggests that many African Americans, especially men, believe that services cannot help them because there is a lack of understanding of what it means to be Black in society. "Invisibility" is the term used to discuss the inner struggle with the feeling that one's personality, values, abilities, and beliefs are not valued or recognized because of prejudice and racism (Franklin, 1999). In other words, the mental healthcare system, and the professionals involved, cannot understand or appreciate the plight of those who are Black in American society. Franklin hints that the mental healthcare system is a byproduct of individual and institutional racism. Racism and invisibility complicate the racial identity of African American men and transcend into the therapeutic setting. Franklin states that these therapists must be able to understand the importance of recognition, validation, and visibility in order to adequately assist African American men.

This notion of a cultural disconnect has been addressed in more recent literature. Briggs, Briggs, Miller, and Paulson (2011) point to institutional inequalities and cultural insensitivities as major contributors to the underutilization of care by African Americans. This alludes to the possibility that the assessments, evaluation processes, psychotherapeutic approaches, and cultural framework are simply not aligned with African American culture and therefore render treatment ineffective (Briggs et al., 2011). Wade (2013) supports the continued development of Black psychology, a subdiscipline of psychology that includes elements of Africa's renaissance and development, with an emphasis on the experience and perspectives of Blacks, as necessary in the restoration of the mind, identity, and healing of Black people. However, Black psychology is not a narrow approach that is not applicable to individuals from other backgrounds. Wade elaborates on Black/African Psychology as follows:

> Relying on the principles of harmony within the universe as a natural order of existence, African-centered psychology recognizes (a) the Spirit that permeates everything, (b) the idea that everything in the universe is interconnected, (c) the value that the collective is the most salient element of existence, and (d) the idea that communal self-knowledge is the key to mental health.

At times it becomes difficult to determine whether or not cultural differences in normalcy versus psychopathology present as a barrier or if the actual barrier is denial. Consider that the research by Murry et al. (2011) notes that the majority of African American mothers in their study endorsed mental health issues in their children such as externalizing behaviors, attention deficit disorder, and depression, but their perception of their children's behavior was typically written off as normal childlike behavior. This is suggestive of denial, cultural differences in normalcy, or a lack of information about mental health problems.

Conclusions

It is clear that there is great diversity within the experience of African American people. The very definition of African American is ever evolving and the experience of being Black in America is often misunderstood. This chapter serves as a relatively brief glimpse into some key experiences that are often present, but there is room for much needed exploration. We are just beginning by increasing the visibility of Black people in America.

References

Alexander, J. C., Eyerman, R., Giesen, B., Smelser, N. J., & Sztompka, P. (2004). *Cultural trauma and collective identity* (1st ed.). Berkeley, CA: University of California Press.

American Psychological Association. (2012). APA Guidelines on Multicultural Education, Training, Research, Practice and Organizational Change for Psychologists. Retrieved from: http://www.apa.org/pi/oema/resources/policy/multicultural-guidelines.aspx

Berlin, I. (2010). Cracking the Code of the Human Genome: The Changing Definition of African-American. http://www.smithsonianmag.com/history/the-changing-definition-of-african-american-4905887/#egspmV7dWZ2egYvR.99

Bowleg, L., English, D., del Rio-Gonzalez, A., Burkholder, G., Teti,

M., & Tschann, J. (2016). Measuring the pros and cons of what it means to be a black man: Development and validation of the black men's experiences scale (BMES). *Psychology of Men & Masculinity, 17*(2), 177-188.

Briggs, H. E. (2011). *Mental health logic model development*. Portland, OR: Portland State University.

Briggs, H. E., Banks, L., & Briggs, A. C. (2014). Increasing knowledge and mental health service use among African Americans through evidence-based practice and cultural injection vector engagement practice approaches. *Best Practices in Mental Health, 10*(2), 1-14.

Briggs, H. E., Briggs, A. C., Miller, K. M., & Paulson, R. I. (2011). Combating persistent cultural incompetence in mental health care systems serving African Americans. *Best Practices in Mental Health, 7*(2), 1-25.

Cruz, M., Pincus, H. A., Harman, J., Reynolds, C. F., & Post, E. P. (2008). Barriers to care-seeking for depressed African Americans. *The International Journal of Psychiatry in Medicine, 38*(1), 71-80. doi:10.2190/PM.38.1.g

Eyerman, R. (2004). The past in the present: Culture and the transmission of memory. *Acta Sociologica, 47*(2), 159-169. doi: 10.1177/0001699304043853

Franklin, A. J. (1999). Invisibility syndrome and racial identity development in psychotherapy and counseling African American men. *The Counseling Psychologist, 27*(6), 761-793. doi:10.1177/0011000099276002

Gump, J. P. (2010). REALITY MATTERS: The shadow of trauma on African American subjectivity. *Psychoanalytic Psychology, 27*(1), 42-54. doi: 10.1037/a0018639

Hankerson, S. H., Watson, K. T., Lukachko, A., Fullilove, M. T., & Weissman, M. (2013). Ministers' perceptions of church-based programs to provide depression care for African Americans. *Journal of Urban Health, 90*(4), 685-698. doi:10.1007/s11524-013-9794-y

Jones, L. V., Hopson, L., Warner, L., Hardiman, E. R., & James, T. (2015). A qualitative study of black Women's experiences in drug abuse and mental health services. *Affilia, 30*(1), 68-82.

Lo, C. C., Cheng, T. C., & Howell, R. J. (2014). Access to and utilization of health services as pathway to racial disparities in serious mental illness. *Community Mental Health Journal, 50*, 251-257.

Murry, V. M., Heflinger, C. A., Suiter, S. V., & Brody, G. H. (2011). Examining perceptions about mental health care and help-seeking among rural African American families of adolescents. *Journal of Youth and Adolescence, 40*(9), 1118-1131. doi:10.1007/s10964-010-9627-1

Sue, D. W., Sue, D. (2008) *Counseling the Culturally Diverse: Theory and Practice* (5th ed.) Hoboken, NJ: Wiley & Sons.

Wade, N. (2013). Fundamental task and challenge of Black Psychology. *Journal of Black Psychology, 39*(3), 292-299.

Wang, P.S., Berglund P.A., Kessler, R. (2003). Patterns and correlates of contacting clergy for mental disorders in the United States. *Health Serv Res. 38*(2), 647-673.

6.

THE ROLE OF JUDAISM AND IDENTITY IN THERAPEUTIC SETTINGS

K. Drorit Gaines, PhD

It is nearly impossible to use one demographic or other category in the classification of Jewish individuals due to their vast and complicated diversity (Langman, 1999). However, in the interest of clarifying the most salient aspects of a Jewish identity as they impact the practice of psychotherapy with the Jewish population, some distinctions will be made. Nevertheless, these should not be considered as conclusive or all-encompassing in the study of Jewish identity. In addition, this chapter will provide some historical details to increase the understanding of cultural country of origin, but will not be providing a historical timeline or other details of the nomadic experience of Jews worldwide and through the numerous persecutions (although those have had a profound impact on the Jewish experience and generational mindset, which will be discussed from a therapeutic perspective).

There are two distinct factors that are central to the development of the identity of American Jews: religious and cultural. Both factors are present in various degrees based on age, upbringing, education, and personal choices. Both interact to create an identity with a specific set of values, worldview, and cultural and religious practices. As noted clearly by Schlosser (2006), "Most Jews are likely to consider being Jewish as a central aspect of their identity because of both internal (e.g., cultural pride) and external (e.g., antisemitism) factors."

Religious Identity

The religious factor refers to the stream of thought and practice the person identifies with, such as Haredi, Hassidic, Litvic, Kippa Seruga, Modern Orthodox, Conservative, Reform, or non-affiliated. Philosophy and practice are two aspects of religious identification. Interestingly, individuals may hold by a philosophy associated with a particular stream of thought but not engage in the practices of that stream, and the opposite may be present as well. In addition, personal interpretation of philosophical concepts often results in personal beliefs of merging philosophies. This complexity is clearly evident in that, within the various streams of thought, there are thousands of religious scholarly publications over thousands of years, discussing and debating the nature, meaning, and application of thousands of religious practices. One of the primary religious practices is the study of the Jewish Written (*De'orayta*) and Oral (*De'rabanan*) law, and another is the fulfillment of 613 commandments (M*itzvot*). These aspects, for example, produced a significantly large amount of scholarly work debating the nature and application of Jewish law, and resulted in daily learning of the traditional laws.

Although Jewish observance levels have a wide spectrum from secular to ultra-Orthodox, American Jews, placed anywhere on the spectrum of observance, may have very strong cultural identities as Jews (Schlosser, 2006).

Fluidity in Religious Identity

Schlosser (2006) describes the Jewish Orthodox denomination primarily by their physical appearance, such as their dress code, and secondarily by what they "can and cannot" do, from an observance standpoint. This approach becomes too simplistic and may even be perceived as superficial, because it fails to address what is central to the individual's choice of membership in the group—the value-based ideology that characterizes the group. Moreover, it fails to account for the many people who philosophically belong to a specific group but may not adhere to the dress code or follow the rituals, and others who may "dress the part" but their ideology is different in many ways from the communally encouraged "dos and don'ts." In fact, studies show that, across religions, individuals are more fluid in their religious ideologies and level of observance and that fluidity continues to change over time and as life's milestones are reached. For example, a typical Hassidic synagogue of the Chabad dynasty includes the clergy family, which adheres more than the rest of the congregation to a modest dress code and level of observance. But then it also includes families who observe some of the practices while dressed in a more relaxed manner, and yet others who are modern followers who are college-educated and live a modern lifestyle. Affinity and interest, during various periods in life, from rituals to philosophy, determine the level of involvement. When Schlosser (2006) describes Hassidic Jews, the description focuses on the dress code and the main laws and restrictions that they follow. There is no description of their deep and wise decades-long ideologies or their core social values. When he describes American Jewish values, he is actually referring to the Hassidic values—healing the world (*Tikun Olam*), performing good deeds (*Mitzvot*), and donating time and resources to charity (*Tzedakah*). These specific values are coined and discussed in length in *Kabbalah* (ancient writings on the structure of Godliness in the world, upon which the Hassidic movement is founded) and the *Tanya*—the core book of conduct and daily life of the Chabad Hassidic movement. The failure to address the origins of these values creates injustice to the Hassidic movement and reduces its teachings to merely behavioral and observable characteristics. It is the philosophy that creates the fundamentals of the movement, and what has attracted Jewish and non-Jewish people of all levels of observance to participate in its services. Therefore, strict religious classification does not hold true in the reality of the individual and should only serve as information to aid the clinical practice, not as an absolute that produces a predictive outcome.

Cultural Identity

The cultural factor refers to the influence of the culture from which the person's parents originated, and the culture in which the person grew up. For example, a Jew whose parents are of Yemeni descent but grew up in the U.S. is likely to resemble varied degrees of both the Yemeni and the American cultures. Frequent migration of Jewish people, often referred to as the "wandering Jew," provides more color to their identity. Jews coming from European countries are often referred to as *Ashkenazi* Jews, while the ones whose families originated from North Africa, the Iberian Peninsula, and west Asia are referred to as *Sefaradi* Jews.

Generational Difference

It is essential to understand that both factors, religion and culture, are fluid in the sense that the intensity of each in terms of impacting the person's values and worldview may vary through age and life experiences; aging, marriage, having children, or obtaining secular education are all life stages that may elicit the intensification or withdrawal from religious observance and cultural affiliation.

Judaism as a Religious Identity

Secularization of society and academia contributed to marked differences in religious affiliation among Jews between generations. Fully 93% of Jews in the aging generation identify as Jewish on the basis of religion (called "Jews by religion" in this report) and just 7% describe themselves as having no religion ("Jews of no religion"). In contrast, among Jews in the youngest generation of U.S. adults—the Millennials—68% identify as Jews by religion, while 32% describe themselves as having no religion and identify as Jewish on the basis of ancestry, ethnicity, or culture (Pew, 2013). Among Jewish leadership, this phenomenon has become a concern, and recently efforts have been

185

made by various Jewish organizations to increase awareness of the Jewish religion among Jewish youth.

Jews have high levels of educational attainment. Most Jews are college graduates (58%), including 28% who say they have earned a post-graduate degree. By comparison, 29% of U.S. adults say they graduated from college, including 10% who have a post-graduate degree (Pew, 2013). Roughly four in 10 U.S. Jewish adults (39%) say they live in a household where at least one person is a member of a synagogue. This includes 31% of Jewish adults (39% of Jews by religion and 4% of Jews of no religion) who say they personally belong to a synagogue, temple, or other congregation (Pew, 2013).

Generations of being subjected to race-based discrimination may account for the sensitivity Jews have toward discrimination. Jews think several other minority groups face more discrimination than they do. Roughly seven in 10 Jews (72%) say gays and lesbians face a lot of discrimination in American society, and an equal number say there is a lot of discrimination against Muslims. More than six in 10 (64%) say Blacks face a lot of discrimination. By comparison, 43% say Jews face a lot of discrimination. Overall, 15% of Jews say that in the past year they personally have been called offensive names or snubbed in a social setting because they are Jewish (Pew, 2013).

Jews are heavily concentrated in certain geographic regions: 43% live in the Northeast, compared with 18% of the public as a whole. Roughly a quarter of Jews reside in the South (23%) and in the West (23%), while 11% live in the Midwest. Half of Jews (49%) reside in urban areas and a similar number (47%) reside in the suburbs; just 4% of Jews reside in rural areas (Pew, 2013).

Orthodox Judaism

Studies suggest that the number of Orthodox Jews is growing as a share of the overall Jewish population. This is at least partially due to higher fertility rates in the Orthodox population. Orthodox Jews tend to be younger and have much higher fertility than the overall Jewish population. On average, Orthodox Jews (ages 40-59) have about 4.1 children, as opposed to 1.9 children per other Jewish adults (Pew, 2013). The other factor that may also contribute to the growing numbers of the Orthodox population is an increasingly higher retention rate (Orthodox individuals continue to stay Orthodox) (Pew, 2013). For mental health clinicians working with the Jewish population, this trend supports the need to understand Orthodox Judaism and the cultural, social, and existential perspectives this group holds.

Scholarship as a lofty pursuit has traditionally been encouraged in the Jewish belief system for thousands of years. Historically, Jews were referred to as "the people of the book" (Esposito, 2014). According to Jewish law, there are three pillars upon which the world stands: Learning of Torah, Divine Service, and Acts of Kindness (Pirkei Avot 1:2). These pillars of the Jewish belief system represent the Jewish life one should aspire to lead. As a core principle, the learning of traditional Jewish text (*Torah*) and wisdom should occur, preferably daily, from infancy to the last day of the person's life. Religious Jewish children are trained in biblical Hebrew reading and comprehension and the reciting of prayers. The study of the Torah, the text that is considered most holy and the main "guide manual" to what is described as holy Jewish life, is held as an utmost valued practice. This is reflected in King David's words, "Your Torah is my inner parts" (Psalm 40:9), equating Torah study to the nourishment of the soul, and good deeds (*Mitzvot*) are equated with the garments of the soul (Etz Chaim, Portal 44, ch. 3). The richness of thousands of books and scriptures of religious Jewish thought produced over thousands of years in all regions of the world will account for the fundamental value of the study of Torah as a core value. This is important to understand from a therapeutic perspective, because Orthodox Jews will consult first and foremost with the Jewish text and with a studious Jewish scholar (often referred to as Rabbi), as the source of life's wisdom and direct guidelines to taking action. Orthodox Jews follow *Halacha*—the Jewish code of law, which has 613 commandments of "Dos" and "Don'ts."

The Torah is where Jewish law originates. The Torah is divided into what is referred to as the Written Law (the text) and the Oral Law (verbally given at the time of Moses and transferred into text later on). Orthodox Jews generally follow these two main sources. However, over time, other secondary sources of legal guidelines were produced, such as the Mishna and the Gemara (one set of text originated in Israel and another in Babylon). In addition to these sources, a third type of source was developed in the various regions of the world that Jews lived in, such as Eastern Europe, Spain, or North Africa. Fundamentally, the secondary and tertiary sources do not contradict the written and oral law, but rather expand and clarify in more specific details of practice the laws established in the Torah. Finally, the fourth type of source is what is referred to as *Minhagim*, which is considered the traditions of various communities in cities and towns. These are not held as laws, but as traditions.

There are several types of Rabbinical leadership in the Orthodox communal system. Some serve as Koshering experts, others specialize in philosophy and thought, and others serve as Jewish legal authority. The latter are called *Dayanim* (*Dayan*, singular); their academic degree is considered the highest, and their educational program is most rigorous (post-high school education that is most often between nine to 15 years of structured learning and examinations by rabbinical credentialing boards). The *Dayanim* are the religious authority to make *Halacha* decisions.

Orthodox Jews routinely reach out to the Dayan in their community to help them decide on a course of action on a variety of matters, from business to family conduct. Because the observance of Jewish law is a daily practice, involving the practice of hundreds of commandments, it is an all-consuming discipline that impacts all areas of life and conduct. Orthodox Jews are significantly more engaged in religious practices than other Jews. Ninety-five percent of them say they fasted on Yom Kippur, while only 53% of Jews overall reported the same. Ninety-two percent say they live in a Kosher home, as opposed to 22% of Jews overall, and roughly 75% of them say they attend synagogue at least once a month, as opposed to 23% of Jews overall (Pew, 2013). As such, in the therapeutic setting, Orthodox Jews will evaluate every educational piece or therapeutic recommendation provided by the clinician in light of what the Jewish law advises them to do. Although Jewish law is heavily focused on healthy psychology and supportive interpersonal and community life, if contradictions arise between the psychological thought of the clinician and the core values of the Jewish laws of the Orthodox Jew, it will likely discourage the client from continuing with therapy or following up with therapy recommendations (Holliman & Wagner, 2015).

In addition, the values of Orthodox Judaism tend to be traditional, such as placing a high value on family life, devotion to a higher purpose, modest clothing, and traditional sexual practices such as monogamy and the requirement of a sexual relationship to be consummated post-maritally. Given that social norms skew toward increased sexual openness and individual-centered values, Orthodox individuals are often suspicious of the clinician's worldview and value system, and whether those will influence them or their family members away from Jewish traditional values. Used to living in an opposed reality, Orthodox individuals tend to quickly pick up on attempts to influence their own value system and often see this as a serious breach of trust with the clinician. Additionally, Orthodox individuals have to practice tremendous discipline in keeping the Jewish Torah law, such as strict Kosher requirements and a daily prayer schedule, and therefore frequently sacrifice their own needs for the sake of compliance with what they believe are higher values. When clinicians show disrespect to that, they fail to validate a core aspect of the client.

These sensitive therapeutic dynamics may account for the unfavorable attitudes toward psychotherapy held by Orthodox Jews as opposed to non-Orthodox Jews (Langman, 2000). Clearly, the significant complexity of the Jewish Orthodox culture and its traditional value system necessitate a careful and thoughtful approach in clinical practice. When working with Orthodox Jews it is therefore important for the clinician to develop and demonstrate respect for the way of life and value system and avoid attempts to change those.

Haredi, Hassidic, Litvic, Benei-Akiva, and Modern Orthodox are all examples of Orthodox Jewish streams of thought that agree on the fundamental laws (the 613 commandments stated in the Torah) but vary in their application of secondary sources of Jewish law and their traditions (*Minhagim*). For example, a dress code of white shirt and black suit for men and a wig for women is often practiced by the Haredi and Hassidic Jews, while a modern but modest dress code is practiced by the Kippa Seruga and Modern Orthodox group members. Typically, the color and type of the *Kippa*, a brimless cap worn by the men, may give information as to what group the person is associating himself with. For example, the Haredi, Hasidic, and Litvic members tend to wear a black or velvet Kippa, while Benei-Akiva and Modern Orthodox will wear a colorful or knitted Kippa. However, in reality, many families may not make a strong distinction to group or clothing identification, see themselves as "plain Orthodox" and will wear different styles interchangeably. As will be discussed further in the fluidity segment, more individuals practice a varied number of religious practices in a variety of degree in different periods during their lifespan.

There is a Jewish saying that says "One Jew, many opinions." Perhaps due to the structure of classical books such as the *Gemara* and *Mishna*, where several opinions for each issue are presented, with

190

several resolutions, Jews tend to traditionally disagree on a variety of topics. When it comes to Orthodox Judaism, one of these topics is secular education. Modern Orthodox Jews tend to have significantly higher levels of secular education (graduated from college, 65%) as compared with Hassidic and Litvic Jews combined (25%) (Pew, 2013).

Conservative Judaism

The attitude toward observing Jewish law is different among the groups. Eight in 10 Orthodox Jews (79%) said that observing Jewish law was essential to their Jewish identity, as opposed to two in 10 (19%) among Jews overall. While that seems to be the case, Conservative Jews still incorporate numerous religious practices into their daily routine. Their level of adherence to the traditional Torah law varies greatly, from individuals who keep the Shabbat or keep the Kosher laws, to others who do not, and often their prayer books contain changes such as omissions, shortening of segments, and additions (Tapper, 2016). Conservative Jews tend to feel a strong affiliation with the traditions and many engage in active learning and services. Here as well, a reductionist approach that focuses only on the technical practice of the "dos and don'ts" does not appropriately describe this group. Although the majority of conservative Jews may not follow the literal translation of Torah law, many may engage in Torah learning, Jewish scholarship, traditional practices, and may have a strong Jewish identity. Here, too, the fluidity of Jewish identity and practice varies over time and during the various life milestones.

Reform and Reconstructionist Judaism

A fundamental guiding principle of Reform Judaism is the autonomy of the individual to choose which commandments or rituals the individual would like to observe or participate in (CCAR, 1937; 1999). Other core values focus on commitment to Jewish life, Jewish identity, and pluralism (CCAR, 1937; 1999). The reconstructionist movement posits that Western morality may take precedence over

Jewish law and, like Reform Judaism, it does not require believers to hold onto specific beliefs or rituals. Both ideologies see Judaism as an evolving tradition that should be updated in accordance with modern trends. Neither ideology promotes adherence to the three core elements of Orthodox Judaism: observing the Shabbat; keeping Kosher; and Family Purity (*mikva*). The major philosophical difference between the Reform/reconstructionist movements and the Orthodox movement is very fundamental and crucial for each system as a driving force. Orthodox Judaism believes in the concept of holiness and sees it as the loftiest pursuit for humans. Its adherents also hold the Torah text as the utmost holy text. Reform and Reconstructionist philosophy does not consider the Torah text as holy or the word of God, and scholars in the movement often entertained the perspective that much of the content and development of the Jewish religion was social and cultural. Because of this fundamental disagreement, non-Godly versus Godly origin, and whether the Torah is timeless or time-constrained, the rift between the movements has been historically deep. Validating one would inevitably destroy the other, and vice versa.

From the perspective of the Jewish religion, which is ancient, the Reform and Reconstructionist movements are relatively new. Their birth originated during 19th century in Germany. This placed the religion's ethical values as the center of focus and emphasized the need for ritualistic practices. As such, many of the core values, such as the three pillars and the concept of *Tikun Olam*, have continued to be handed down in families. The same holds true for studiousness, which continued to be applied in secular fields such as the sciences, as opposed to the study of Torah.

Individuals who identify as Reform/Reconstructionist generally do not spend nearly as much time during their typical schedule in religious practices, with the exception of the ones who serve as clergy or as educators. With the exception of clergy or religious activities, they may or may not attend religious services for a long duration of time and may or may not participate in holiday celebrations. As such, they tend to be more involved in professional pursuits and other organizations of purpose, and apply Jewish values through these pursuits and in those settings. Seventy-six percent of American Jews report that they made a charitable contribution in 2012; median annual giving was $1,250 (NSAJG, 2013). Among Jews who make charitable contributions, nearly all of them (92%) give to a non-Jewish organization and the vast majority (79%) also give to a Jewish organization.

Social justice has been a modern trend since the 19th century and is taking an increasingly central place in modern development. Gender, ethnic, and sexual orientation equality and other issues have become important pursuits for the Reform and re-constructionist movements. Jewish traditional rituals that were perceived as discriminatory in any way were eliminated or augmented to achieve a type of equality. As such, separation between men and women during prayer services has been eliminated; ordination as rabbinical authority and prayer cantorship was offered to women, not just men; and women could choose to wear *Kippa* and *Talit* (ritualistic clothing traditionally worn by men). Social conformity and comfort became higher values than the adherence to Torah law, and ritualistic artifacts were seen as tools to affect a desired social experience.

The Non-Affiliated Jewish Person

Uniformity in any religious group is a fallacy. Some say it is because of the dynamic joining and leaving of members of the group (Chaves, 2013), but there is more to it. Surveys show that it is actually fairly common for people to vary in religious ideas, values, and practices within their group, and those variations are multi-factorial, and bi-directional (Chaves, 2013, p. 3). For example, 7% of Orthodox Jews do not keep a Kosher home, and 7% of Reform Jews do keep a Kosher home (Pew, 2013).

After the Holocaust, a macro-traumatic event with post-traumatic implications for Jewish individuals and the Jewish nation as a whole, survivors chose to cope with the horror of ethnic persecution in different ways. Some chose to disown their cultural and religious origins and embrace assimilation, and some of these chose to do so out of anger with the Almighty or loss of faith. As a result, their children were often provided with minimal to no Jewish education, and were raised outside the Jewish community. At least in part, this resulted in an increased number of Jewish people who are not affiliated with their Jewish roots. The Pew Research Center completed interviews with 3,475 Jewish respondents, including 2,786 Jews by religion and 689 Jews of no religion, and found that the number of non-affiliated Jews is as high as one-third. Fairchild (2010) indicates that Judaism is not a religion but a culture or a community, because non-religious Jews consider themselves Jewish, and religious Jews will consider non-religious Jews to still be Jews. It is important to clarify a distinction in worldview on this matter when it comes to religious orientation. Religious Jews do consider their practices religious, not a culture or a community. They consider all Jews by birth as Jews, regardless of whether they observe the religious laws, because the religion believes in four fundamental ideas: (1) The Right of Passage: a Jewish mother gives birth to Jewish souls, and it is the birth of the soul that determines the identity; (2) Level of observance is a matter of free will, a right given to the Jew by G-d, and it is up to the Jew to choose their own level of participation; (3) Reincarnation and the journey of each soul: during each lifetime the person's soul refines itself and grows, and so one's level of observance is a part of that process; and (4) the process of grappling with spiritual and religious doubt and questioning values and ideas is part of the soul's process of growth, and by itself does not rob the person of their identity.

Cultural Identity

The Jewish population in the United States, as of 2016, is estimated at 6.1 million, which is about 3% of the overall U.S. population (US Census, 2016; Sheskin & Dashefsky, 2015). More than one-third of American Jews live in large urban centers, and the three U.S. cities with the largest Jewish populations are New York, Miami, and Los Angeles (Singer & Grossman, 2005). Jewish history is marked by dynamic migration of Jewish people all over the world, across seas and continents. It is likely impossible for many Jews to trace their family origin for multiple reasons: determining the historical starting point; the high frequency of migration throughout history; and the loss of valuable Jewry due to political upheavals. In reality, Jewish men and women migrated to varied degrees. Some married within their family circle or their community, and others married Jews from other countries, and yet others married converts and out of the faith. This heightened complexity makes tracing the roots of the family a nearly impossible task. And yet, a certain number of families maintained knowledge of their lineage, and many are able to identify their tribal orientation in temple and prayer (*Cohen, Levi,* or *Israel*) due to the prayer services that have been maintained for generations. With that complexity in mind, there is a general cultural classification of Jews based on their recent, most identified, country of origin.

This classification, described by Schlosser (2006), identifies Jews coming from European countries (*Ashkenazim*), Jews coming from Spain and Portugal (*Sefaradim*), Jews coming from North Africa and Western Asia (*Mizrachim*), and other smaller groups such as Jews coming from Yemen, Italy, and Greece. This classification is not always used colloquially within the general Jewish population, and is instead distilled to Ashkenazi for all Europeans, and Sefaradi for nearly everyone else. Schlosser (2006) refers to Mizrachim as non-White by saying: "The Mizrachim shatter the erroneous assumption that all Jews are White." However, the genetic evidence suggests something more detailed than a division of "White" versus "non-White." Interestingly, Jewish populations (Ashkenazi, Sefaradi, Mizrachi, etc.) have retained their genetic coherence along with retaining their unique cultural and religious traditions. Isolated practices of marriage within the group means that each Diaspora group has maintained common genetic threads that reflect their shared ancestry. Furthermore, these various ethnic groups within the Jewish population are genetically closer to each other than to non-Jewish genetic makeup. Within each group, individuals shared as much of their genome as equivalent to what would normally be expected of a shared genome of two fourth or fifth cousins (Ostrer & Skorecki, 2013). In addition, the closer the geographical origin between two groups, the more similar their genomic makeup was (Ostrer & Skorecki, 2013).

The Sefaradi and Mizrachi Jew Versus the Ashkenazi Jew

For the purposes of practicing therapy with Jewish individuals, what often becomes a central issue of ethnic identity is the secular-cultural practices associated with the geographical origin of the person. For example, the Sefaradi and Mizrahi Jew comes from countries with an Arabic or Muslim cultural background and therefore may display cultural norms that are practiced in Muslim countries, such as male-dominated leadership of the home and the community, laws of modesty in clothing, and separation between men and women. The highest value is family loyalty. Devotion to the elders of the family and submission to the family's needs come before the individual's needs. When it comes to education, Jewish individuals of Mizrahi origins lived for generations in Northern African and Middle Eastern countries, which were dominated by Muslim laws. Much like the non-Jewish population in these countries, Jewish people, and women in particular, lacked exposure to secular education. Women were not permitted to learn how to read or write, and many did not receive formal education.

Marriages were arranged at a young age to avoid kidnapping of girls, but marriage was generally consummated when the girl reached the age of 16 or 17. Jewish prayers and music absorbed the tunes of the geographic origins of the community. Jewish Yemen prayers have Yemeni tunes, and Jewish Moroccan prayers are distinguished by Moroccan tunes. In contrast with Sefaradi or Mizrahi Jews, Ashkenazi Jews carry cultural characteristics that are European in nature. Higher education and secular knowledge for both genders are held in high value; individualism and modernism have a stronger presence, and dress code is less restrictive.

In therapy, differences in cultural background can present generational and marital issues. Common generational issues are differences in cultural norms between parents and children. For example, the parents may have been raised in Iraq before migrating to the U.S., with cultural values characteristic of a Muslim society, but their children have been primarily exposed to American values. In addition, the parents may be more religiously traditional than their children. These various layers of their identity make therapy more complicated. Their relationship dynamics are enriched with identity development but also require higher levels of interpersonal awareness and communication skills.

The American Jew

American Jews reported that they feel bicultural (i.e., both Jewish and American) (Friedman et al., 2005). While the majority of American Jews do not practice traditional observance rituals, many carry fundamental Jewish values and worldviews in their daily lives. Thousands of Jewish scholarly teachings identify the most important values of a Jewish life to be: (1) the sanctity of life; (2) the importance of family; (3) the need for justice in the world and support for its existence; and (4) the obligation to repair the world (improve the world) (Kertzer, 1993). To serve these goals, American Jews may choose professions in the healing arts, such as medicine and science, and often engage in charitable and humanitarian activities. The American Jew often continues to carry on the value of studiousness and scholarship through activities such as learning, contemplation, discussion, and introspection. Several of the main scholarly Jewish texts that have been studied in Jewish institutions for thousands of years (*Gemara* and *Mishnah*) are structured around the presentation of opposing views about a wide range of topics and an in-depth analysis of the pros and cons of the various points of view. This style of learning has translated to positive study habits implemented in the pursuit of secular education as well. The practice of debate often results in various opposing views within the Jewish population on a wide range of topics, from politics to religion.

The Israeli-American Jew

Israeli Jews have distinct cultural characteristics. Historically and today, Israelis fight for their right to exist as a nation, and to do so with safety. Just shy of 70 years old, the State of Israel was primarily built by Jews who immigrated from all over the world, while leaving all their possessions behind in their countries of origin. By necessity, they had to be brave and innovative and build a country from inception, with few resources, and with significant opposition and threat from neighboring countries. Israeli children grow up knowing that their parents and siblings served in the military and fought in wars (and those occur in every generation) and therefore may not come home. Israeli children are born into the reality of daily threats of terrorism and death, and quickly become aware of the presence of the ever-growing antisemitism in the world. These realities teach an Israeli person to realize that their success depends primarily on them, and that accomplishments may have to be earned by efforts of their own, and theirs alone, despite opposition or even denial of rights. Israelis have also learned to negotiate; sometimes one has to make something from nothing, because nothing is what the individual has. Negotiation skills are also the common way of conducting business in the Middle East (Greaves, 2012). These cultural characteristics have often resulted in Israelis being described as aggressive, potentially rude or pushy, but also strong, smart, and innovative.

Because of the realities of a small country, surrounded by enemies, that has to deal with existential and financial survival on its own, Israelis also describe other Israelis as "family." Israelis often feel comfortable reaching out to other Israelis and have a strong sense of commitment to their people and the land. Family values and cultural realities often make them a people proud of their history and home.

Depending on their age when they relocated from Israel to the United States, and on the extent of their involvement outside of the Israeli community, Israelis may augment their cultural traits to various degrees. When their children attend American schools, they naturally become a unique blend of the two cultures. Due to the long history of a positive relationship between the U.S. and Israel, American-Israelis are often very proud of becoming Americans and take great pride in participating in the American culture. They often celebrate American holidays with great enthusiasm.

Growing Trends of Antisemitism

An astute therapist will not shy away from addressing the deepest issues their client is dealing with. For Jewish people, their safety as a people and as a nation is one of these core issues.

Negative stereotypes about Jewish people, such as having long noses or loving money, still exist. One need only to search the Internet or visit social media sites to be faced with the large number of sites that perpetuate these ridiculous beliefs and promote dangerous ideologies to justify the extermination of the Jewish people or the Jewish State of Israel. Antisemitism has been a problem in the existence of Jewish people for thousands of years, and numerous periods of pogroms and persecutions account for that. Despite the establishment of centers of tolerance and formal education about the Holocaust in the United States, recent and alarming trends of Antisemitism are on the rise in the United States and the world at large (ADL, 2017; FBI, 2015). For example, from 2014 to 2015, violent anti-Semitic assaults rose by 3%, and anti-Semitic incidents at colleges and universities nearly doubled (ADL, 2017). When working with Jewish people in therapy, it is important to understand that the concern Jewish people have about Antisemitism is deep and valid. It has generations of evidence. Political changes and personal experiences impact this concern in various ways. The persistence of negative Jewish stereotypes and antisemitism requires capable clinicians to be knowledgeable about the topic and respectful of the issue (Schlosser & MacDonald-Dennis, 2006).

Recommendations for Effective Therapy With Jewish Clients

1. When working with a Jewish client or looking to understand the Jewish faith, direct interaction and experience with Jewish communities will provide far better insight than reviewing the scholarly facts (Fairchild, 2010).

2. Respect a set of values that is different than our own, and in particular values that focus on a divine involvement in the person's decisions and course of life is essential in affective therapy. Allow, in a non-judgmental way, for individuals to not only incorporate but also utilize their religious orientation for the benefit of the therapeutic goals.

3. Keep in mind the considerable diversity within the Jewish population and the varied complexity of religious orientation along with cultural background.

4. Appreciate the affiliation and connection many Jewish individuals have to the state of Israel and the Jewish community as a whole and allow in a non-judgmental way for the individual to express their issues within this identity and affiliation.

5. In particular during times of political changes or terrorism, appreciate

the intense emotions, concerns, and fears Jewish individuals may feel and express in therapy and allow for those to be addressed appropriately within the therapeutic process should the individual desire to do so.

References

ADL, American Defamation League. (2017). Anti-Semitism in the U.S.—Audit. Retrieved on 5/18/2017 from: https://www.adl.org/anti-semitism

CCAR, Central Conference of American Rabbis. (1937). "The Guiding Principles of Reform Judaism—"The Columbus Platform." The Central Conference of American Rabbis. Retrieved on 04/20/2017 from: https://www.jewishvirtuallibrary.org/the-columbus-platform-1937

CCAR, Central Conference of American Rabbis (1999). "A Statement of Principles for Reform Judaism." The Central Conference of American Rabbis. Retrieved on 04/20/2017 from: https://www.jewishvirtuallibrary.org/reform-judaism-modern-statement-of-principles-1999

Esposito, J. L. (2014). "Ahl al-Kitab." The Oxford Dictionary of Islam. Oxford: Oxford University Press.

Chaves, M. (2013). American Religion: Contemporary Trends (2nd ed.). Princeton, NJ: Princeton University Press.

Vital, C. (1573). Etz Chaim. A summary of the teachings of Isaac Luria, the Arizal (1534-1572). Publisher: Rabbi Yosef ben Yitzchak Hacohen / Barazani | Language: Hebrew.

Fairchild, E. (2010). An Overview of Jewish Beliefs and Traditions for Counselors. James Madison University, JMU Scholarly Commons

FBI, Federal Bureau of Investigation. (2015). Hate Crime Statistics, 2015. Retrieved on 5/18/17 from: https://ucr.fbi.gov/hate-crime/2015

Friedman, M. L., Friedlander, M. L., & Blustein, D. L. (2005). Toward an understanding of Jewish identity: A phenomenological study. *Journal of Counseling Psychology, 52*, 77-83.

Greaves, S. (2012). *A Primer of Middle Eastern Leadership Culture*, Vol. 5, No. 4.

Holliman, R. P., & Wagner, A. A. (2015). Responsive Counseling in Jewish Orthodox Communities. *Journal of Counselor Practice, 6*(2):56-75.

Kertzer, M. N. (1993) What is a Jew? *A guide to the beliefs, traditions, and practices of Judaism that answers questions for both Jew and non-Jew* (5th ed.). New York: Simon & Schuster.

Langman, P. F. (1999). *Jewish issues in multiculturalism*. Northvale, NJ: Aronson.

Langman, P. F. (2000). Assessment issues with Jewish clients. In R. H. Dana (Ed.), *Handbook of Cross-Cultural and Multicultural Personality Assessment* (pp. 647-668). Mahwah, NJ: Laurence Erlbaum Associates.

NSAJG, The National Study of American Jewish Giving. (2013). Connected to Give: Key Findings. Retrieved on 5/20/17 from: http://connectedtogive.org

Ostrer, H., & Skorecki, K. (2013). The population genetics of the Jewish people. *Human Genetics, 132*(2), 119-127. http://doi.org/10.1007/s00439-012-1235-6

Pew Research Center. (2013). Pew Research Center Survey of U.S. Jews: A Portrait of Jewish Americans. Retrieved 3/20/2017 from http://www.jewishdatabank.org/studies/downloadFile.cfm?FileID=3088

Pirkei Avot—Ethics of the fathers. Retrieved on 4/1/2017 from: http://www.chabad.org/library/article_cdo/aid/5708/jewish/Translated-Text.htm

Psalm 40:9.

Schlosser, L. Z. (2006). Affirmative psychotherapy for American Jews. *Psychotherapy: Theory, Research, Practice, Training, 43*(4), 424-435.

Schlosser, L. Z., & MacDonald-Dennis, C. (2006). Antisemitism. In Y. Jackson (Ed.), *Encyclopedia of multicultural psychology* (pp. 44-45). Thousand Oaks, CA: SAGE.

Sheskin, I. M., & Dashefsky, A. (2015). Jewish Population in the United States. Retrieved on 4/20/17 from: http://www.jewishdatabank. org/Studies/downloadFile.cfm?FileID=3393

Singer, D., & Grossman, L. (Eds.). (2005). *American Jewish year book 2005*. New York: American Jewish Committee.

Tapper, A. J. (2016). *Judaisms: A Twenty-First-Century Introduction to Jews and Jewish Identities*. University of California Press

United States Census. (2016). U.S. Population. Retrieved on 4/20/17 from:https://www.census.gov/quickfacts/fact/table/US/ PST045218#

Section II:
Case Studies and First Person Accounts

7.

Asian Americans

Whillma Quenicke, MA and Margaret Loo, PhD

In this chapter we have two presentations from quite different situations. The first is from someone who was not born in the United States but immigrated here as an adult. She tells you her story from her position, and provides us with many ideas to consider when developing sensitivity to the Asian cultures. The second presentation is from someone whose family has lived in this country for over a century and it tells us of the many subcultures and the effect generation has on her culture and some of the difficulties of living in a foreign hostile environment. Together they provide us with great insights into the cultures involved and an appreciation for the diversity within these cultures.

As a Chinese-Dutch-Indonesian (WQ) who migrated to the United States at the age of 18 and became American citizen, my phenotype and accent tend to make people wonder and want to guess my ethnic background. Within the same day, different people came up to me and told me that they think I am Vietnamese, Filipina, and Thai. A barista at Starbucks asked if the name I gave her for my order was my original name, meaning that I was born with that name. She then explained that my name was not a common Asian name. In my mind, I thought: I do not even know if there is a common name for Asians as people from Japan do not have the same name as people from Korea or China. I recommend not asking an Asian with a Western name about their "other [original] name" as this question can be perceived as inappropriate if not offensive.

I was born and grew up in Indonesia, however; the native Indonesian does not see me as Indonesian because my ancestry was from China. When I told Chinese people that I am Chinese, they told me that I am not Chinese, although my ancestors were from China. Growing up, I did not fully identify myself with either Indonesian or Chinese as I know that they do not identify themselves with me. By immigrating to the United States and becoming a U.S. citizen, somehow, I was hoping that now I finally can feel that I belong to a country. However, when people ask me questions about what my nationality is due to my accent, I found this question annoying because I am an American citizen and my nationality is U.S.A. as it is clearly printed on my U.S. passport. Another question that blows my mind that I sometimes receive is whether I eat dog or cat. I often answer that I have never eaten dog or cat but I love eating chicken feet and frog legs. While eating dog may still exist in certain regions of Asia, this practice has been declining. Eating chicken feet and frog legs come from the fact that there is poverty in many Asian regions and limited access to food. People do not want to waste resources and food such as chicken feet has become a tradition. I really want to say that I eat fried children's fingers dipped in ranch dressing,

Having the above experiences, I am writing this to share some of my perspectives as a first-generation Asian American in hope to help mental health clinicians be more mindful about the complexities and richness of Asian culture, or, more accurately, of Asian cultures. For our purposes here, the first generation of Asian American is defined as an Asian person who is not born and raised here and who comes to United States. As I write this, I realize further the value of diversities and complexities among different Asian subcultures and their influence on mental health function, symptoms, diagnosis, and treatment among the first generation of Asian Americans.

Although the research suggests that some generalizations can be made for the characteristics of people with Asian descent, it is important to be very aware of and mindful about the fact that "Asian American is the most diverse group in terms of cultural background, country of origin, and circumstances for coming to the United States" (Sue & Sue, 2003). (There are varieties within Asian cultures depending on the region and ethnic group. Looking at physical characteristics, people from India, Bangladesh, or Pakistan are different from people from Malaysia, Thailand, Cambodia, the Philippines, Taiwan, China, Korea, Japan, and Pacific Islanders. Asian people from different regions also speak completely different languages and dialects, and they have different names, music, dance, food, and traditions. In addition, there are always individual differences within each ethnic group.

While Asian people from different part of Asia tend to share similar cultural values, it is important to remember that there are differences within Asian cultures as well as individual differences among Asians. However, questioning Asian Americans who were born and raised here about where they come from originally may be more or less offensive to some as we do not really hear similar question toward Caucasians although we know Caucasians come from different parts of Europe. It is wise to be mindful about certain feelings that are triggered by asking this question. After all, in general, people are likely to appreciate when they are identified as a unique individual first rather than being associated with a certain ethnic group.

Immigration, Education, and Types of Careers

The historical background and reasons for different Asian groups immigrating to the United States may influence the development of cultural identity of each Asian American group. They also affect how each member of this group is perceived in society. Due to language barriers, it is common among the first generation to have less prestigious jobs such as waitresses, maids, manicurists, and dry cleaners. However, Asian parents in general strongly and highly emphasize the importance of pursuing higher education that leads to prestigious careers such as psychologists, physicians, engineers, and lawyers. Asians, in general, highly value education because education reflects positively on family and is viewed as an investment in the family's well-being. Getting a higher degree of education and having certain types of careers puts pressure on and creates a high expectation among Asian students. The vast majority of international students who come from Asia tend to major in science, engineering, medicine, and Business. Many of these students come from very well-off families and they are not expected to work while in school. Tuition for international student is multiple times higher than for residents and citizens of the United States. Their parents fully financially support them while they are in school because international students in general are not allowed to work off campus and are not qualified for financial assistance such as student loans, grants, or scholarships.

When financial issues strike home, it can create a great amount of stress and a sense of powerlessness, as financial assistance and resources for these students are either not available or very limited. Because getting a degree from an American university is prestigious for their family and it opens many doors and opportunities, many Asian parents sacrifice and do whatever they can to continue supporting their children in higher education in the United States. This comes with a great expectation for their children to choose a career that is approved by their parents. Writers, artists, and musicians are among unconventional careers that do not necessarily get support and approval from Asian parents in general. Thus, unconventional careers of choice may become a source of conflict and tension between Asian parents and their adult children. It is common for adult children with unconventional careers to experience inner conflict between their desire to be truthful about their aspirations and feeling obligated to satisfy their parents' desire for having children with prestigious careers after all the sacrifice and financial support they provided. There is this notion of unspoken rules that, after all the hard work and sacrifice Asian parents have done, their adult children should meet their parents' expectations. Choice of a career that is different from what is expected by his or her parents can result in loss of emotional and financial support.

The financial pressure that often forces the first generation of Asian American couples to work tends to change the couple's dynamics and challenges of traditional gender roles. Typically, the first generation of Asian American males do not participate much in performing household chores. However, when their wives work fulltime due to financial pressure and ask for their husbands to help with household chores, this can create tension and conflict within the relationship. Confucianism strongly influences traditional gender roles for some Asians as it teaches that wives must be submissive to their husbands. For some Asian American women, when the wife is the breadwinner, she tends to feel guilty because she feels as if she is emasculating her husband. As a result, she does not demand that her husband do household chores.

Conflicts Between and Within Asian Groups

People from Southeast Asia are different from people from China or India, and they are different from people from Korea or Japan. Within Korean culture, North Korean people are different from South Korean people as North Vietnamese people are different from South Vietnamese people. Due to the history of World War II, Japanese and Korean, and Japanese and Chinese may still have some hostile feelings toward each other, depending on the generation. A psychologist may have a second-generation Korean client who experiences relationship distress because her or his parents are against her or his romantic involvement with a Japanese American because of World War II-related history that greatly affected the family more than a half century ago.

Another example of animosity is Taiwanese and Chinese. Taiwanese people do not want to be called Chinese. When they encounter this type of problem in therapy, the encapsulated psychologist may think, "Geez, what is the difference between Taiwanese and Chinese, or between Japanese and Korean; you guys all look the same to me." This psychologist only focuses on the physical characteristics and similarities between these two different ethnic groups, and fails to recognize the major impact of their history that influences how these two groups perceive and construct their reality. Sue and Sue (2003) stated that one of their research conclusions is that, in general, Asian Americans value restraining strong emotions that might otherwise disrupt peace and harmony and/or bring shame to the family. This conclusion does not necessarily apply for people from North Sumatra or East Timor (Indonesia) if they immigrate to the United States, as they are known to be very vocal in expressing their strong emotions and opinions compared to people from Java or Bali. Therefore, it is important for a psychologist to be aware of and sensitive to differences in historical background and the level of acculturation among Asian American clients. It is not realistic to expect clinicians to be familiar with every single culture among Asian ethnic groups. However, being aware of the fact that there are differences and being willing to familiarize oneself to clients' cultures is part of practicing psychology mindfully.

Religion

There are several different religions and beliefs shared among Asian people throughout different regions. Indonesia is the largest Muslim country in the world; however, there are a good number of people whose religion is Christian Protestant, Catholic, Hindu, or Buddhist. In Malaysia, the major religion is Islam; in the Philippine, their major religion is Catholic; and Thailand's major religion is Buddhism. In China, although many are atheist, there are people practicing Buddhism, which promotes spiritual understanding of disease causation, Christianity, Taoism (the basis for yin and yang theory), Islam, and ancestor worship. Within these countries, persecution against groups with minor religions exists that people from other parts of the world may not necessarily be familiar with. In Myanmar, Muslims from a region called Ronghya have been persecuted. While in North Korea independent religious practices are discouraged, the majority of people in South Korea are Catholic, Protestant, or Buddhist.

Other Asians practice Confucianism, which is a belief system that stresses respect for authority, filial piety, justice, benevolence, fidelity, scholarship, and self-development; and animism, which is the belief that human beings, animals, and inanimate objects possess souls and spirits. Confucianism also influences stereotypical and patriarchal gender roles within certain Asian communities. According to Confucianism, before marriage, a woman needs to be submissive to her father; after marriage she has to be submissive to her husband; and to be submissive to her son after her father and husband have passed away.

Differences in religious views can be the source of tension and conflict within the same ethnic group, as these people share different values and traditions influenced by their religious belief. When these persecuted Muslims immigrate to the United States and they see and hear negative stereotypes that Muslims are terrorists, it may significantly affect their mental health. While religious belief and spirituality practice can often serve as a protective factor to buffer psychological stressors, having a perception or experience of religious persecution can be very detrimental to mental health functioning.

Aging

Getting older is not necessarily feared as a bad thing among Asians. Perhaps it may be because Asian culture encourages filial piety due to the influence of Confucianism. Therefore, although there are some concerns regarding the declining of this value due to modernization, generally and typically elderly people are still well respected within the community. Elder people are perceived as wise because of their life experience. It is probably safe to say that collectivism and respecting the elderly are common values shared by the majority if not all different Asian groups. Elderly Asians usually hold power in making important financial decisions, and whether they will live with their children or not. They typically are looking forward to be taken care of by their adult children and they play a major role in caring for their grandchildren.

The value of respecting older people carries over to non-parental figures. It is a common practice for Asians to refer to someone older than they with "big brother" or "big sister" terms instead of using their first name. For example, Korean people called an older male person *opa*; Chinese and Vietnamese people called an older female person *cie*; Indonesians call an older female and male person *kakak*. However, the degree of these values tends to vary among individuals. For example, people from a major big city such as Jakarta (the capital of Indonesia) are likely to value individualism more than people from smaller city in Indonesia. This is due to more exposure of Jakarta's people to the influence of Western values.

Mental Health and Acculturation

It is strongly recommended for clinicians to ask patients and their family members to share their cultural views on the cause and understanding of the problem, coping strategies, barriers, health care-seeking attitudes and behaviors, and treatment expectations.

An important factor that determines mental health is the degree of integration of one's cultural origin with the current dominant culture. One example I want to discuss here is women's postpartum experiences, and parenting values and practices. I am going to use my own personal experience. In most if not every South-East country such as Indonesia, Vietnam, Thailand, after a woman gives birth, she is not allowed to shower, let alone to wash her hair for 30 to 40 days. She is not allowed to leave the house for the same amount of time and she must wear long pants, long sleeve t-shirt, and socks all day despite 90-degree heat outside. These practices and reasons for doing them do not make sense for people from the mainstream American culture. The cultural reason for doing this is to prevent the woman from getting sick or aging prematurely. There is no scientific explanation or research as far as I know to support this argument. However, it has been a tradition that is passed from generation to generation. When I asked my mom, aunts, and my friends' moms, all they say is "I don't know, that's what my mom and grandma told me." In the U.S., women take showers and wash their hair after labor. I am thinking: How do you not feel depressed from being isolated at home, and not taking a shower or washing your hair after being in labor for hours? Sometimes taking a shower is just enough to refresh your body and clear your mind. Sometimes what new moms need is going to their girlfriends to chat and share their tired and overwhelming feelings as new moms. As psychologists know that when women share their feelings with other women, the brain releases oxytocin and it makes you feel supported and better about your feelings. So if you have Asian female clients who are the first generation and they came to see you for postpartum depression, it is important to consider their degree of acculturation in assessing how it affects their mental health functioning.

Some common stereotypes about Asian patients are that men tend to hold anger in and that females are usually shy, quiet, and soft-spoken.

A good virtue held by many Asians is the importance of having total control over emotions. One of this author's friends shared that when she told her psychologist that the reason she has therapy is to learn how to be more outspoken and assertive in communicating her needs, her psychologist seemed to be surprised because it was not matching with the psychologist's stereotypical belief. The psychologist implied that he did not really understand why would she want to be more outspoken because she is Asian. The psychologist failed to recognize that the client did not consider her lack of assertiveness as something to do with the nature of her ethnicity. Thus, she never returned to therapy because she felt judged and completely misunderstood. One wonders how prevalent this incident is and whether it contributes to the low level of satisfaction experienced by Asian American women. It is strongly recommended for mental health clinicians to be aware of their own cultural bias and to put extra effort into being mindful about the importance of cultural sensitivity.

Another interesting client-psychologist relationship dynamic that may be worthy of research is when the client is an older first-generation Asian male client and the psychologist a young female, second or third generation. The client may well be reluctant to become vulnerable and less actively engage in therapy, as he is likely to see the psychologist as someone close to the age of his daughter or grand-daughter. On the other hand, from the psychologist's perspective, since respecting the elderly is highly valued within Asian culture, the psychologist may struggle in confronting her elderly client's issues.

The literature often discusses how common it is for Asians to manifest their mental health issues as somatic symptoms. While this is common, it is not always the case. Further, personality traits and coping styles could buffer and may be the moderating factors for the manifestation of somatic symptoms. It is hypothesized that the virtue of maintaining control over the expression of negative emotion is one of the reasons for somatization symptoms. Expressing an unwell feeling in a form of physical illness or discomfort is safer, more acceptable, and less stigmatizing.

We just said it is known that Asian people often manifest psychological distress in somatic complaint. In addition, cold and flu-like symptoms are interpreted as "the body is getting bad wind." And it is a common practice to do "coining" to get rid of the bad wind in the body and to treat maladies. Coining is a technique of using a coin and cream/oil to scratch and press the body part which leaves bruises, red/black marks like welts. Coining is to make the blood flow and circulate better; it is to open the stuck "chi" (good energy). When this traditional practice is carried to the United States and parents do coining to their children or adult children to their elderly parents, it most likely warrants teachers and other people with good intentions but who are not familiar with this practice to make a child abuse or adult abuse report. This traditional practice leads to a great misunderstanding, with legal consequences. The question is how to be culturally sensitive and tolerant while certain cultural practices conflict with mainstream societal value and law.

It is recommended for psychologists to be more open in exploring differences among values, beliefs, and traditions among different generations. These differences are due to historical backgrounds, socialization, and the level of acculturation. For example, the first generation of Asian as parents, will not charge their children rent and utility bills as soon as they turn 18. However, the second and third generation are more likely to do so. These differences in values and expectations are likely to create intergenerational conflicts.

Different reasons for immigrating to the U.S. influence the level of acculturation, mental health, and degree of functioning. Asian refugees do not experience privileges as Asians who come to study or to work. The circumstances around the time of immigration lead to different schemas, different levels of self-esteem and self-efficacy, and a different sense of control and belonging. It is suggested that clinicians always conduct a biopsychosocial assessment while being aware of and sensitive to individual differences related to historical background among Asian clients.

Parenting Practices

Another interesting thing about parenting values and practices is that teachers and most parents in the U.S. encourage independence in their children starting at a very young age. For example, it is a common practice to stop giving bottles when the babies reach 12 to 15 months old and to encourage a toddler to start eating by her/himself. In Indonesia, kids aged four, five, and sometimes even six still drink milk from a bottle. Kids these ages also still have their parents feed them. When I visited Indonesia and let my three-year-old son eat by himself, I had everyone staring at me and asking: How can you let your son eat by himself? You are his mom; you should feed him. He is too young to eat by himself. When I had a parent-teacher conference for my almost five-year-old son at his transitional kindergarten, his teacher suggested that I should foster more independence in him just because my son still struggles to hook and zip his pants as I always do it for him at home. First-generation Asian American parents do not necessarily encourage early independence in their young children. In general, Asian parents do not expect their children to move out of the house once they turn 18. It is not uncommon for adult children to stay at their parent's home until they are married. Co-sleeping is also a common practice among Asian parents. What's considered as attentive parenting styles can be viewed as enabling an over-protective parenting style. The questions are: Is there such a thing called the right parenting style? If yes, what is the right way of parenting? Based on criteria or cultural perspective, what would you do as a psychologist and how do you help your distressed clients find the balance integrating between the culture of origin beliefs and the mainstream culture in regard to child rearing practice?

While it is a common tradition for children to defer important and big decision such as type of career to their parents, the number of the younger generation following this practice varies depending on their personalities, level of acculturation, and exposure to mainstream culture. The tendency for the second and third generation of Asian Americans to embrace the mainstream American culture can be the source of tension, confusion, and familial conflict, which increases the risk for experiencing mental health problems. Moreover, Asian Americans are typically reluctant to share about their family's problems, or they tend to deny that their family's problems exist, which can lead to feelings of isolation.

Psychotherapy

There is still a strong stigma against mental illness and its treatment within most Asian cultures. This stigma is likely to make Asian clients self-isolate from their close family members, which can worsen their prognosis. Providing psychoeducation to close family members and involving them in treatment planning can be crucial. In psychotherapy, sometimes therapeutic confrontation is needed. However, therapists may want to do it carefully when they have Asian clients because of the notion of "save face" and "lose face" among Asians, especially if the therapist is a lot younger. When the need to "save face" is great, confrontation may lead to early, premature termination and clients will drop out of treatment. Therapists should also be aware of the possibility that model minority myths may affect the client's attitude toward psychotherapy.

There is literature suggesting that there is the tendency for Asian Americans to be confused about feeling well and doing well. For example, just because some Asian American students can graduate cum laude, it does not mean that they are not suffering from psychological disorders such as depression, anxiety, and bipolar disorders. It seems that hidden depression is prevalent and is well covered by what seems to be high functioning among Asian Americans.

Typically, the first and second generation of Asian Americans who experience mental illness are likely to use psychological services less than Caucasian Americans, and they are more likely to seek spiritual counseling. The American Psychological Association says that Asian American college students are far more likely to experience suicidal thoughts than their White counterparts. A relatively recent article stated that the second generation of Asian Americans are more likely to suffer from mental health disorders (Laurie Meyers *Monitor* Staff February 2006, Vol 37, No. 2). Other literature suggests that Asian Americans born in America have a higher suicide rate than foreign born Asian Americans. One possible explanation for this may be because second-generation Asian Americans are more exposed to the mainstream culture and information on mental illness through socialization and have more access to treatment. Because second-generation Asian Americans are born and raised here, language is not a barrier for them compared to their parents. As such, they can access treatment relatively more easily compared to their foreign-born parents.

Another important thing to remember when treating Asian clients is that, typically, Asian clients expect and want their therapist to be direct in giving them advice or concrete suggestions on what to do to solve their problems. When therapists use too much and or too often Socratic Questioning or Guided Discovery, they are likely to be perceived as incompetent, unskilled, and not trustworthy.

Asian cultures in general also emphasize the importance of being humble and not to be boastful. However, being humble may be misinterpreted as having low self-esteem. Individual personalities create a variety of expressions of humility and of achievement. It is important for the therapist to be mindful and to not necessarily interpret being humble and quiet as a sign of having low self-esteem.

Japanese Americans

In order to understand the psychology of Asian American people, a knowledge of their background and what their families have endured is necessary. The term "Asian American" was first used in the 1960s to refer to Chinese, Japanese, and Filipinos who immigrated to the United States from around the mid-1800s to early 1900s. The first largest Asian group to immigrate to the United States was Chinese men seeking to find gold. Gold was discovered in California, which was known to them as "the Golden Mountain," and they had high hopes of striking it rich, but most did not achieve their goal. They were followed by impoverished Chinese women seeking to marry these "rich" Chinese men who came back to China from the Golden Mountain. In the 1860s, many Chinese men were recruited to build the Transcontinental Railroad. To put this into a time context, my husband's grandfather, at age 18, came to the United States and was one of the men who worked on the railroad. The reason my husband was the only one out of all the siblings who did not speak Chinese was because his grandfather took care of him when he was growing up and only spoke English to him, whereas my husband's parents had just come from China and took care of the other siblings and spoke only Chinese to them (due to not being able to understand or speak English). As a result, his other siblings are able to speak Chinese. All of the children in my husband's family were born in the United States and are second-generation Asian Americans. Chinese people immigrated to the United States to escape the poor political and financial situation in Communist China. One of my husband's uncles was shot and killed trying to escape China.

Asians faced racism, harassment, and violence by Whites in America from the beginning. Because the Chinese laborers worked harder for lower wages, thus were more prone to be hired, the White workers became resentful of them for taking their jobs, and often resorted to violence against them. Dennis Kearny, who immigrated from Ireland at age 34 in 1868 (United States Census, 1880), was a zealous speaker against the Chinese, drawing thousands of people who listened to his speeches calling for lynching and setting fire to Chinese homes and businesses. The large crowds would chant "The Chinese must go!" before and after his speeches (Carlsson,1995).

In 1882, Congress passed a bill called the Chinese Exclusion Act that prohibited Chinese workers, skilled and unskilled from entering the United States for 10 years and was renewed in 1892 for another 10 years. The Chinese who were already in the United States were treated with severe prejudice and violence. One such event was the Chinese Massacre, which occurred in Los Angeles, California in 1881, when a mob of about 500 non-Asian people hunted down and attacked any Chinese people they could find and, within only six hours, 18 Chinese men were lynched (Dorland, 1894). Chinese people in cities across the United States were driven out of their homes and forced out of town. In 1888, Congress passed the Scott Act, which prohibited Chinese people's reentry into the United States after visiting China. Congress later extended the Chinese Exclusion Act indefinitely and it was finally repealed in1943.

Because of such treatment, and because they were not allowed to own homes or having access to education and certain jobs, not allowed to intermarry with whites or become American citizens, the Chinese people tended to stick together in Chinese communities for safety, support, and the ability to earn a living among themselves. As such, Chinese culture and traditions were perpetuated. One tradition is that relatives are referred to by their titles that describe their position in the family. For example, an older brother would be called "Goh" (older brother) by the younger siblings, and the older brother would call younger siblings by their first names. The second brother would call an older sister *Jeh* (older sister) and a younger sister by her first name, whereas a younger sister would call the second brother *Ngee-goh* (second brother). Aunts and uncles would not only have rankings in terms of their position in the family, but their titles would also include whether they are maternal or paternal relatives.

This ranking system can be significant when conducting therapy with a Chinese American client. For example, a client who was gay got tired of his parents trying to find him a wife so that he can have many children, which is important to traditional Chinese parents. He wanted to come out to his parents, but was afraid of what their reaction would be. He believed that it would be better for his oldest brother to tell them because, since the first son is revered in a traditional Chinese family, his parents would listen to him more than the client who was the second son and not respected the same way. A therapist, not understanding the dynamics of the Chinese family, may consider this "passing the buck" and not taking charge of oneself.

Further, when a parent dies, all relatives are called to his or her bedside and are positioned by rank in the family. The first son stands closest to the deceased parent even ahead of the mother. In addition, at the funeral, wearing red is strictly forbidden because the color red represents happiness. Likewise, brides do not wear white because the white color symbolizes death so they instead wear red. The importance of the symbolic meaning of colors is often very important for Chinese people especially for first-generation Chinese American parents and grandparents. These customs may be unfamiliar to non-Chinese therapists and, as a consequence, they may misinterpret certain behaviors of their Chinese American clients—not understanding that although they are highly acculturated, they still respect their parent's beliefs.

Chinese parents usually have an authoritative style of parenting and they encourage actions that benefit the family, especially excelling in school and getting high-paying jobs, and they discourage actions that would shame the family. As such, Chinese American people raised by traditional parents learn to be passive ("don't rock the boat" and "the nail that sticks out gets hammered down"). This passive tendency might lead to two issues: In therapy, these clients might not want to freely reveal things that might be perceived as short-comings, and they might meekly acquiesce to whatever the therapist suggests without question, even if they disagree, because they were trained from childhood to obey their parents and people in authority. Thus, the therapist should be aware that the initial response of the passive Chinese American client may not be authentic and the client should be put at ease and probed further.

The Japanese were the second largest group of immigrants in the United States seeking fortune between 1885 and 1924 and, within a short period of time, violence and discrimination laws forced them to struggle for survival. The first generation of Japanese immigrants were called Issei and, like the Chinese immigrants, Japanese men came to the United States seeking work, many working as farm laborers and fishermen. After a while, pictures of potential brides were sent to the men by matchmakers and relatives in Japan. The pictures that were exchanged between the men and women often did not match their present selves and both parties were often disappointed. However, as a result of this exchange, 20,000 "picture brides," as they were called, came to the United States from 1908 to 1920. Again, to put this into a time context, my grandmother was one of the picture brides who traveled from Japan to Los Angeles. She married my grandfather, and together they opened a Mom and Pop grocery store. By the early 1900s, the Issei were settled, many becoming farmers and small business owners.

Because of naturalization laws, the Issei were not allowed to become

223

citizens; however their American-born children were automatically American citizens. During this time, the Issei were not allowed to buy property unless they were citizens and since they were not allowed to become citizens, many bought property in their children's names. For example, my maternal grandfather and grandmother worked as farm workers until they saved enough money and had the opportunity to buy land, which they put in their oldest son's name because he was an American citizen by birth. They turned the land into farmland and, when they passed away, their oldest son took over the management of the farm. It is also traditional for the oldest son to inherit the parents' estate because he is expected to care for the parents in their old age.

When World War II broke out and Japan attacked Pearl Harbor, hysteria broke out, and all Japanese were racially profiled as possible spies without any evidence. It is especially important to have knowledge about this when treating clients who are the children of parents who were imprisoned in the internment camps, because it highly affected them as well. There is research on Japanese American children of internees that has found that they are indeed affected by their parent's traumatic experience. After President Truman signed Executive Order 9066 on February 19, 1942, approximately 120,000 people of Japanese ancestry living on the West Coast, whether U.S. citizens or not, simply because they looked like the enemy, were given a few days' notice before they were rounded up, forced to sell their possessions for pennies, and give away their family pets. They were only allowed to take with them what they could carry, and were sent to remote prison camps made up of hastily built barracks shared by many families, with no partitions or walls for privacy, even to use the toilet. As a holding area during the roundup, the internees had to sleep in horse stalls at race tracks such as at Santa Anita Park in Los Angeles until the trains were ready to take them to their unknown destinations.

There have been studies on how this imprisonment of Issei and

Nisei affected the next generation (Nagata, 1993). To illustrate how this affects potential Asian American clients, my father, who was in his second year of college at the University of Southern California studying business, was not allowed to finish his degree and instead was incarcerated in the Manzanar internment camp. As he neared the compound, surrounded by barbed wire, he said to himself "They're not putting me in there! I did nothing wrong." He was very bitter when the war was over and he was able to leave the camp. He did not trust anyone after his experience except those of Japanese descent for all matters, business and recreation. He also did not allow his children to associate with non-Japanese American people, which can cause stress and anxiety, because they had to go to American schools that comprised mixed races.

Of course, nonverbal and verbal race-related messages to their children varied among the internees. Many Nisei did not talk about their experience with their children, which often caused confusion, void, and a feeling of detachment. It often gave the message that "Well, we came back from discrimination and we're OK" but, as one Sansei put it, "the message I *felt* was that no, we are not OK" (Nagata, 1993, p. 96). This behavior is influenced by the cultural belief of *Gaman* (enduring the unbearable with fortitude, dignity, patience, perseverance, tolerance, self-control, self-denial). However, many of the Nisei and Sansei did become activists involved in promoting awareness and pride in their cultural heritage and history.

The Japanese Americans had no choice about going to the camps, which were surrounded by barbed wire and guard towers. They were herded by armed guards who would shoot anyone who tried to escape. My mother talked about some of the men having to wear targets on their backs while living in the prison camps so they can be easily shot if they tried to escape. My mother, an American citizen, who had dreams of graduating from a university and having a career, had her dreams taken away from her, and she was forced to live in imprisonment in the compound built in the remote barren desert in Poston, Arizona. She was also very bitter, especially about being forced into low income status by the circumstances of losing property and possessions, while the Japanese Americans who were not incarcerated were able to achieve a higher social economic standard. Internees reintegrating into society and reestablishing businesses and livelihoods were met with extreme racial tension, making it very difficult to start over.

The internees' whole way of life changed. Many Japanese families, who were mostly private people and did not know each other, were forced to live together in one barrack with no walls for privacy. Cultural customs were tossed aside in order to survive living under these paltry and miserable circumstances. Even their meals were government rations and surplus castoffs from Army surplus meats such as Vienna sausages, hot dogs, Spam, ketchup, and kidneys, with potatoes and no rice—far from the Japanese foods they were used to. The meat was rationed. They were served very little meat, and often pieces of it were mixed with lots of gravy to seem like more. One internee remembered, on one occasion, a thin slice of meat they were served that was thickly covered in breading to look like a big portion of meat. After eating rice everyday of their lives and now forced to be without, they rebelled, and rice was finally added but cooked very badly—often burnt or undercooked. The Japanese internees did not waste the rice, but dug holes in the ground, putting the burnt rice in a container they found and allowing it to ferment, becoming homemade sake (NPRb, 2007).

They were served their meals in a mess hall and all the internees ate together, which caused families to break up because the teens would run off to hang out with their friends, making it difficult for parents to control their children. The Issei would eat together and their children, the Nisei (second generation), would eat together by

226

default. I remember my grandfather saying, "It was no good place for *kodomo* (children)," referring to his youngest son, a teenager then, who would run off and meet with his buddies and not listen to his parents. It disrupted traditional family life. Mothers could not cook for their families, and the family unit began to break apart. Louise Kashino (NPRa, 2007) remembers,

> . . . after being served Vienna sausages for four days in a row, many internees developed diarrhea and had to run to the latrine. We then had to stand in line, but spotlights would come on with guns pointed at us like we were planning a riot or escape or something, creating fear in the residents.

The children internees growing up on this diet acquired a taste for Spam, Vienna sausages, and hot dogs. I remember my friend's father, a Nisei, would often make teriyaki spam or teriyaki hot dogs for dinner.

Similar to Chinese tradition, the first son is very important and is usually the one to care for the parents in old age, therefore often inheriting everything. My father, a Nisei (children of Issei who were born in the United States), took care of his parents, so I lived with my parents and my grandparents. It is very common to have several generations within the same household. This is important for therapists to know because the Issei and Nisei are very connected to traditional beliefs and culture, whereas the Sansei (children of Nisei who were born in the United States) and later generations were more ingrained in American culture, which may conflict with traditional Japanese ways, causing problems.

The Sansei are mostly in their sixties now, many serving as caregivers for their Issei parents who would be in their eighties or nineties. Often it is not understood why they do not just put their parents in assisted living homes instead of assuming the arduous task of taking care of a parent who often has dementia or Alzheimer's disease, but it is strongly ingrained in the culture that children care of their elderly parents when they are unable to care for themselves.

The Sansei grew up in American neighborhoods and went to American schools and were more removed from the traditional Japanese culture. Many did not speak Japanese and often felt unaccepted by Japanese and White Americans. For example, as I was paying a White cashier in California (where I was born and grew up, never having been to Japan), she asked me if I missed my country. She did not think that the U.S. was my country. In addition, Japanese nationals do not consider me truly Japanese because I do not speak the language and have never been to Japan. The Sansei often experienced culture clash and, as a result, had conflict with their parents and grandparents who had traditional beliefs and customs. Yet many Sansei, despite a history of troubled relationships, strongly feel the duty to care for their elderly parents.

It is important to refrain from assuming that Sansei Japanese American clients conform to stereotypes. Each is an individual, and their personalities are influenced more by American standards than Japanese standards. For example, a Sansei woman sought the help of a White therapist to help her with a social phobia that has disabled her throughout her life. Her quietness from fear of making a mistake or being embarrassed had cost her jobs and she was often reprimanded by teachers in school. However, the therapist made a comment, maybe to help normalize her concerns by saying, "But aren't all Japanese women quiet?" which she thought was a very insensitive comment and made her realize that the therapist had preconceived stereotypes about Japanese women and had no clue about her situation. The therapist did not differentiate her as an American and assumed she just fit the stereotype of a traditional Japanese woman. This triggered other racial microaggressions she had experienced growing up and turned her off to therapy.

Many of the Yonsei (American-born children of Sansei) feel even less of a tie to Japanese traditions and culture. They grew up in communities across the United States, went to American schools, often do not understand the Japanese language, and feel as American as non-Japanese Americans. However, they still experience prejudice and discrimination and may feel they are not accepted as Americans by non-Asians, nor are they accepted as Japanese by Japanese nationals. Many Yonsei describe racist bullying from other children in school and being mocked by others making "Bruce Lee sounds" and children chanting "Ching-chong Chinaman." One Yonsei described an experience when his fourth-grade teacher was choosing roles for the children to play in a Gold Rush video the class was making, and he was forced to play the "foreigner" despite his declining the role. He described how hurtful this was and damaging to his self-esteem, because he was constantly being bullied for his "foreignness" even though he was not a foreigner.

Often it is assumed that all Asians know each other or it is assumed that they can be grouped together, such as Yonsei and the immigrant Asian students, and will make friends automatically because "they are alike." One Yonsei described that although there were more Asians on campus than before, the other Asians were immigrants and she could not relate to them. She stated that it was easier for her to get along with non-Asian children who were also American. She described how less assimilated Asians would have a hard time understanding her "unAsianness" and would call her a "race-traitor", "wannabe white" "Twinkie," or "banana." Another Yonsei spoke about going to a predominantly White school and being bullied for his small size and "slanted eyes." He stated that the students who bullied him were mostly White and, as a result, his friends were mostly Hispanic students who were the only other minority group at school, because he was the only Asian student in his class.

Some other stereotypes Asian Americans may have encountered

229

are: They are good with computers; they are good at math; Asian males are physically inferior, lack masculine qualities, and are not attractive, but they know martial arts; they keep to themselves; and they are conniving and often self-serving. Actually, one Yonsei man stated "Bruce Lee was a pioneer in transforming the stereotypes of Asian men." For instance, an Asian American man described one incident when he was working as a police officer in which three White police officers were trying to arrest a man for a drug offense when he came to help them and pulled out his baton as he approached the group assuming a fighting stance. The offender thought the Yonsei was going to use Kung Fu with his baton (influenced by popular Kung Fu film stars at the time such as Bruce Lee, Jackie Chan, and Jet Li) and became genuinely scared and submissive. However, this Asian American man experienced many disadvantages of these stereotypes, such as being put in the role of computer tech and having a difficult time persuading his superiors to train for the SWAT rifle team that he preferred. The feelings triggered by these experiences are often misunderstood by therapists who have not had such experiences and are often the reason for not seeking mental health services.

References

Carlsson, C. (1995). The working man's party & The Denis Kearny agitation: Historical essay. Retrieved February 23, 2017 from www.foundsf.org/index.php?title=The_Workingmen's_ Party_%26_The_Denis_Kearney_Agitation

Dorland, C. P. (1894). Chinese Massacre at Los Angeles in 1871. *Annual Publication of the Historical Society, 3,* 22-26. Retrieved February 23, 2017 from https://www.jstor.org/ stable/41167579?seq=3#page_scan_tab_contents

Lee., E. (2015). *The making of Asian America: A history.* New York:

Simon & Schuster, Inc.

Nagata, D. (1993). *Legacy of injustice: Exploring the cross-generational impact of the Japanese American internment.* New York: Plenum Press.

Nagata, D. & Cheng, W. (2003). Intergenerational communication of race-related trauma by Japanese American former internees. *American Journal of Orthopsychiatry, 73,* 266-278.

NPR. (2007a). Louise Kashino describes the fear in the Minidoka Incarceration Camp when internees became ill. Retrieved April 1, 2017 from http://www.npr.org/2007/12/20/17335538/weenie-royale-food-and-the-japanese-internment

NPR. (2007b). Weenie royale: Food and the Japanese internment. The Kitchen Sisters, morning edition. Retrieved May 1, 2007 from http://www.npr.org/2007/12/20/17335538/weenie-royale-food-and-the-japanese-internment

United States Census, 1880. (2017). Family search. Retrieved February 23, 2017 from https://familysearch.org/ark:/61903/1:1:M6PD-WNN

8.

FIRST NATIONS PEOPLES

Heather Sorenson

Prodigious amounts of literature, scholarly and otherwise, refer to indigenous First Nations people as "American Indians." For the purpose of this chapter, and clarity throughout, indigenous First Nations people (FNP) will be utilized as a general term for individuals who identify as a FNP and with ancestors who lived in the Americas before European contact. It is challenging to define and provide a general descriptor for FNP because FNP are not a homogenous group. There are a plethora of various descriptors and, when trying to determine how to be culturally sensitive and accurate in describing someone's ethnicity, it is most acceptable to just ask that individual what terminology they would prefer. Personally, when identification is needed to describe my heritage I prefer the term indigenous First Nations person. However, I do not speak for all FNP and as such encourage individuals working with this population to be mindful that everyone is unique and if you do not know something about someone's cultural identity or preferred terminology—just ask them rather than guess. Much of this chapter will weave personal experiences as well as scholarly literature in an effort to encourage readers to be more culturally sensitive and competent, as well as to inspire individuals to seek more understanding outside their own microcosm.

I utilize terminology that I find appropriate for me, as well as terminology that might be more effective for readers who were not raised in my community or within my culture. Additionally, my "experience" as a FNP is not generalizable to the whole of FNP. Presently, there are 562 federally recognized tribes in the United States alone and each nation is "ethnically, culturally, and linguistically diverse" (National Congress of American Indians, 2017, p. 2). Furthermore, as a "white-passing" FNP, I experience a degree of privilege that sets my experiences apart from those who are not so "passing." White-passing is a term loosely used to describe a person of color (POC) who appears, or passes, as Caucasian (Zumba, 2016). To discuss white-passing, an understanding of white privilege must be identified, because passing as Caucasian provides POC a modicum of privileges (i.e., potentially not being followed by security in a store, a reduced reaction time for a police officer firing their weapon, etc.) that our "non-passing" brothers and sisters are not privy to. It is important to understand, and for me to identify myself as white-passing because not to do so would do FNP culture and diversity a potential disservice.

Concomitantly, my experience is not typical, in that I was raised within various tribal/FNP communities. However, identification of who I am and where I come from is an important facet of my experience as an FNP. When someone asks, "What do you identify as?" or "Where do you come from?" there is a specific way I was raised to introduce myself. For example, during ceremonies, such as sweat lodge (or *inipi*), when we are to speak, I was taught to introduce myself by my legal name, my indigenous name, my tribal affiliation and location, and the parent my FN ancestors originate from. I am *Lenca* from Honduras on my father's side. I was raised on several reservations and rancherias in central California and much of my understanding of ceremonies were taught to me by my brother Carl who was Chukchansi Yokut. Further, my indigenous name was given to me by a Lakota medicine woman.

The term *medicine man* or *medicine woman* is often used to identify a FNP who is a healer and active in providing traditional ceremonies, such as *inipi*, awakening of the bears, weddings, Chanupa blessings, etc. (Cherokee Nation, 2017; Hartmann & Gone, 2014). Many times I hear non-FNP inappropriately refer to our medicine people as *shamans*, which is a term that I think is incorrect. Incidentally, the word "shaman" is not a FN word and in fact comes from Turkish-Tungusian languages (Laufer, 1917). Using non-FN words to describe an aspect of our culture involves a major degree of erasure of our culture, history, and identity.

A great deal of symbolism is intertwined within FNP oral culture. Words carry a great weight as well. For many FNP that I know, when we tell someone this seemingly unrequested list of information it is because we feel all of it is important when identifying our heritage, who we are, and where we come from. The legacy, culture, languages, and much of the history of FNP was nearly erased through the horrors of colonization and, as such, the aforementioned oral record and our storytelling is the primary and traditional way we preserve our history.

Although I was fortunate enough to go to a preschool for FNP, I quickly learned how isolating it feels when someone is culturally insensitive or offensive. I was often called "exotic-looking," and whenever asked to identify my ethnicity, I would get these responses, "No, you don't look Indian. What percentage are you?" or "Oh yeah, I can see it now in your cheekbones!" Or "Me too! My great-grandmother was a Cherokee princess" or "So you own a Casino?" or "Better stay away from that 'firewater' then." When working with communities and cultures one is not familiar with, it is important for professionals to ask themselves whether they would ask a specific question of someone who is Caucasian or African American/Black, and their reasoning behind that. For instance, during the uncertain times that I am writing this, it is generally unlikely that one would ask a Caucasian individual what percentage of their blood is European or a Mexican American what percentage of their blood is "Mexican," or any other ethnicity/culture for that matter. This is inappropriate for a number of reasons. Primarily, this is an abnormal way to communicate with individuals and is quite ostracizing—not to mention that FNP are the only ethnicity in America that must prove their percentage of blood to obtain recognition, services, and protection under the federal government (Schmidt, 2011).

It is offensive to ask about blood quantum because it is not relevant to how most FNP I know identify ourselves. Additionally, blood quantum is an area of contention, disagreement, and dislike among many FNP (Ellinghaus, 2008; Schmidt, 2011). Incidentally, the application of blood quantum is not how FNP established tribal affiliation precolonization (Ellinghaus, 2008; Schmidt, 2011). The use of blood quantum began in 1705 in an effort to restrict the civil rights of FNP (Ellinghaus, 2008; Schmidt, 2011). Therefore, when an individual asks a FNP a question regarding blood quantum they are, in essence, pushing an ideology and understanding of what it means to be a FNP that is not founded in many FNP cultural and historical perspectives regarding lineage. This is to say that blood quantum is an external label used to identify FNP. Often what follows after blood quantum lines of questioning involves ignorant and ethnocentric commentary such "Oh, you're 49%? So you're not a real Indian."

The aforementioned type of erasure and ignorance has continued throughout my life and even within employment in behavioral health professions. For example, I have long experienced colleagues who would unintentionally say offensive things to me such as referring to me as "Pocahontas Barbie" and arguing with me about their desire to preserve "artwork" that was disparaging to FNP. Oftentimes, during these situations individuals would become very upset when I would share with them that something is offensive to me as a FNP. Instead of taking my word for it as someone who is a FNP who was raised

235

within indigenous culture, I have, more often than not, been told that their Google search says otherwise, they know a "real Indian who says it's okay," or I should choose not to be offended because they have a right to have a good time. It is funny how they know more about me, my culture, and my history than I do. There are countless other experiences I could share that range from microaggressions to direct racism, but for the purpose of this chapter I will focus primarily on scholarly sources rather than personal experience. I want to provide a better understanding of FNP through scholarly sources, the personal experiences that shaped my views, and through the iteration of other FNPs' stories, so that mental health professionals and researchers alike can be more mindful and effective when working with this population. For those working in the mental health field and otherwise, it is important to comprehend that an individual's culture and their place in that culture are incredibly important to understand and best help them.

First Nations people are not a homogeneous group from which one can generalize one tribe or band's experiences to others. However, there are many values that are commonly instilled and followed, as well as a shared history regarding colonization. As an interdependent culture, the collective good is often held in higher esteem and value than individual success (Yeh, Hunter, Madan-Bahel, Chiang, & Arora, 2004). Research has substantiated the importance of clinician and client equity regarding racial identity perspectives, as well as the clinician's multicultural competence (Yeh et al., 2004). In addition, a substantial body of research is focused on how to establish an effective and collaborative partnership with psychology and indigenous FN healing perspectives (Hodge, Limb, & Cross, 2009; Rasmus, Charles, & Mohatt, 2014).

A History of Violence and Trauma

To understand some FNP better, the professional must be aware of the history of violence perpetrated against indigenous people as its place within the culture. As discussed, erasure of FNP and our history is still a considerable concern and injustice that continues to proliferate. Many history textbooks provide an inaccurate, nationalistic retelling of European contact and conquest in the Americas (Fenelon & Trafzer, 2014). The fact that "Columbus Day" is still an observed holiday for many public schools is a testament to this revisionist history (Desai, 2014). The genocide of FNP is often denied even though the FN lives that were ended by colonization are estimated to be between 95,000,000 to 114,000,000 (Stannard, 1992). Even at the lowest estimates, colonization deaths overtake those from the holocaust approximately 16 times over (Stannard, 1992). However, the Holocaust is always considered a terrible genocide and taught as such, whereas the genocide of indigenous FNP is not considered with the same gravity (Stannard, 1992). Concomitantly, Adolf Hitler reported that he learned much from "America's extermination [of First Nations people]" and utilized the genocide of FNP as a template for his concept of concentration camps (Toland, 2014). When working with FNP it can be important to appreciate the perplexing and disparaging experience of having one's history rewritten, nearly erased, and often debated; all the while living in a society that was usurped by foreign invaders who annually celebrate an individual's crimes against humanity—crimes that still directly and indirectly affect us as individuals.

Theory of Historical Trauma Among First Nations People

The theory of historical trauma (HT) explains that some FNP contend with psychiatric symptoms from historical loss (Brave Heart & Debruyn, 1998; Gone, 2009). Some of these symptoms present as general psychological distress, substance use disorders (SUDs), poverty, depression, and diabetes, to name a few (Brave Heart & Debruyn, 1998; Gone, 2009). In addition, the symptomatology is similar in nature to previous criteria and conceptualizations of unresolved grief, complicated bereavement, and complex post-traumatic stress disorder (Brave Heart & Debruyn, 1998; Gone, 2009). Historical trauma is not necessarily trauma that one has experienced physically, but rather "intergenerational accumulation of risk for poor mental health status" among FNP that derive from colonial oppression, subjugation, racism, and related polices (Gone, 2009, p. 752). Due to the historical trauma, certain sectors of the culture view themselves as "less than" and not competent. Culturally competent mental health professionals serving FNP know all too well the effects of colonization on FNP (Gone, 2009).

Boarding Schools

Residential schools were known for not providing adequate nutrition or learning modalities, as well as forcing manual labor and subjecting FN children to "sadistic acts of torture;" along with corporal punishment, sexual, physical, and emotional abuse, cultural assimilation, and Christian indoctrination (Gone, 2009, p. 752). Additionally, there are numerous research findings substantiating the negative psychosocial consequences resulting from FNP in boarding schools (Charbonneau-Dahlen, Lowe, & Morris, 2016; Corrado & Cohen, 2003; Gone, 2009). The boarding schools are frequently referred to as a clear example of the intergenerational effects of HT (Charbonneau-Dahlen, Lowe, & Morris, 2016; Gone, 2009). Anecdotally, a FN friend of mine who has had her share of adverse psychosocial impairments was sharing about her grandmother whom she loved had been in a boarding school as a child. My friend, Dara, told a story about when she was younger and learning her people's language. Dara recounted being excited to repeat the words she had learned that day to her grandmother. However, when Dara spoke her traditional language, her grandmother reacted physically toward her and then distanced her for the rest of that night. Dara said she was upset, shocked, and confused regarding her grandmother's reaction.

Later on in Dara's life, her grandmother made amends to her and explained that early on in her boarding schools experience, before she had learned English, all she knew was her native tongue. Consequently, in the boarding schools every time a FNP spoke their native language, they were punished. Dara continued to explain that her grandmother told her that the boarding school cut off one of her grandmother's fingers due to using her native tongue. Her grandmother was reportedly very apologetic and explained that it was a knee-jerk reaction due to her experiences at the boarding school. I do not know what became of Dara but her grandmother's story is not an abnormality or outlier in FN communities.

The boarding schools had an obvious goal, to assimilate FNP into Anglo-European homogeneity (Graham, 2012; Gram, 2016). First Nations children were dressed in clothing not accustomed to them or to FNP culture (Graham, 2012; Gram, 2016). Spiritual and cultural practices were prohibited and demonized (Kelsey, 2013). FN children were militarized in the way they were treated in these boarding schools (Graham, 2012; Gram, 2016; Kelsey, 2013). These boarding schools not only abused FN children but they attempted to remove every trace of who they were and where they came from (Graham, 2012; Gram, 2016). These attempts to eradicate FNP from America through murder, genocide, rape, forced sterilizations, and assimilation of FN children were the result of federal directives (Graham, 2012; Gram, 2016). Graham (2012) reports that the boarding school substantially impacted social development and as a result these "schools have historically been used as tools for reinforcing power relationships and cultural identities" (p. 467). Professionals working with FNP should be mindful of HT and how it not only may affect the patient, but also how it affects the power dynamic within the patient-clinician relationship.

Negative Health Outcomes for First Nations People

Along these same lines, the statistics regarding the disproportional

239

negative health outcomes FNP experience are staggering (Dickerson, Spear, Marinelli-Casey, & Rawson, 2011; Hedden, Kennet, Lipari, Medley, & Tice, 2015; Jiang, Mitran, Minino, & Hanyu, 2015; Lyons, Fowler, Jack, Betz, & Blair, 2016; Males, 2014; Macartney, Bishaw, & Fontenot, 2013; Tjaden & Thoennes, 2000). Indigenous FNP have the highest risk of being sexually assaulted of any group. Furthermore, FNP experience increased poverty and unemployment rates when compared to the national average (US Census Bureau, 2015). First Nations teens and young adults have one of the highest suicide rates (Jiang, Mitran, Minino, & Hanyu, 2015). First Nations people have one of the highest substance use disorder rates (Hedden, Kennet, Lipari, Medley, & Tice, 2015; Results from the 2007 national survey on drug use and health: National findings, 2008) and drug-induced death rates (Hedden et al., 2015). Additionally, FNP are more likely to be killed by police (Lyons, Fowler, Jack, Betz, & Blair, 2016; Males, 2014). Concomitantly, FNP typically have very poor treatment outcomes as well (Dickerson, Spear, Marinelli-Casey, & Rawson, 2011).

Sexual Assault Crimes

Indigenous First Nations (FN) women are more likely than any other race or cultural group to be sexually assaulted (Tjaden & Thoennes, 2000). In fact, one in three FN women will be raped in her lifetime (Tjaden & Thoennes, 2000). First Nations people are 2.5 times more likely to be the victim of a sexual assault crime than any other race (Tjaden & Thoennes, 2000). Additionally, these sexual assaults are most commonly perpetrated by non-FNP (Tjaden & Thoennes, 2000). It is important to understand the way FN women are romanticized by non-FNP, which interferes with the appropriate interventions needed to address the related crimes committed against FNP (Ono & Buescher, 2001).

Fetishizing First Nation Women

When FN women are romanticized, fetishized, and overly sexualized in the media it effects the way individuals view FN women. If FN women are romantic and sexualized characters, then our personhood is affected both in our minds as well as in the perspectives of those who might capitalize on this dehumanization. In addition, the sexualization and dehumanization of FN women for the purpose of dressing up on Halloween is a glaring example of this Western propensity. Every year for Halloween many FN women are offended and depersonalized by individuals wearing "Pocahottie" costumes and the like. The practice of dressing up as a person who is alive as if they are a mythical creature is dehumanizing. In addition, sexualizing FN women only compounds our risk for sexual assault.

The Role of Cultural Appropriation

For some indigenous FN people, it is disparaging to have individuals adorn themselves with pseudo-FN regalia without any idea of its cultural significance. For example, a war bonnet or traditional headdress is spiritually and culturally sacred. Although there are variations in appearance, symbolism, and ways in which a headdress is earned, the wearing of one is not taken lightly (Killsback, 2013). For tribes whose regalia involves headdresses, more typical of American Plains tribes, it is an honor that is often earned through a great degree of work and dedication (Killsback, 2013). Traditionally, Cheyenne warriors wore a *mámaa'e*, war bonnet, when battling an honorable opponent or during ceremonies (Killsback, 2013). The wearing of pseudo-headdresses and war bonnets as a costume is akin to wearing a dress-up Purple Heart from the Dollar Tree.

Many tribes consider an eagle feather to be one of the highest symbols of respect and honor and many headdresses utilize eagle feathers (Killsback, 2013). Each feather is sacred and typically requires great sacrifice to earn or be honored with (Killsback, 2013). I, myself, did not receive my first eagle feather until I was 24 years old and graduating cum laude with a bachelor's degree. Similarly, the branding and commodification of FNP through logos and mascots perpetuates the marginalization and oppression of FNP (Turner, 2015). Professionals in the field should be aware of how the cultural commodification and museumification of FNP can impact our self-esteem, identity, cognitive schemas, relationship with the dominant Western culture, and self-efficacy (Turner, 2015).

Substance Use Disorders

First Nations people experience some of the highest rates of SUDs (Hedden et al., 2015). There are various hypotheses regarding the cause of increased incidence of SUDs among FNP; however, a comprehensive understanding of the various risk factors for FNP provides the most advantageous conceptualization of this epidemic (Hedden et al., 2015). A common misconception or myth is that FNP are more sensitive to the effects of alcohol (Garcia-Andrade, Wall, & Ehlers, 1997; Gonzalez & Skewes, 2016). This misconception is based on a racially charged myth often referred to as the "firewater theory" that proposes FNP are physiologically less able to manage the effects of alcohol (Garcia-Andrade, Wall, & Ehlers, 1997; Gonzalez & Skewes, 2016). Another myth is that "the culture" of FNP involves frequent intoxication (Gonzalez & Skewes, 2016; Prussing, 2007). In fact, quite the opposite is true.

At every ceremony and cultural gathering I have ever attended, it is announced that if someone has used any substances of abuse that day they should not participate. I was taught that you carry your medicine (your intensions that have the power to heal or cause sickness) with you and if you are not "on the red road" (meaning in recovery from SUDs or maintaining abstinence during ceremonies) your medicine can negatively affect others. It is important that we try to affect others and our environment in *a good way* and if our medicine is sick we must cleanse ourselves instead of potentially harming the whole. Although

242

FNP suffer from SUDs at an increased rate, it does not mean our principles or cultural practices are responsible for that. The most likely culprit involves historical trauma, socioeconomic status, systematic oppression, and the various related negative factors FNP are more susceptible to (Crawford, 2014).

Considering the expectations of abstinence during many ceremonies and related activities across various tribes, it is relevant to consider the cultural implications of FNP with SUDs. Identifying abstinence requirements during ceremonies has become a more and more common occurrence among many FNP. However, given the nature of SUDs, it is no easy feat for those afflicted by the brain disease of addiction to simply cease using substances of abuse. For FNP, it can become increasingly difficult to seek community support through ceremonies when still using substances of abuse. Conversely, many FN communities integrate and support SUD recovery activities. When I was working for the tribal government in a residential treatment facility, we would frequently transport our clients to ceremonies and community gatherings. Engaging FN clients in cultural activities while receiving residential treatment in FN-run treatment centers is a common practice (BigFoot & Schmidt, 2010).

Clients shared that it benefitted their recovery to be able to participate in ceremonies again or, for some, the first time. Every week this treatment center would have an open 12-step community support meeting that began with drumming and smudging, then an hour long Alcoholics Anonymous meeting, and would end in the *Great Spirit Prayer* (Translated by Lakota Sioux Chief Yellow Lark, 1887). Many clients found this cultural adaptation of 12-step meetings encouraging, given that many 12-step meetings were predominantly Caucasian. Another example of the encouragement of recovery from SUDs among FNP was the New Year's Eve Powwows we would take our clients to. These Powwows involved typical Powwow activities along with 12-

step meetings that occurred several times a day for two days. There are countless examples of ways many FN communities are particularly supportive in recovery from SUDs for FNP.

Other than the obvious ways that many FN communities support recovery from SUDs, it is important to understand interdependent aspects of FNP culture in providing culturally specific interventions. Respect for elders and supporting one's community are common themes in the way I was raised as an FNP. There is considerable research that substantiates the positive effects of altruistic behaviors in improving affect, happiness, remission from SUDs, reducing severity of symptoms of mental illnesses, etc. (Post, 2005; Seligman & Csikszentmihalyi, 2014). A particularly useful intervention with FNP in treatment for SUDs involves such behaviors. During my employment at that FN treatment center, clients and staff alike would provide volunteer services during community gatherings. Volunteering would often involve assisting elders with their food, setting up, breaking down, teaching the youth how to make prayer ties, and drumming during FN conferences, to name a few. The clients I worked with always shared how impactful their "giving back" or volunteer work was to their remission from SUDs. During these outings, our clients were accepted by FN community members regardless of tribal affiliation (though all of our clients were from federally recognized tribes, their specific tribal membership did not seem to cause in-group/out-group effects). There are many culturally sensitive therapies that are particularly useful among many FNP (BigFoot & Schmidt, 2010; Kinsey & Reed, 2015). As a mental health professional, it is especially important to be aware of these therapies and whether or not FNP you may be treating would benefit from such culturally specific treatments.

Cultural and Custom Differences Among First Nations People

A great deal of this chapter has thus far described many similarities among FNP; however, it is important to understand differences among tribes. For the purpose of this chapter, I will describe five different indigenous First Nations tribes to highlight how diverse one FNP can be from another. To begin, even among one tribe, there may many separate bands that make up that Nation, each with their own customs, beliefs, iconography, etc. (Pass, 2009). Additionally, due to the horrors of colonization, information is limited and often disputed regarding tribal practices, customs, beliefs, ceremonial regalia and relics, and every other potential facet of cultural identification. Even among FNP, there is false information passed on regarding FN culture, history, and the like. Furthermore, the present FN Zeitgeist seems to combine various FN tribal customs and ceremonies that further obfuscate present understandings of contrasting customs among FNP. Our culture is not static; we are allowed to change the way we practice our ceremonies. Where the practice of inipi is no longer specific to one FN tribe, one might hear Lakota, Cherokee, Mono, or other FNP songs during a sweat. An understanding of the challenges of identifying historical information or present tribal customs is important in consuming any documentation regarding FNP. Though this section will be supported by reliable sources, it is important to understand the aforementioned discrepancies.

Lakota History and Culture

Although many tribes lived in one place, the Lakota people, for instance, were predominantly nomadic after the introduction of horses (Littlefield, 2003; Modaff, 2016; North Dakota State Government, 2017). In addition, Lakota people consist of seven related tribes or bands: Sičháŋǧu, Oglála, Itázipčho, Húŋkpapȟa, Mnikȟówožu, Sihásapa, and Oóhenuŋpa (Littlefield, 2003; Modaff, 2016; North Dakota State Government, 2017). Lakota people are often grouped into the Great Plains Tribes (North Dakota State Government, 2017). The buffalo is of particular importance to Lakota culture and history as much of Lakota life historically involved following buffalo migration (Littlefield, 2003; Modaff, 2016; North Dakota State Government, 2017). In addition, traditionally Lakota people used every part of the buffalo, as the buffalo was the primary source of food and was used to make shelter, tools, and clothing (Littlefield, 2003; Modaff, 2016; North Dakota State Government, 2017). Historically, Lakota people often lived in tipis because they were easy to set up, break down, and travel with (Littlefield, 2003; Modaff, 2016; North Dakota State Government, 2017).

The most sacred ceremonial object specific to Lakota people is the sacred pipe or *chanupa* (Littlefield, 2003; Modaff, 2016; North Dakota State Government, 2017). The Lakota have a story of *Ptesanwin*, the White Buffalo Calf Woman, which explains how the sacred pipe came to them and how it is practiced (Littlefield, 2003; Modaff, 2016; North Dakota State Government, 2017). A misnomer used by U.S. military involved calling it a "peace pipe" and another that still persists is that it is used to smoke marijuana and "get high" (North Dakota State Government, 2017). However, tobacco is a common sacred herb medicine used by many FNP and is what is commonly used during *chanupa* ceremonies (Littlefield, 2003; Modaff, 2016; North Dakota State Government, 2017). Another ceremony that is now widely participated in by various FNP but is traditionally accepted as having been given to the Lakota/Dakota people is the Sun Dance (Littlefield, 2003; Modaff, 2016; North Dakota State Government, 2017).

Sun Dance is a ceremony that lasts a week and involves flesh offerings through piercings, dancing, and *inipi* (Littlefield, 2003; Modaff, 2016; North Dakota State Government, 2017). Concomitantly, *inipi* ceremonies are purification ceremonies that are sacred to Lakota/Dakota people (Littlefield, 2003; Modaff, 2016; North Dakota State

Government, 2017). During these ceremonies, water is poured over hot rocks in a lodge, which causes steam to rise and is considered one part of the purification and cleansing process occurring during the *inipi* (Littlefield, 2003; Modaff, 2016; North Dakota State Government, 2017). Another sacred Lakota/Dakota ceremony is the vision quest or *hanbleca* (Littlefield, 2003; North Dakota State Government, 2017). During the vision quest, the individual fasts and prays for a vision while staying on a hill fasting until that vision arrives (Littlefield, 2003; Modaff, 2016; North Dakota State Government, 2017). There are so many specific ceremonies brought to other FNP by the Lakota people and, while many other FN tribes now utilize these ceremonies, it is always important to identify where the sacred medicine one is using comes from.

Iroquois Confederacy History and Culture

The Iroquois Confederacy was a group of five tribes that originally lived in close proximity to each other in what is now New York, spoke homologous languages, and developed a non-aggression agreement among themselves (Abler, 2000; Milwaukee Public Museum, 2017). These five tribes included the Seneca, Cayuga, Onondaga, Oneida, and Mohawk people (Abler, 2000; Milwaukee Public Museum, 2017). During the 1700s, the Tuscarora tribe joined the Iroquois Confederacy as the sixth tribe (Abler, 2000; Milwaukee Public Museum, 2017). The non-aggression agreement also involved the institution of a representative government and an iteration of inalienable rights that the present United States Bill of Rights was founded on (Abler, 2000; Milwaukee Public Museum, 2017). The Six Nations of the Iroquois Confederacy are matrilineal and, historically, female tribal members were incredibly influential, from selecting chiefs to act as representatives for the people, to decisions about whether or not to go to war (Abler, 2000; Milwaukee Public Museum, 2017).

A primarily important symbol to the Iroquois was *wampum* beads

247

and belts which joined all significant events and decisions (Abler, 2000; Milwaukee Public Museum, 2017). *Wampum* brings up another misunderstood and often retold conceptualization of FNP culture. Many colonists falsely assumed that *wampum* was "Indian money" (Keagle, 2013, p. 221; Otto, 2017). However, *wampum* was much more involved than that unsavory simile. *Wampum* was not used by most FN tribes, primarily being used by the Iroquois (Keagle, 2013; Otto, 2017).

Wampum was often shaped from shells and grouped as strings and/or made into belts (Keagle, 2013; Otto, 2017). Symbolism is traditionally a primary component of FN culture and *wampum* is no different (Keagle, 2013; Otto, 2017). It was often combined with trade and other important matters as a way to highlight the truth of one's words (Keagle, 2013; Otto, 2017). Additionally, the beads' color represented a variety of meanings (Keagle, 2013; Otto, 2017). Although the Iroquois are not understood as a traditional First Nations tribe, much of their practices and principles influence the way many FNP practice and share customs and ceremonies today.

Incan History and Culture

The Inca tribe may be the most different from any other FN tribe in its customs and government. Concomitantly, the Incan Empire established a totalitarian government that involved incredibly strict rules for its citizens (Kulmar, 2003). It is reported that the Incan government controlled its people through fear and punishment. Incans were reported, prior to European contact, to have had no privacy in that at any moment their home could be searched (Besom, 2013; Ceruti, 2015). Punishments historically involved being thrown off a cliff to one's death, having one's hands cut off, or other forms of torture that led to death (Besom, 2013; Ceruti, 2015). Additionally, ceremonies were performed by priests, and these ceremonies sometimes involved animal or human sacrifices (Besom, 2013; Ceruti, 2015). There is much controversy regarding the accuracy of historical record regarding the brutality of the ancient Incan people (Julien, 2009). Further, there is even more controversy regarding the teaching of Incan history in schools (Julien, 2009). Regardless of these controversies, the reported history of Incan people seems very different than most other FN tribes.

Inuit History and Culture

Inuit FNP lived in the Arctic, Canada, Labrador, Alaska, and related Northwest Territories (Henitiuk, 2017; Meis Mason, Anderson, & Dana, 2012). Inuit people are the aboriginal people that developed and implemented the first autonomous territorial government in Canada (Henitiuk, 2017; Meis Mason et al., 2012). Many non-FNP call Inuit people by another term, "Eskimos," that is generally considered inappropriate and offensive. However, controversy exists on this terminology as well (Henitiuk, 2017; Meis Mason et al., 2012). Inuit societies are reported to historically have no class system (Henitiuk, 2017; Meis Mason et al., 2012). Additionally, Inuit people had limited property rights, where much was considered the property of the tribe as opposed to the property of one individual. The caribou was a primary source for health care (Henitiuk, 2017; Meis Mason et al., 2012). Inuit people have continued to be marginalized, with their treaties and land rights continually being broken (Henitiuk, 2017; Meis Mason et al., 2012). Due to the cold and harsh climates of northern Canada, Inuit culture revolves highly around aspects needed for survival in these extreme climates (Henitiuk, 2017; Meis Mason et al., 2012). Many Inuit practices and traditions are shared across tribes and continue to change somewhat to adapt to the ever-changing climate and engagement with other FNP.

First Nations People share many commonalities but we are not a homogeneous group. Several variations in cultural and traditional practices and customs have been described. Even within each tribe, every individual had their own practices and adherence to cultural norms.

Concomitantly, FNP still share our customs with indigenous tribes and with some non-FNP. Historically, FNP also have an interrelated experience in regard to surviving the horrors of colonization. There are so many aspects of FN culture, and this chapter barely enters an overview of some practices. Aspects that are of paramount importance to those in the field of psychology and related mental health areas who aspire to be effective clinicians and researchers are openness to the effects of one's own culture and how that, and specifically colonization, shapes one's worldview.

References

Abler, T. S. (2000). Iroquois policy and Iroquois culture: Two histories and an anthropological ethnohistory. *Ethnohistory, 47*, 483-491. Retrieved from https://fgul.idm.oclc.org/login?url=http://search.proquest.com.fgul.idm.oclc.org/docview/209751782?accountid=10868

Besom, T. (2013). Inka human sacrifice and mountain worship: Strategies for empire unification. Albuquerque, NM: University of New Mexico Press. Retrieved from http://www.ebrary.com.fgul.idm.oclc.org

BigFoot, D., & Schmidt, S. (2010). Honoring children, mending the circle: Cultural adaptation of trauma-focused cognitive-behavioral therapy for American Indian and Alaska Native children. *Journal of Clinical Psychology, 66*, 847-856. doi:10.1002/jclp.20707

Ceruti, M. C. (2015). Frozen mummies from Andean mountaintop shrines: Bioarchaeology and ethnohistory of Inca human sacrifice. *BioMed Research International*, (2015), Article 439428, 1-12. doi:10.1155/2015/43942

Charbonneau-Dahlen, B. K., Lowe, J., & Morris, S. L. (2016). Giving voice to historical trauma through storytelling: The impact of boarding school experience on American Indians. *Journal of Aggression, Maltreatment & Trauma, 25*, 598-617. doi:10.108 0/10926771.2016.1157843

Cherokee Nation. (2017). Cherokee medicine men and women. Cherokee Nation. Retrieved 1 April 2017, from http://www. cherokee.org/About-The-Nation/Culture/General/Cherokee-Medicine-Men-and-Women

Corrado, R. R., & Cohen, I. M. (2003). *Mental health profiles for a sample of British Columbia's Aboriginal survivors of the Canadian residential school system*. Ottawa, Ontario, Canada: Aboriginal Healing Foundation.

Crawford, A. (2014). The trauma experienced by generations past having an effect in their descendants: Narrative and historical trauma among Inuit in Nunavut, Canada. *Transcultural Psychiatry, 51*, 339-369. doi:10.1177/1363461512467161

Desai, C. M. (2014). The Columbus myth: Power and ideology in picturebooks about Christopher Columbus. *Children's Literature in Education, 45*, 179-196. doi:10.1007/s10583-014-9216-0

Dickerson, D. L., Spear, S., Marinelli-Casey, P., Rawson, R., Li, L., Methamphetamine Treatment Project Corporate Authors, & Hser, Y. (2011). American Indians/Alaska Natives and substance abuse treatment outcomes: Positive signs and continuing challenges. *Journal of Addictive Diseases, 30*, 63-74. http://doi.org/10.1080/10550887.2010.531665

Ellinghaus, K. (2008). The benefits of being Indian: Blood quanta, intermarriage, and allotment policy on the white earth reservation, 1889-1920. Frontiers: *A Journal of Women Studies, 29*, 81-105. doi:10.1353/fro.0.0012

Fenelon, J. V., & Trafzer, C. E. (2014). From colonialism to denial of California genocide to misrepresentations: Special issue on indigenous struggles in the Americas. *American Behavioral Scientist, 58*, 3-29. doi:10.1177/0002764213495045

Garcia-Andrade, C., Wall, T., & Ehlers, C. (1997). The firewater myth and response to alcohol in Mission Indians. *American Journal of Psychiatry, 154*, 983-988. http://dx.doi.org/10.1176/ajp.154.7.983

Gonzalez, V. M., & Skewes, M. C. (2016). Association of the firewater myth with drinking behavior among American Indian and Alaska Native college students. *Psychology of Addictive Behaviors, 30*, 838-849. doi:http://dx.doi.org.fgul.idm.oclc.org/10.1037/adb0000226

Gram, J. R. (2016). Acting out assimilation: Playing Indian and becoming American in the federal Indian boarding schools. *American Indian Quarterly, 40*, 251-273. Retrieved from https://fgul.idm.oclc.org/login?url=http://search.proquest.com.fgul.idm.oclc.org/docview/1826877080?accountid=10868

Hartmann, W. E., & Gone, J. P. (2014). American Indian historical trauma: Community perspectives from two great plains medicine men. *American Journal of Community Psychology, 54*, 274-288. doi:http://dx.doi.org.fgul.idm.oclc.org/10.1007/s10464-014-9671-1

Hedden, S. L., Kennet, J., Lipari, R., Medley, G., & Tice, P. (2015). Behavioral health trends in the United States: Results from the 2014 national survey on drug use and health. *Center for Behavioral Health Statistics and Quality.* Retrieved from https://www.samhsa.gov/data/sites/default/files/NSDUH-FRR1-2014/NSDUH-FRR1-2014.pdf

Henitiuk, V. (2017). 'Memory is so different now': The translation and circulation of Inuit-Canadian literature in English and French. *Perspectives, 25*, 245-15. doi:10.1080/090767

6X.2016.1197956

Hodge, D. R., Limb, G. E., & Cross, T. L. (2009). Moving from colonization toward balance and harmony: A native American perspective on wellness. *Social Work, 54*(3), 211-219. doi:10.1093/sw/54.3.211

Jiang, C., Mitran, A., Minino, A., & Hanyu, N. (2015). Racial and gender disparities in suicide among young adults aged 18-24: United States, 2009-2013. *Centers for Disease Control and Prevention*, 1-4. Retrieved from https://www.cdc.gov/nchs/data/hestat/suicide/racial_and_gender_2009_2013.pdf

Julien, C. (2009). Reading Inca History. Iowa City, IA: University of Iowa Press. Retrieved from http://www.ebrary.com.fgul.idm.oclc.org

Keagle, J. (2013). Eastern beads, Western applications: Wampum among plains tribes. *Great Plains Quarterly, 33*, 221-235. Retrieved from https://fgul.idm.oclc.org/login?url=http://search.proquest.com.fgul.idm.oclc.org/docview/1449498301?accountid=10868

Kelsey, P. (2013). Disability and native North American boarding school narratives: Madonna Swan and Sioux sanatorium. *Journal of Literary & Cultural Disability Studies, 7*, 195-211. Retrieved from https://fgul.idm.oclc.org/login?url=http://search.proquest.com.fgul.idm.oclc.org/docview/1426059396?accountid=10868

Killsback, L. (2013). Crowns of honor: Sacred laws of eagle-feather war bonnets and repatriating the icon of the great plains. *Great Plains Quarterly, 33*, 1-23. Retrieved from https://fgul.idm.oclc.org/login?url=http://search.proquest.com.fgul.idm.oclc.org/docview/1326772177?accountid=10868

Kinsey, K., & Reed, P. G. (2015). Linking Native American tribal policy to practice in mental health care. *Nursing Science Quarterly,*

28, 82-87. doi:10.1177/0894318414558616

Kulmar, T. (2003). Totalitarianism and the role of religion in the Inca state. *Folklore: Electronic Journal of Folklore, 23,* 25-39. http://dx.doi.org/10.7592/fejf2003.23.incastate

Laufer, B. (1917). Origin of the word shaman. *American Anthropologist, 19*, 361-371. Retrieved from http://www.jstor.org/stable/660223

Littlefield, A. (2003). Lakota culture, world economy. *American Anthropologist, 105*, 453. Retrieved from https://fgul.idm.oclc.org/login?url=http://search.proquest.com.fgul.idm.oclc.org/docview/198195555?accountid=10868

Lyons, B. H., Fowler, K. A., Jack, S. P., Betz, C. J., & Blair, J. M. (2016). Surveillance for violent deaths—National violent death reporting system, 17 states, 2013. *Surveillance Summaries, 65,* 1-42. doi:http://dx.doi.org/10.15585/mmwr.ss6510a1

Macartney, S., Bishaw, A., Fontenot, K. (2013). Poverty rates for selected detailed race and Hispanic groups by state and place: 2007-2011. *American Community Survey Briefs*, 1-20. Retrieved from http://www.census.gov/prod/2013pubs/acsbr11-17.pdf

Males, M. (2014). Who are the police killing? *Center on Juvenile and Criminal Justice*. Retrieved from http://www.cjcj.org/news/8113

Meis Mason, A. H., Anderson, R. B., & Dana, L. (2012). Inuit culture and opportunity recognition for commercial caribou harvests in the bio economy. *Journal of Enterprising Communities: People and Places in the Global Economy, 6*, 194-212. doi:10.1108/17506201211258388

Milwaukee Public Museum. (2017). The league of the Iroquois: Indian country Wisconsin. Indian Country. Retrieved 2 April 2017, from https://www.mpm.edu/wirp/ICW-155.html#related

Modaff, D. P. (2016). Just-in-time: Organizing the Lakota Sun Dance. *Journal of Organizational Ethnography, 5*, 13-27. doi:10.1108/JOE-01-2015-0008

National Congress of American Indians. (2017). An introduction to Indian Nations in the United States. Ncai.org. Retrieved 28 March 2017, from http://www.ncai.org/about-tribes

North Dakota State Government. (2017). Cultural overview—Ways of believing. North Dakota Studies. Retrieved 1 April 2017, from http://www.ndstudies.org/resources/IndianStudies/standingrock/culture_believe.html

Ono, K. A., & Buescher, D. T. (2001). Deciphering Pocahontas: Unpackaging the commodification of a Native American woman. *Critical Studies in Media Communication, 18*, 23-43. doi:10.1080/15295030109367122

Pass, S. (2009). Teaching respect for diversity: The Oglala Lakota. *The Social Studies, 100*, 212-217. Retrieved from https://fgul.idm.oclc.org/login?url=http://search.proquest.com.fgul.idm.oclc.org/docview/596622088?accountid=10868

Post, S. G. (2005). Altruism, happiness, and health: It's good to be good. *International Journal of Behavioral Medicine, 12*, 66-77. doi:10.1207/s15327558ijbm1202_4

Prussing, E. (2007). Reconfiguring the empty center: Drinking, sobriety, and identity in Native American women's narratives. *Culture, Medicine and Psychiatry, 31*, 499-526. doi:http://dx.doi.org.fgul.idm.oclc.org/10.1007/s11013-007-9064-0

Rasmus, S. M., Charles, B., & Mohatt, G. V. (2014). Creating qungasvik (A yup'ik intervention "toolbox"): Case examples from a community-developed and culturally-driven intervention. *American Journal of Community Psychology, 54*, 140-52. doi:http://dx.doi.org.fgul.idm.oclc.org/10.1007/s10464-014-9651-5

Results from the 2007 national survey on drug use and health: National findings. (2008). *Medical Benefits, 25*, 9-10. Retrieved from https://fgul.idm.oclc.org/login?url=http://search.proquest. com.fgul.idm.oclc.org/docview/207125721?accountid=10868

Schmidt, R. (2011). American Indian identity and blood quantum in the 21st century: A critical review. *Journal of Anthropology, 2011*, 1-9. http://dx.doi.org/10.1155/2011/549521

Seligman, M. E., & Csikszentmihalyi, M. (2014). *Positive psychology: An introduction* (pp. 279-298). Springer Netherlands.

Stannard, D. (1992). *American Holocaust: Columbus and the Conquest of the New World* (1st ed.). New York [u.a.]: Oxford University Press.

Tjaden, P., & Thoennes, N. (2000). Full report of the prevalence, incidence, and consequences of violence against women. *US Department of Justice*, 1-61. Retrieved from https://www. ncjrs.gov/pdffiles1/nij/183781.pdf

Toland, J. (2014). *Adolf Hitler: The Definitive Biography* (1st ed., p. 202). New York: Anchor Books.

Turner, J. S. (2015). The semiotics of a Native American sports logo: The signification of the "screaming savage". *Journal of Sports Media, 10*, 89-114. Retrieved from https://fgul.idm.oclc. org/login?url=http://search.proquest.com.fgul.idm.oclc.org/ docview/1716966857?accountid=10868

United States Census Bureau. (2015). American Indian and Alaska Native heritage month: November 2015. *United States Census Bureau, CB15-FF.22*. Retrieved 1 April 2017, from https:// www.census.gov/newsroom/facts-for-features/2015/cb15-ff22.html

Yeh, C. J., Hunter, C. D., Madan-Bahel, A., Chiang, L., & Arora, A. K. (2004). Indigenous and interdependent perspectives of healing: Implications for counseling and research. *Journal of*

Counseling and Development, 82, 410-419. Retrieved from https://fgul.idm.oclc.org/login?url=http://search.proquest. com.fgul.idm.oclc.org/docview/219036964?accountid=10868

Zumba, S. (2016, Apr 05). White passing privilege. University Wire Retrieved from https://fgul.idm.oclc.org/ login?url=http://search.proquest.com.fgul.idm.oclc.org/ docview/1778552258?accountid=10868

9.

ON MONKEYS, TEXANS, AND PORTUGUESE WOMEN

Aspects and Examples of Cultural Development
Henry V. Soper, PhD

Culture. Everyone agrees that it is important in understanding people. There is a plethora of talk about it, much of not very useful, and a dearth of knowledge about it. Many push a sensitivity to culture, which is good, but it is still all too easy to generalize from one incident called a part of culture across many cultures. We have all heard something to the effect of "I knew someone with autism, so I know all about it." To go on, I knew someone from Ghana [actually born in New Haven and never has been to Ghana], so I know all about their culture." Or even, "I am tall," meaning I understand the culture of those who are tall.

One can understand the absurdity of our government naming just four minorities as the various ethnic groups. Although ethnicity and culture are hardly the same, the concept of ethnicity has many of the same shortcomings as the terms race and culture. We are told that there are five ethnic groups in our country (Wong, Strickland, Fletcher-Jensen, Ardila, & Reynolds, 2000): Caucasian (or European American/ Anglo American) and the four federally designated ethnic minorities of African American; Hispanic/Latino Americans; American Indians/ Alaskan Natives; and Asian/Pacific Islander Americans. This kind of subdivision, admittedly based on ethnicity—whatever that is—and not culture is basically of no value in trying to understand the biological underpinnings of these groups of peoples, and as such are next to worthless. Wong et al. (2000) go on to say,

> For example, there are at least ten distinct groups under the category Asian residing in the United States, not including Pacific Islander Americans. One of these groups, Chinese, is comprised of individuals who may be from distinct cultures (e.g., China, Taiwan, Hong Kong) and whose primary language/dialect may be different (i.e., Mandarin, Cantonese).

One of the problems, of course, is the lack of a clear definition of the words, and also a lack of clarity of many of their aspects. Can a culture contain only one person, or two, or 10? Furthermore, can one person belong to more than one culture? Several years ago, a charge nurse, a very well-respected woman, was sent to me for depression. Though she knew she was depressed, she had no idea why. She had been born in the Philippines, earned her nursing degree, and came to the States to find employment. She had slowly brought her family over and moved them into a house she bought some 30 miles from work. After I counseled with several Philippine friends it turns out that though she was well respected as a charge nurse at work, at home she was a young daughter and expected to keep the house, prepare meals, and essentially wait on her elders. As I explained this to her, she could see the source of her depression. In fact, she had started feeling guilty for resenting the treatment she received at home. Moving to an apartment nearer work solved the problem, and she told me that now when she went to the house she was treated more like a respected visitor. The source of her problem was clearly the clashing of the cultures.

The Concept of Culture

Many of the comments about "race" can also be applied to "culture," except that few think there is a biological basis for culture. The human cultures we observe are clearly made by humans, and are not based on some genetically based difference between peoples. Although not the focus of our attention, the same can be said of specific skills. Although it appears that certain abilities run in certain families, there are other explanations, environmental ones, to explain, for example, why the women in certain families tend to be more skilled in making clothing. An example I heard some time ago centers on the ability of certain Australian aborigines to excel in processing spatial information so that they can travel many miles across open spaces at nighttime and wind up at the village they were seeking. Yet those raised in London would have trouble avoiding walking into trees, let alone heading off in a direction that would have them end up where they want to be. With one of my graduate students (Diaz, 2005) I decided to look into this. We assessed a group of First Nation individuals who had not lived in an urban environment on various spatial and non-spatial tasks. We found that there was effectively no difference in these abilities between them and their brethren who had live a large portion of their lives in urban environments. Later I found that those "Australian aborigines" who were raised in London did not have this special spatial ability, yet some "Londoners" who were raised in Australia with aborigines did have the ability. I was sure that after so many generations in Australia natural selection would have selected for such an ability; however, my hypothesis was totally wrong, as evidenced by my latter findings and the formal dissertation research.

Wong, Strickland, Fletcher-Janzen, Ardila, and Reynolds (2000) stated that:

> Culture is a broad and overarching concept that refers to a body of customary beliefs and social norms that are shared by a particular group of people. It includes behaviors, beliefs and values, and other

shared elements. Some have defined it as "a way of the people," which includes beliefs and behaviors, as well as other social characteristics that are common to a group. Alternatively, is could be simply defined as the specific way of living of a human group.

Culture is a complex concept that, potentially, can have ethnic, geographic, generational, linguistic, and social determinants. Unfortunately, culture is often used interchangeably with ethnicity or race and, to a lesser extent, with language. Such confusion can impede serious theoretical understanding and investigation in cross-cultural study. Wong et al. (2000) go on to say, "As with all cases in empirical research, unless the relevant independent variable is defined and isolated, a moderating variable may lead to a confoundment and muddle the explanation of the results."

Two Portuguese Women

To show how two similarly named cultures can become very divergent, I would like to provide the following examples drawn from an exercise when I asked two students to give their culture and tell us about it. Both were women over 30 and graduate students in clinical psychology. Here are their responses.

Student A. Being a Portuguese woman I, like many Americans, can claim a varied cultural background. My father's father is Native American (Apache) and Scottish; my father's mother is Scottish and English; my mother's father is French Canadian; and my mother's mother is Portuguese. Growing up I most identified with my Portuguese roots. As a child I participated in Portuguese celebrations, and family gatherings on my mother's side were rich in Portuguese culture. Most of the celebrations occurred at the Portuguese Hall in our area.

One thing about the Portuguese culture that always stuck out to me was the strength of the women; they always appeared to be in charge

261

of everything. Most of my female relatives worked in addition to being in charge of the house. The women always seemed to be in the foreground, while the men always seemed to be in the background. The women planned everything and dished out appropriate jobs to the men. Whenever we had a family gathering or celebration the women were always directing the activity.

On the surface both men and women took on "traditional" male/ female roles. In reality, the women had a lot of control over what happened. This is in contrast to my father's side of the family. My grandmother was always in the kitchen while my grandfather would bark orders to her. She sometimes seemed more a slave than a partner. My father's mother would be in the kitchen doing dishes and my grandfather would want the channel on the television changed. He would whistle for my grandmother and she would drop what she was doing to do as he wished. This is part of why my parents' marriage did not last. My father wanted someone like my grandmother, yet my mother grew up in an atmosphere where women had more control than to just be somebody's servant.

Student B. This was my experience growing up Portuguese. I feel a sense of great pride being a woman of Portuguese descent. My experience of the Portuguese women in my particular family has been that they believe that, in order to be a decent human being, one must be a martyr of sorts. My grandmother never learned to drive or manage finances, although she had quite a strong and stubborn personality in many other respects. She put an inordinate amount of time and energy into Catholicism, with icons and candles around the house and daily visits to church at dawn, where she would do her rosary several times. Thus, she was quite provincial in many respects. My grandfather, more sophisticated, traveled the world and was an active member in literary groups and business organizations.

Edith was very attentive and affectionate, and a staunch Catholic.

However, she has been doing Charismatic healing with a group of Catholics, including a priest, for many years. I remember her showing me a rather large kidney stone that she had stored in a glass jar that she had extracted from Uncle Tommy simply by putting him in a hot bath and speaking in tongues. When my mother was in intensive care, Edith did a healing group. I found out later that it was the exact same hour that I was doing one with two "professional" healers. My mother's organs were shut down, she was in a comatose state, on a respirator, and we were told she had less than a few hours to live. The next day my mother came out of the comatose state. Soon she got off the respirator. She lived a couple more months, with me as her hospice caretaker.

Part of the constellation of personality factors that my mother and aunts shared was a result of a combination of Catholic fear-based lessons and understandings regarding the role of the typical Portuguese wife and mother, which was to put others' needs before her own and to keep passions and dreams at bay. Indeed, they were all masters at managing other people's lives, but could not nurture their own souls. In my mother's case, she was the chief financial provider with her teacher's salary, neglecting to even take herself to the doctor for a physical. She had an intense and overprotective interest in her offspring, yet her lack of attention to her own needs and her worrying and chain-smoking led to her early death of lung cancer.

The most prevalent theme I see in the Portuguese women from my background is that of martyrdom. They were strong, intelligent, creative women who could have fared much better outside of thankless marriages, yet they remained enslaved out of a sense of duty and guilt. Perhaps this has little to do with being Portuguese per se, and much more to do with the psychological tendencies of my particular family tree. However, part of the construction of the meaning of what it is to be female has to do with observing the lives of these women who happened to have been Portuguese and, more than that, Catholic.

Provincial Latin Catholicism is a culture all in itself.

Animal Examples

A wonderful book by Hans Kummer (1971) provides us with a few examples of the development of culture or, in the second case, adaptation to a culture by moving animals into groups where the culture and the rules were different.

Adoptive Baboons. In the hamadryas male, a high motivation to associate with females merely had to be extended to the anoestrous female to make him the intolerant permanent mate he now is. To own more than one female, however, required an innovation, the herding technique. The repertoire of baboons already included its behavioral components, that is, brow-raising and neck-biting.

The hamadryas, however, are the only baboon species that built these behaviors into a tool for keeping females close by timing their attack to the female's behavior. Anubis males never herd their females even when they consort with them. Even an adult anubis male who lived for several months in a wild hamadryas troop did not adopt the herding technique, and this completely deprived him of female company.

While the behavioral and morphological dispositions of baboons prepared the way for the one-male group, the new system also required some secondary social adaptations. For one thing, hamadryas females have to respond to a male threat by approaching the aggressor, whereas any other primate female, including anubis, takes flight in the same situation. This paradoxical reversal of the "normal" response stimulated a series of field experiments in which adult anubis females were transferred to hamadryas troops. The results were quite impressive.

First, the anubis females were eagerly accepted and herded by resident hamadryas males despite the females' different appearance. Second, the species difference did not prevent the animals from communicating successfully. Furthermore, the anubis females learned, within one hour on the average, to follow the one hamadryas male who would threaten and attack them, and to interact with no other male. In fact, their scores for following reached the same level as the hamadryas control females that were transferred into the same troop.

In the reverse experiments, hamadryas females readily adapted to the independent life in the anubis group; they groomed several males in succession and ceased to follow any particular male.

Potatoes and Wheat. This is also extracted from Kummer (1971). The little island of Koshima is a wooded, precipitous mountain surrounded by sandy beaches and the sea. Until recently only the mountain and its forest had any ecological significance for the group of Japanese macaques (Macaca fuscuta) inhabiting the island; they had so far not foraged on the beach and they had never entered the water.

In 1952, however, researchers from the Japan Monkey Center began to feed the troop on the island's beach and thus triggered an ecological expansion that provided some fascinating insights into the adaptive potential of primates. The following description is based on a detailed report by Kawai (1965):

> The artificial feeding consisted of throwing sweet potatoes onto the beach. The group soon got used to leaving the forest and to eating potatoes as free of adhering sand as possible. The beach became not only a new foraging ground, but also the breeding ground of what the Japanese researchers call a "preculture." Among the most interesting aspects of the Koshima events are the secondary effects of the new traditions. The changes in feeding behavior reverberated into superficially remote parts of the socioecological system. The habit of washing primarily facilitated the rapid ingestion of food, but beyond this it opened the way to a hitherto irrelevant part of the habitat, the sea.

One year after the feeding was started, a nearly two-year-old female named Imo was observed carrying a sweet potato to the edge of a brook. With one hand she dipped the potato into the water while she brushed off the sand with the other. In the years to follow, the technique slowly spread throughout the group. In addition, the washing was gradually transferred from the brook to the sea. Today potato-washing in salt water is an established tradition which infants learn from their mothers as a natural adjunct to eating potatoes.

The second way of acquiring the behavior had an interesting secondary effect: All of the potatoes that the new infants ate were seasoned with salt water, and the taste of salt apparently became associated with potatoes. Many of the new generation now not only washed their potatoes, but also seasoned them by dipping them into the sea between bites.

The Koshima group had still more surprises in store. When the scientists began to scatter wheat on the beach, the female Imo, now four years old, invented another trick. Instead of picking the grains singly out of the sand, she carried handfuls of mixed sand and wheat to shore, threw the whole mess into the water, and waited for the sand to sink and the wheat to float; then she collected the wheat and ate it.

The youngsters of the new generations took up bathing as part of their playful and exploratory activities. Splashing became a preferred pastime in hot weather. The juveniles learned to swim; some of them began to dive and brought up seaweed from the bottom. At least one of them left Koshima and swam to a neighboring island. The sea then became a potential food source, and it was no longer an absolute barrier to would-be migrators or to socially hard-pressed refugees from the island group.

We can see in this example how the monkeys, when their environment changed, changed their behavior substantially. When we look for the origins of behaviors in certain tribes or troops, the actual explanation may be something as simple as a minor environmental change, or one incident, as in the example below.

Nice Guys. One example comes from the work of Sapolski, who is well known for his work with baboons to study stress. He had been studying this one troop, the Kikkorock troop, for years. The troop culture at the time was stratified, with very aggressive males often taking out their tempers on the females. They were foraging for food waste at a dump near a tourist lodge that included meat that was tainted with tuberculosis. The result was that nearly half the males died, but the deaths were not random. Those males who were aggressive and not socially connected with the females and other males were the ones who died. The result was that there were twice as many females as males, and the males who survived were the "good guys" who were not aggressive but were kind to the females and would groom and hang out with others—very socially affiliated. This changed the culture of the troop, because male aggressiveness would not be tolerated. Adolescent male baboons would leave their home troop and join another, and when outside adolescents came to join this group and acted aggressively toward the females, the group would send the message "we don't act like that here." It took six months for the outside adolescents to assimilate this culture. The group still maintains this culture after 20 years, quite different not only from what they had been, but also quite different from the other baboon troops in the area. Sapolski also found that markers for stress were noticeably reduced in this troop.

In this example, the culture of the troop changed drastically, for the betterment of both the troop's stress levels and for the females. This was brought on by, one could say, an accident of nature. But still, new members had to go through a learning curve to adapt to this culture quite different than their "home" one.

East Texas. In this final example, a human one, when I first presented it to a class there were several who had difficulty believing that there could be a human culture so different from what they were used to. At the end of this section, I have included a brief email exchange we had on the topic. This was similar to a discussion I had with an otherwise bright woman who could not understand why the warring parties in the Middle East do not just sit down at a table and iron out their differences. She became upset when I told her this would be like sitting down with a hornet and explaining why it should not bite you. Below is the transcript from the woman, my research assistant, who came from this area in Texas.

My Town

I just read a book about my town. It was called A Death in Texas, by some lady I've never heard of from, of all places, New York City. It was a good book and would have been great for one of those Whodunit mystery novels. Of course, to me it was mostly fiction anyway, because I know the truth. I'm not some conspiracy nut or someone who is looking for attention. Like most people in my town, I feel it is just better if it goes away and we can forget about it. Unfortunately, the press just won't let a sleeping dog lie. Every now and again I hear it come up or someone refers to "the incident in Texas" when there is a beating or shooting of a Black man. Each and every time I cringe and wonder how much of the stuff we hear and see on the news is totally false, like our story in Jasper.

I'm not sure how to begin a tale that most people will not believe. I could start with "Once upon a time" or some other such nonsense, I suppose. The fact is, once the general public sees something on the news, they pretty much take it as fact. After all, wouldn't you believe Dan Rather? You can read my story and take it with a grain of salt. I suppose that's your God-given right. Maybe you might just read this and question those heartfelt and scathing in-depth reports you see on 60 Minutes from now on.

Once upon a time in a land far, far away (How's that?) there was a small town very much isolated from the outside world, Jasper, Texas. I grew up here, actually on the outskirts in a community called Roganville. When people ask me where I'm from, I always get that weird look, you know the one that would make you think I actually have leprosy. But I am proud to be from my town. We are good people with good morals who got drug through the mud because it was better entertainment than the home-run race. I can tell already you are either saying "I have no idea what she is talking" about, or "Yeah, right, I remember that story." Here is the deal: In 1998 a man in my town was killed in a really gruesome manner. He was tied behind a truck and drug down the street until he was dismembered. Now everyone is on the same page: the "Oh-yeah-that-racist-killing-in-Texas" page.

To understand the real story, you have to understand our town. Jasper is the big city to most of us in the county. I actually attended Kirbyville School in the neighboring town about 30 miles away (population 1,972), but I worked in Jasper because I lived right in between the two and Jasper was the only place to work. Now Jasper has about 7,000 people, and I am pretty sure some of those were counted twice because I don't think we have 7,000 people within 100 square miles of Jasper.

Anyway, my town is dirt poor on a good day. Most of the people that have jobs are working at the lumber mill, the grocery store, bank, school, Pizza Hut, or the like. What I am trying to say is that there is not much opportunity. You can't work your way up the social ladder. There are no big companies, and any good job is pretty much taken, and when people retire, their kid gets the job. Good jobs are with Southwestern Bell running cable [or] the Super Walmart, and we have

269

some lawyers, and some doctors, and the veterinarian—oh, yeah, and politicians. How come no matter how small your town is you always have at least one politician? Back on track, to say the least, we are not going to be holding a lot of cotillions in the near future (for you Yankees that's a sixteenth birthday party for rich folks).

Now, I am a firm believer that classism exists far beyond and more often than racism. Maybe it was how I was raised (my folks were part of the 27% unemployed in our county), but I never saw racism growing up; the only differences in my town were how much money you made, and what religion you happen to be. Jasper sits right on the buckle of the Bible belt, so if you want to be an out-of-the-ordinary religion too far from Baptist, watch out. Some people always ask me when I tell them this: "How do people know what religion you are or how much you make?" This is when I can tell people who have never lived in a small town (city folk): Everyone knows everything about everybody else in our town. There are no secrets. If you had an affair, stayed out past curfew, snuck in alcohol to our dry county, had a party, or went on a date, your mama or spouse will know about it before you even set foot in the door. This is how I know about what really happened to James Byrd, Jr.

A couple of weeks before the death of James Byrd there was a drug deal in Jasper. Jamie Byrd was selling some drugs (I don't know what kind) to a friend of Shawn Berry's (the one that got life in prison). Now, this friend, whose name I won't say—call him Billy—did not pay for his drugs in a timely fashion. A couple of days later Billy's dad gets beat up and sent to the hospital in a coma. This I know is fact because Billy's dad is best friends with my grandpa, who told me what happened. So Billy tells his best friend Shawn Berry what happened, and Shawn Berry tells some drinking buddies about it one night and they decide to get justice. In East Texas we still follow the law of eye-for-an-eye and also that you do not involve other people in your disputes. If you got

270

a problem with someone you take it out on them, not family members. This keeps us from dissolving into the old "Hatfield and McCoy" problem. I am not saying what they did was right. As a matter of fact they should have never been involved in the dispute, either.

Back to the story: Shawn Berry and his drinking buddies decide to get justice. Being that one of these "buddies" was Bill King, maybe this was not such a good idea. Bill King was from Jasper as well, but everybody knew he was bad news. He had been a bad kid, a horror as a teen, and finally someone came to their senses and put the guy in jail when he dropped out of school. Unfortunately, he kept getting out and getting worse. The other guy involved [was] a guy by the last name of Brewer. No one knew him; he wasn't a local. So these three bad kids go out looking to serve up a little justice for Shawn's friend. Lo and behold, who do they find but Jamie Byrd's dad—drunk and walking down the side of the road. They coax him into the truck and then tie him to the bumper to inflict a little hurt on the guy. (Attaching someone to a horse by their feet and dragging them a while is not an uncommon practice in our town, usually for serious offenses that are not readily handled by the sheriff.)

The press hears how these three white guys killed a black guy in the rural South and off to the races they go. So the story you hear from the Klan members (who were from Georgia, by the way) and the Black Panthers (who had come down from Chicago), Jessie Jackson (I don't know where he is from), and some sort of militant Black Islamic Leader named Quannell X (we were not even sure why he was there) is the wonderful spin that looked good on TV. As far as I know there is no KKK in our town, nor did any people from our town show up for the rally. The only Klan I knew of was almost 100 miles away in Vidor. Of course, there is no Black Panther Society and the funniest thing was when my uncle (who happens to be a Black man) asked why basketball teams were coming to march on the town when we told him

271

*the NAACP was coming. The fights you saw on your television, and
the speeches spewed by officials (the sheriff told me that the speeches
he read to the cameras were written by the FBI), all were designed to
give you at home a good show, and it worked. Just something for you
to think about.*

I think it is easy to see the differences in culture coming into play,
as this case is presented. This person, my assistant, is a friend of mine
who happened to come from that area. She had no agenda but to tell
the truth as she saw it. However, as you can see below, not everyone
bought it:

Henry,

I was the one in class who said that the story you read (*My Town*)
could also be viewed as one person's perspective and that, since I grew
up in a very small town, I know that personal views can get shaped by
the attitude in the community. Following your advice, I have thought
about the article from a scientific point of view and it has led to my
having questions that maybe you can answer. Who wrote the article?
Why is a name not attached to it? How can anyone grow up anywhere
in America and not experience racism, as she implied in her article
(maybe not overt, but at least covert)? Why was the victim's body
left by a black church or cemetery? Why do so many in the same
community believe that it was an act that had overtones of racism?

Now, I am hoping that we can have a friendly exchange about this.
Educate me. But let me play the devil's advocate for you. Remember. .
. I said I come from a small town (even smaller than Jasper. . . my town
was only around 1,400) and so I take issue with some of the things said
in the article. It kind of has the tone of "Aw, shucks." She makes some
pretty unbelievable statements in the article (such as saying there are
no secrets. . . or that everything you do is talked about immediately).
I even wondered if this is a real article. I know that at least some of
it is an exaggeration. Yet, then I wonder. . . how did this article get

272

circulated? By some form of media?

Fidel

(These types of things were true in my small town, and because it falls outside her realm of reality, to her it must be a fake or exaggeration.)
Dear Fidel,

As you noticed, I really did not want to get into an in-depth discussion on *My Town* at the time. These tend to be incendiary topics, and I wanted to consider the possibility that there could have been another point of view. In research you ask a question and then find out the answer. In a demonstration you have the answer and show how it is true. In this case the latter is what happened, and, as you can see even in the class, to suggest otherwise leads to crucifixion. It was very difficult for the people to be open to the possibility that there could be another explanation. Things were simple, organized, and understandable, and why did Dr. Henry have to complicate things? How can there be a reality other than mine?

Some things I am willing to do, others I am not. I know the author of the article very well, and trust her very well. She came out with these comments, and more, about how the whole town knew far better than the newspapers what was going on, but also knew that was not going to sell. She wrote the article for me because I asked her to and for this class. She has no agenda of her own. Her name will never be associated with it for her protection. I know fully well what happens when one disagrees with something politically correct. There is a saying I have used in the past. The general gist is that you can say and believe whatever you want, without any bounds, as long as you agree with me. In other words, you agree with me or there is something wrong with you. I have seen this since I first grew up, but I am not willing to say that my environment is unique in this. You can imagine how this stifles academic freedom. Anyhow, *My Town* is a straightforward and honest representation. There is no other agenda. There is certainly no promise that it might improve understanding between peoples. Be careful of the Lucy phenomenon. Lucy was one of our ancestors many of whose bones we have uncovered. From this we have an idea of what all Australopithecines were like. Except, we have found, Lucy was not representative of all of them. I too grew up in a small town, but in New England, not East Texas. Although some things may have been the same, many were not. Prejudice can take many forms, and those found in some communities are quite different from those found elsewhere.

It is one thing to state that there is no racism in that town. That would be absurd, I agree. However, to conclude therefore that this crime was racially motivated is not warranted. Symbolism, intended or not, can be found in anything, but not necessarily intended by the perpetrators. I think there is little question about the idea that these were pretty dumb antisocial people. I would hesitate to give them too much credit. To state that something would be inconceivable to me is not to prove that the opposite would be true.

A part of this comes from an old personal problem. It bothers me to see people wax professional on topics they have no idea about, from ADD to Vietnam to mental health to Jasper. This is a part of our problem in the Middle East right now. Some people just do not live in the real world, and when you point that out to them, they say you do not know what you are talking about. The millions of people killed by the Pathet Lao did not exist. (Their relatives tell me differently, but who are they to know.)

You might want to look at the book by Burkett (*Stolen Valor*) as an elucidation of misrepresentation. What you believe happened in East Texas is not so important. What is important is that you be open to views stemming from cultures and experiences different from yours. Not that you understand them, or agree with them, but that you appreciate them for what they are. Hope this clarifies somewhat what we run into when we treat people of quite different perspectives. They have to live in their world, not ours.

References

Chang, T. (2012). Personalizing medicine: beyond race. *AMA Journal of Ethics, 8*, 628-634.

Diaz, S. H. (2005). Differences in Cognitive Strengths between Native North Americans Living in Rural versus Urban Environments (unpublished doctoral dissertation), Fielding Graduate University, Santa Barbara, CA.

Gibbons, A. (2009). How we lost our diversity, *Science NOW Daily News*, 8 October

Jensen, A. R. (1969). How much can we boost IQ and academic achievement? *Harvard Educational Review, 39*, 1-123.

Herrnstein, R. J., & Murray, C. (1994). *The Bell Curve: Intelligence and Class Structure in American Life*. New York: The Free Press.

Howells, W. (1959). *Mankind in the Making: The Story of Human Evolution*. Garden City, NY: Doubleday.

Kawai, M. (1965). Newly acquired precultural behavior of the natural troupe of Japanese Macaques on Koshima Islet: A detailed report of the beginnings of a primate tradition (food-washing). *Primates, 6*, 1-30.

Kummer, H. (1971). *Primate Societies: Group Techniques of Ecological Adaptation*. Chicago: Aldine.

Sapolski, R. M.) National Geographic Society and Stanford University (producer), (2008). *Stress: Portrait of a killer*. Country of Origin, U.S.A.

Temple-Raston, D. (2002). *A Death in Texas*. New York: Henry Hold and Company.

Wong, T., Strickland, T. R., Fletcher-Jensen, E. A., Artila, & Reynolds,

C. R. (2000). Theoretical and practical issues and the neuropsychological assessment and treatment of culturally dissimilar patients. In E. Fletcher-Jensen, T. L. Strickland, and C.R. Reynolds, Eds.), *Handbook of Cross-Cultural Neuropsychology*. New York: Springer-Science.

10.

WORKING WITH HISPANICS

Laura Rieffel, Ph.D.

As a Spanish-speaking psychologist who immigrated to the United States with my immediate family when I was seven years old, I have had the benefit of rich cultural experiences many people have not. I distinctly recall the optimism of the days just prior to our move from Uruguay, thinking of our new life in the United States as one might think of Oz, even though, of course, I had never heard of the *Wizard of Oz* at the time. I also recall the disillusion as I came to find out that everything familiar to me, my language, food, and lifestyle, were immediately and profoundly impacted. For example, as a new reader who no longer had any access to reading material in Spanish, I determinedly translated the newspaper comics with a dictionary, only to find out with dismay that the joke was lost in the translation. I can remember crying in frustration that "I would never learn English," as I sit here writing this chapter.

This chapter seeks to provide not only pragmatic information that I hope providers will find useful in working with Hispanic clients and families, but also a personal characterization of these facts based on my own experience, as well as the amalgamation of experiences from treating Spanish-speaking individuals over my 25 years of practice. Information presented regarding client experiences has been disguised to maintain client confidentiality.

Hispanic Versus Latino/Latina

Not infrequently when discussing professional matters, I encounter a question from fellow practitioners, almost in a whisper, asking whether it is more respectful to use the term Hispanic or Latino/Latina. Growing up, I became accustomed to using the term Hispanic simply because it was the direct translation of the term *Hispano*, which was the word used within our family context. Much later, as I came to learn of the controversy between the terms, I made a more determined effort to understand the differences and make a conscious choice. I identify most with the term Hispanic, probably in part because of my familiarity with the term, but also because, having grown up in the U.S., I culturally identify with being part of a group of individuals who speak Spanish and, secondly with my country of origin.

As someone born in Uruguay, it is appropriate to refer to myself as either Hispanic or Latina. Professionally speaking, I have never found any of my Spanish-speaking clients to be offended by a reference to being *Hispano* (Hispanic), primarily because the meaning as it is commonly understood within Spanish-speaking communities is simply that of being Spanish speaking, without any ethnic, racial, or sociopolitical connotations. However, I have found that for individuals who are generationally more distant from the Hispanic culture, such as those who reside in the U.S. and most often do not speak Spanish, a specific identification with Hispanic or Latino/Latina may have a stronger valence.

Hispanic is the official term used by the U.S. Census to refer to individuals with a cultural, linguistic, and historical relationship to Spain, which can include individuals from any number races who have a wide range of physical characteristics such as both light/dark skin and blonde/dark brunette hair. As such, an individual from Brazil would not be considered "Hispanic" because the country was settled by the Portuguese, even though Brazilians share many cultural similarities with their bordering neighbors, such as Argentina, Bolivia, Columbia, French Guyana, Guyana, Suriname, Paraguay, Peru, Uruguay, and Venezuela. However, Brazilians could correctly be referred to as Latinos/Latinas, as the term denotes individuals who trace their nationality to Latin American countries, which would include Mexico, the Caribbean, as well as Central and South America. Individuals who identify as Hispanic or Latino/Latina can be of any race.

The term Chicano/Chicana is chosen by individuals of Mexican descent who identify with the Civil Rights movement of the 1960s. Although it was originally a derogatory term, the use of the term has come to signify pride in their indigenous ancestry. A related term, Tejano, is used by Texans of Mexican descent, a term that derives from the name given to citizens of the Mexican State of Coahuila y Tejas (*Coahuiltejano*), which is modern-day Texas.

For practitioners seeking clarity with regard to this issue with their clients it can be helpful to listen to the client's language. What term does he or she use? If this fails, *ask,* as it can be more insulting to make assumptions than to be direct.

Hispanic Diversity

Hispanics share some similarities that create a sense of kinship, leading to increased flexibility in the definition of in-group status when residing in an outgroup majority culture. That is, even though in their native countries, individuals may not regard bordering neighbors as "kin," these same individuals are viewed with much more affinity when the outgroup contrast is more significant. Most Hispanics are Spanish speaking, Roman Catholic, and share common values and beliefs that are rooted in a history of conquest and colonization.

However, despite similarities, it is important to also understand differences. Hispanics are the fastest growing ethnic group in America, comprising 17% of the U.S. population, up from 13% in the year 2000. Mexicans are by far the largest of the Hispanic groups, making up approximately two-thirds of the Hispanics in the U.S., followed by Puerto Ricans at 9%. Salvadorans and Cubans make up the next largest group at 4%. Differences in land, climate, and degrees of cultural influence by Europeans are some of the factors responsible for the differences among Hispanic groups. For example, Costa Ricans and Colombians share cultural similarities because of their geographical location on the Caribbean coast, as well as the effect of slavery on their cultures. Argentina, Chile, and Uruguay tend to have the strongest European influence on their culture. Argentinians and Uruguayans speak Spanish that contains a strong Italian influence on the language; for example, it is just as common in these countries to say "adios" as it is to say "chau" (*ciao in Italian*). Ecuador, Bolivia, and Peru consist of much larger indigenous populations that influence their culture. Others, such as Hispanics residing in the Southwestern U.S. acquired a new language, culture, and government after the peace treaty of 1848 subsequent to the U.S.-Mexico war. Similarly, Puerto Ricans were granted U.S. citizenship in 1917 after the Spanish-American War ended in 1898 and Spain ceded Puerto Rico to the U.S.

While it is easy to assume that all Hispanics eat tacos and beans, I can attest as an Uruguayan that I have never even seen a Mexican restaurant in Uruguay. The geopolitical roots of each country also influence differences in regional cuisines. Argentinian and Uruguayan cuisine is a mix of indigenous, Spanish, and Italian food, while for most countries in the Caribbean and on the coasts, cuisines consist of fish and seafood. Characteristic cuisines are also strongly influenced by ingredients and spices that are indigenous to the area. For example, Hispanic countries differ widely in their use of peppers for spiciness.

First Versus Second Generation

A crucially important element to understanding the influence of culture on a client's presentation is their generational status. The term first generation is confusing because it is used to refer both to a foreign-born individual who immigrates to the U.S., as well as a native-born citizen of a country whose parents are foreign born. By these definitions not only would I be considered first generation, but also my children who have been born in the U.S. would be. Despite the ambiguous use of the term, the impact of the Hispanic culture has been profoundly different for me and my children. Understanding an individual's use of the term becomes crucial and is only the first step toward clarity regarding the influence of culture on a specific person's experience. For example, the experience of acculturating to another culture has been immensely impactful in my life in many positive, and some negative ways. This is not an experience my children have had; nevertheless, they identify as Hispanic. Ethnic identification can be an important element of identity formation, particularly during the formative years of individuation. I recall an young adolescent woman who was of Mexican descent. While her mother had been born in the U.S. from Mexican parents, her father had been born in Mexico. She grew up in a predominantly Mexican neighborhood and attended a school with a high population of adolescents of Mexican descent of varying generations. I recall how she struggled to make sense of her identification as being "Mexican." In particular, she mentioned being teased by her friends for liking sushi and good naturedly and not so good naturedly being taunted that she was trying to act "white." Her constellation of beliefs about being "Mexican" included not only what foods she could eat, but extended to her beliefs about being academically successful, and expectations for career achievements.

Level of Acculturation

Generation is one form of assessing the level of acculturation to a new culture. However, even within the same generation there can be monumental differences in levels of acculturation. Even if my parents and I can be considered to be first generation, there is no denying the fact that having moved here as middle-aged adults, the influence of

281

my parents' Uruguayan culture is much stronger than mine. Like most adolescents, I paid little attention to the cultural differences between my household and those of my friends. I knew they existed, but I did not see them as very impactful. It's with amusement that I recall trying to figure out how I was going to get permission to date, at the age of 16. I decided to enlist my oldest brother because his level of understanding of American norms made him a useful bridge between my norms and those of my parents. Although I could sense my parents' worry and consternation as they gave me permission to date, it wasn't until the relationship ended that I realized their definition of "dating" was grossly different from mine. I thought of it as someone to go to the movies with; they thought I was going to marry him. I remember my mother's anguish, "What are the neighbors going to think when they see you going out with someone else?" My eternally sharp adolescent response was "They are going to think I went to the movies with one person and now I'm going to the movies with someone else!"

Educational Levels

Total population literacy rates among Latin American countries range from 98% in Uruguay to 67.5% in Nicaragua. Poverty levels and access to education play an important role in educational achievement. In Uruguay, education through professional levels is free, although it is quite academically challenging to weed out less dedicated or talented individuals. For example, it is not unusual for university students to be unable to afford necessary textbooks, and therefore they must rely on public access in libraries, sharing their textbook times with many other individuals in the class. There are private universities as well, where families who are financially better off can afford to send their children. Education is regarded as important in many Latin American countries with strong literacy rates and many parents sacrifice a great deal to give their children access to the best educational experience they can afford. Consequently, a small country like Uruguay is filled with many professionals who are unable to find work in their area of expertise because small economies cannot support such a high number of professionals. High education levels are not unusual for immigrants to the U.S. from among the range of Latin American countries. It is common to find individuals from Spanish-speaking countries who have come to the U.S. for better economic opportunities and who are degreed as engineers, accountants, and teachers but who are employed here as laborers and housekeepers.

Despite a strong emphasis on education, there is an equally strong emphasis on practical knowledge and being " street smart." Academic knowledge is not viewed as useful for making your way in the world, particularly in situations where economic hardship creates a society accustomed to scarcity of resources rather than bountiful resources. My sense is that others unfamiliar with the culture of scarcity can have a tendency to misjudge the emphasis on the practical nature of Spanish-speaking individuals as lacking an emphasis on education. If you are a single mother trying to raise eight children and work, you are faced with making practical choices that you might not otherwise choose to make. It may become a luxury to have your 14-year-old daughter go on to high school when the care of the other children in the household is at stake.

Not only is it not unusual to find individuals who have immigrated to the U.S. who hold advanced degrees working as laborers and housekeepers, it is also not unusual to find Spanish-speaking individuals with relatively low levels of education who are quite bright and adaptable. It is important not to equate low education with low intelligence, as many individuals have lacked the opportunity to fully realize their academic potential. Both of my parents had a sixth-grade education, yet I was always aware that they were very bright and capable despite educational experiences that were limited due to poverty and unfortunate life circumstances. In turn, when talking with clients regarding their educational background, it is important to understand the specifics. This can be a difficult conversation to have with clients. I have found that disclosing that my own parents had a limited education and that I am fully aware that everyone does not have the same opportunities and circumstances helps alleviate discomfort and embarrassment my clients may have about their own low educational backgrounds. Engaging the client in a conversation about their own educational experiences, strengths, weaknesses, and family circumstances can add rich information to a provider's knowledge about their current life circumstance. Educational experiences are extremely varied. An individual may state that they have a sixth-grade education, but upon further questioning may reveal that they attended school for only three of those years. They were in sixth grade only because they were placed with same-aged peers. I have also encountered the opposite, a mentally challenged individual who was retained in third grade for the bulk of his educational experience because of those mental challenges, despite growing into adolescence. Many others stop at sixth grade because advanced schooling was not accessible in their small towns unless they moved out of the area. Still others may drop out in third grade, yet questioning about their siblings' educational experiences reveals that they attained much higher levels. I suspect that often these individuals who drop out during their elementary years, while others in the family have attained higher levels, have suffered from unidentified disorders such as ADHD or reading disorders. While Latin American countries are making progress by leaps and bounds in identifying these individuals and providing access to limited resources, individuals in smaller communities continue to suffer the bulk of the disadvantages.

Cultural Barriers to Treatment

Just as there are stereotypes of Hispanic individuals, they, in turn, also have stereotypes of the U.S. culture. These beliefs about the majority culture can negatively impact seeking treatment. Spanish-speaking individuals come to me hoping to be "understood," feeling that those in the mainstream U.S. culture are not likely to understand the nuances of the Hispanic culture.

Hispanics expect and have a preference for a more personal, less formal approach. Recently, a client described his struggles with his American physician who, on more than one occasion, called him by the wrong name, and couldn't seem to keep his injuries straight. He expressed an intense feeling of representing "one of those Mexicans who are all alike."

The Spanish language has two forms of " you"; the formal " you" is used to communicate respect to individuals one does not know well. This differentiation exists to varying degrees in all Hispanic countries. For example, people from Argentina and Uruguay will expect to be addressed formally for a longer period of time, while Mexicans will quickly revert to the informal " you" once they begin to feel comfortable. This distinction can vary by level of education as well, with more highly educated individuals expecting and providing a more formal tone for longer periods.

Practitioners may also sense an initial guardedness that arises from an individual's hesitation about " what you really want to know." In general, more questions and curiosity are expected. Hispanics are also aware that they often relate stories and information in much greater detail than Anglos do and so may be cautious about causing impatience in their provider.

Hispanics are also keenly aware of the Anglo culture's strong emphasis on the individual and may perceive that they "only care about themselves." This can make them hesitant to have a family member, such as an adolescent child or a wife, engage in treatment for fear that they will be encouraged to distance from the family. In general, there is a deep sense of family commitment, obligation, and responsibility. It is not unusual for the youngest child, particularly females, to become responsible for taking care of their parents in old age, even at the expense of sacrificing their own opportunities to start their own families or careers. In turn, there is a high degree of social support and sense of belonging provided by the family, which is thought to be responsible for the longer life expectancy of Hispanics. The family system is quite extended and includes almost anyone of any degree of relation. Sometimes even friends of the family become " adopted" into the family as " aunts/uncles" or " madrina/padrino." Often what looks like enmeshment is actually quite common and normal for Hispanic individuals. For example, it is not unusual for an adult Hispanic individual to call their parents every day, even multiple times a day, if finances allow for this.

Parenting practices differ, as well. In some ways Hispanics can be viewed as stricter than Anglo parents, and in others, they are much more lenient. Within the Hispanic culture, *respect* is extremely important; as such, socialization to be good means that the child will be conforming and respectful. In general, conformity to external standards is considered much more important than developing autonomy. As such, a practitioner that encourages an adolescent to be verbally or behaviorally assertive may be interpreted by the parents as showing disrespectful behavior. Consistent with a lack of emphasis on autonomy, Hispanics tend to be more permissive and tolerant of "immature" behaviors and are less concerned about meeting timelines regarding independence. I recalled my shock when my female cousin went about what she considered to be the routine task of bathing her 8-year-old nephew. Hispanics also tend to have closer mother-child relationships and will be more open about verbal and physical expression of affection.

Time sense for Hispanics is *very* different. I can recall a conversation with a client regarding the stresses of acculturating to the dominant culture where he identified *having to be on time* as the greatest cultural stressor he faced. To an Anglo provider, a client's chronic lateness may be perceived as a failure to take the appointments seriously. At the same time, Hispanics do not mind nearly as much when they have to wait. In fact, in Uruguay, doctor's offices do not even attempt to set up an appointment system because they simply do not work. It is expected, by all parties, that one just shows up and is waited on in due turn. I find that my own time sense is some blend of these two perspectives. I am not strongly impacted by clients who are five or 10 minutes late who come rushing in and are very apologetic as they enter> Neither am I so time-bound as to end sessions at the 45-minute point, and routinely run a few minutes over.

Although advances in equality between the sexes are continuously being made, *machismo*, and more traditional male/female roles, are still widespread. Although more educated women may resist traditional roles, those that have been more sheltered are socialized to tolerate a lot of inappropriate behavior from their husbands. *Individual* therapy can mean two people, (and sometimes a whole family), as spouses usually accompany each other. I usually structure sessions to allow individuals time without their partner, while also providing some time for the partner to come into the session so that they can feel included in the treatment process.

Things to Keep in Mind

As this chapter demonstrates, "Hispanics" refers to many diverse nationalities that include South America, Central America, and the Caribbean. Asking individuals to identify their country of origin is a great way to demonstrate interest and gain a better understanding about individual differences. Families and couples can struggle with conflicting cultural values due to differing levels of acculturation. Helping to generate discussions about how their lives have been impacted by living in this country, as well as the pros/cons of the culture of origin versus the new culture. Adolescents, in particular, can feel caught between two worlds as they learn about the cultural rules of this society but are also expected to adhere to the cultural traditions of their homes.

11.

ECCE HOMO

Henry V. Soper, PhD and Heather Sorensen

This is a very difficult chapter to write, but an essential one. We would like to think that now we live at our moral acme but, in some ways, we are nearer our nadir. It is a horrible and despicable situation that many are not ready to relieve ourselves of. Some gender stereotypes have proven very resistant to change, such as who decides on vacations and such. We often feel that money is power, and we also have the presumption that in a heterosexual cis-gender relationship—for this example a marriage—the husband makes more money than the wife. Relatedly the wife is placed in a less powerful position for making serious life-changing decisions and even more relatively minor ones. Such gender roles may make life simpler for some, but cause more trouble than they are worth. I asked Louise if she had any plans for Thanksgiving, and her response was that she would do whatever Jeff, her husband, decides. I should have known better, for Jeff loved to put together dinners and parties, and was an expert at it. How often have we seen women, at a dinner with a male, given the check at the end (or anticipated the fear of the waiter who violated this "rule"), or the man being served the "man" food (e.g., a slab of steak) regardless of who ordered it. I have a friend who is an outstanding neurobiologist who presented a paper at a convention in the South, and the hotel refused to make out the bill to her (so her school would pay for it), but instead to her husband. Suffice it to say it involved a lawyer to get that resolved. She complained about this in a professional magazine, and the next month there was a letter stating that she simply did not understand the "gentlemanliness and culture" of the Southern states. I pointed out that the letter was signed by M. Chauvin Porker. There are varying cultural powers acting on what sports, movies, or television shows the family will watch together. Most have probably noticed the gender of the driver when couples go driving. And along with that, whose car they are driving.

The presumptions people make about men and women they encounter, in trying to put her or him into a role (wife, teacher, etc.), go beyond the realm of condescending (or is it colondescending?) but into the realm of rude. The escape is often just as humorous. Once my boss and I were working with an anatomist, and we were all using first names. Later he asked my boss where he had found such a knowledgeable technician; my boss said that I was not a technician but a postdoc. I am not sure which held more prestige, but when next we met he always referred to me as "Doctor."

It is true that, until at least very recently, different expectations are made for women and men, none worse than in academia. We have all heard that women are more gifted in languages and literature, whereas men are generically stronger in mathematics and sciences. How such a thing could be established or proven (or disproven) is beyond me. When I was at an all-male college I was shocked to learn that many of my contemporary female friends went to colleges that taught courses closer to what I would call home economics during their training course to become "perfect young ladies." (I was also told that the only degree that counted was the Mrs. degree.) I never knew there was such a science to serving tea at a reception, or even serving the sugar. I do remember the wives of the faculty in high school getting snitty about who was going to do what at the post-game teas.

Locally we have an automobile dealer (a male), and a professional linebacker would come and shoot advertisements for him. On one shoot, the two of them—both dressed in very dirty coveralls—had their heads under the hood of a vehicle trying to figure out why the engine was running so rough. Then this objectively physically attractive woman came up and asked what was going on. She gruffly and condescendingly told them what they were doing wrong. She picked up a wrench, tapped the distributor cap, and the whole engine calmed down. Her boss looked after her growling, and the linebacker lifted his head and smashed it on the hood of the car. We need more ads like that.

An area of concern is the woman who feels sexually confident in herself, as a person and as a woman, who is not afraid to go up and talk to a person, a man, as an equal with no sexual agenda. The concern is not the woman herself or her confidence but rather that many observers see a hidden agenda and that can be very disturbing. Of course, many men would not approach a woman without such an agenda. This kind of hidden attitude can make it very difficult for women. As a Broadway song of years ago said, this woman approaching a man might be thought of as a whore, but the man doing the exact same thing toward a woman might be thought as a man about town or a bon vivant. Hardly fair, but it is our society.

Women who excel in anything often have their gender or sexual orientation questioned. Top female athletes are often assumed to be lesbian, as are effective leaders, and this is not an experience specific to U.S. athletes and worldviews. The argument goes with an ignorant hypothesis, that male, or stereotypical "male" qualities, are better and associated with success. Therefore, if someone is good and/or successful, they must have an inordinate amount of stereotypical male qualities about them. And the beat goes on.

Woman are constantly reinforced with a message that they are less than or not as good as men, from the dress worn on television advertisements to the higher costs (i.e., the "pink tax") for goods that are labeled for women as opposed to those that are either generic or identified as for men. Women are expected to remain polite and accepting no matter what, including making room for men on sidewalks. Men will invariably try not to share a space. Women are taught to make themselves as small and as quiet as possible, while men are rewarded for being loud and taking up space. Women are expected to be appreciative of sexual harassment such as catcalling from strangers. If the response from a woman is unappreciative, yelling increases and threats can be made. Women are often told by peers to ignore it, but that is just wrong, wrong, wrong. A pat on the stomach, low and hard with a shoe, might be more effective.

Women in leadership roles who are assertive or engaging—in other words, those who are doing their jobs—are called bossy or worse and are often undermined by both male and female colleagues. Stereotypes that have been attached to women include that they are illogical, overly emotional, hysterical, and not credible, especially in regard to rape, assault, or abuse (women are blamed as being vindictive and delegitimized based on a demeaning perspective of their sexuality).

In general, men do not have any appreciation for the feelings of being a woman walking in a large and dark parking lot or even a large store with trepidation surrounding the very real possibility of being violated, in any way, by unseen persons around them. A man can be old, ugly, disabled or out of shape, but he did not grow up with this fear, so he does not experience it now. A very powerful force not appreciated by men includes the treatments after an attack. In addition to the obvious, the woman will be persistently viewed as someone who just made it up for their 15 minutes of fame. Although many will believe this to be true, knowing many of these women has assured me that this is a psychological impossibility; maybe some sociopaths who do not care can carry it off, but no one from the normal population can do so. Women are often forced to consider what normal aspect of their life (i.e., going out with friends to dance, expressing their political beliefs, choice of clothing) might be used to discredit them.

I know a 17-year-old woman who went to trial to get her violator to do time and exact some justice. However, the judge decided that she had made the whole thing up and threw the case out. This young woman also expressed that the assault and the resulting aftermath have stayed with her, making it hard to make close friends.

I remember getting a little more than a bit upset when a new movie about Cinderella came out and, as I understood it, her evaluation as a princess, as a person, as a potential queen, rested on how good a party she could throw. Someday I hope someone can explain this to me, but this flick was not parent-approved in my family.

I am thankful that now there is more emphasis in schools, and consequent freedom, for those of us with a strange number of chromosomes—be all that you can be, I believe in you, now you believe in you. Recognizing and understanding the imbalance is a first step in alleviating its pain.

It is curious how illogical are the generalizations that can be made. A woman stole my retirement, and therefore all women are bad. This man cheated on me, and therefore all men are bad and not to be trusted. Growing up I heard these statements made as facts, plus many that were more innocuous, such as "men can never learn to fold shirts." Counter-evidence never carried any weight, for these people knew these "truths" to be true. We highly question how far gender discrimination, both ways, has progressed since those good old days of yore (when we knew what we knew and no one questioned it). At times it almost seems as if athletic teams, in which one team (i.e., women) can do no good, and, of course, the other team (i.e., men) will win in the end, or the other way around.

It has been tied into sexual harassment of many forms, where the intent of the perpetrator does not matter. Although currently men may be the recipients more often than not, it is equally serious when directed against women. It is equally harmful, as there is seemingly nothing one can do that will not promulgate further accusations of retaliation. A young girl who has been accused of having sex with the captain of the football team can be psychologically just as impaired as this captain if he is falsely accused. In either case the accused is left helpless, and if one accused the other of lying, it does not matter if they are actually lying. The assumption is that the reported action is the truth, and if someone denies it, they are then considered guilty of retaliation. The logical conclusion is that it does not matter whether the deed was committed, but only whether the person was accused of it, and many have been told that by the investigators. It is also all right for the investigator to treat the accuser as a criminal, distort what you say, then accuse you of lying for not substantiating the distortion they came up with. This is an equal-opportunity sin, for anyone regardless of gender in this situation can be equally devastated. And, for our purposes, the accused individual who is not "guilty" of said accusation is often subsequently left needing therapy to just get their feet on the ground again. Often those most trusted as friends and relations will abandon the individual, and certainly this will be the fear of the individual. There is also the fear that they will never again be treated with the trust and compassion they were prior to the (false) accusation. Those more sociopathic individuals who do not care about the accusations will likely not be damaged as much as the others.

Regardless of the specific circumstances, all of these people will probably need therapy. The girl who was accurately accused of sleeping with the football captain most likely had no idea that the word would get out and that she would be ridiculed for it. Whether she is actually ridiculed or not does not matter if she believes that is what is going on. Also, she will feel that her reputation is gone, and no one will even think of her again as a nice girl, but rather as some slut. Certainly, much of her punishment is self-induced, but that does not make it that much less troublesome. Such an individual historically has had a great deal of difficulty finding a therapist whom she believes she can connect with—one who will not judge her; one who is interested in getting her to feel better.

Another person is the girl who is falsely accused. She will invariably believe that most will believe the accusation and not her. A certain sense of paranoia can set in, such as: Why is this happening to her? I have heard some say "No one would falsely accuse someone of sexual assault or indiscretions." The accused will also have a great deal of trouble finding a therapist who believes her or in her, and she may give up before she finds someone who can take her side, believing that everyone must be like that.

On the other hand, there are people who have committed acts that cannot just be brushed off, such as rape or pedophilia. Those accused of or guilty of these crimes will often need therapy too, and this can be difficult for the therapist. Being honest with the client is a good practice, stating that their actions are something you cannot personally accept. During my training, I was doing some counterconditioning with mild shock therapy with a pedophile, and I went to my supervisor to be relieved of it because I felt I was shocking him too much. His response was that he had three young daughters, and what did I think he would do? Point made.

Sometimes tough decisions must be made. I have had students who have tried but just cannot work with certain people. The basis may be their criminal history or their culture or something else. I had one associate who said she could not work with suicidal patients, and she would tell them that if they expressed such ideation they would be transferred to me. (I warned her that that could be considered inhumane punishment.)

Many years ago, when I was working in a hospital, the "examiners" wanted to use my room and an adjacent one for some testing. Therefore, we had to do our work in the hall. At one point after this, my neighbor got a letter from personnel who wanted to discuss his sexually inappropriate harassment behavior. He asked if I knew anything about it, and I did not. All I could say was say little. It turned out that a woman some 40 feet down the hall had witnessed him hugging a young girl, which had left the witness feeling very uncomfortable.

The accused man said nothing but that he had not intended to offend anyone. As the details unfolded, information surfaced that the young woman who was the recipient of the accused man's hug was his daughter, who came to be consoled because she had just broken up with a boyfriend of three years' standing. When the man told the investigator the aforementioned information, he was promptly told that his father-daughter embrace had nothing to do with this investigation, but rather that his behavior (the hug) had made a female co-worker feel uncomfortable. Feeling as if he was on *Candid Camera*, he did not make a big to-do about it, but when he was punished by being effectively fired, (which lasted for two weeks before he was returned to work), he became upset, got a very good lawyer, got his money back and then some, and the hospital was warned about being irresponsible for acting in such a capricious and irresponsible manner.

At a meeting of interns, one young woman was sitting at the edge of a table, and the male next to her later complained that she was making him feel uncomfortable. When I heard of the report I wrote that nothing distasteful had occurred. Her husband was quite upset about it, and neither of them trusted the hospital again. I was warned that my actions in her defense could adversely affect my position. I did ask her if they wanted the name of a good lawyer.

A friend of mine invited me to his trial. He was accused of giving a young woman the key to his room and following her some 10 minutes later. Another member of the faculty witnessed this. The "witness" specifically accused him of giving his room key to a "young blonde." My friend fully admitted to giving his key to said women, and then asked this faculty member if they were willing to take responsibility for their accusations. He then launched into a tirade, accusing this faculty member of trying to poison his marriage, for it seems this "young blonde" woman was in fact his wife. And though she was not happy about the accusation of his playing around on her, she was perfectly happy to be tabbed a "young blonde" who was trying to take advantage of her husband.

A teacher was once accused of keeping female students in the lecture room for three hours without a chance to use the bathroom. He carefully tried to explain that, with an enlarged prostate, he could not last himself for more than 45 minutes; after that if he could not leave they would need a bucket and a mop. To this he was told that it did not matter what, or if, he had done anything, but only that he was accused of it. In this egregious situation, one of the students knew of the plans to bring the false accusations against him. On telling the investigators the plan to bring these false accusations, she was told unceremoniously to shut up or she would be kicked out of the school and, at the time of her dissertation, she did come very close to leaving the program.

Back at the hospital, a supervisor was warned about some serious accusations being brought against him. He taught Tuesday and Thursday mornings and Thursdays he would bring in some doughnuts. He was informed that bringing these donuts was considered sexual harassment, because if a woman did not want to eat them, this would put pressure on her to eat them or get a bad letter from him (though he did not write those letters, but no matter). The irony of this situation was how sexist the assumption was that women must be hypervigilant about their weight and lack the ability to simply resist the donuts for fear of repercussions. Even though this entire situation was based on sexist presuppositions, the supervisor ceased bringing in donuts, though other students brought in donuts in his donut absence. No one complained about their weight or any possible relation of their weight to the aforementioned clandestine donuts.

Around that same time, this supervisor was asked the perpetual question of whether males or females make better neuropsychologists. I don't know what possessed him, but he said: "Look at the evidence. Who are the three top neuropsychologists—Edith Kaplan, Brenda Milner, and Muriel Lezak. This too seemed to get a rise out of people, though for some the expectations were so great they could not hear the response.

Working with battered women opens other doors of vulnerability. I asked one such woman about the chores for her and her three brothers growing up. They did, she said, the "boy" things such as cutting the grass, which took about an hour a week, but with three boys it came out to an hour every three weeks. Whereas she did the "girl" things, including cleaning the dishes in the evening and after lunch on weekends—nine hours a week.

When rephrasing this discrepancy, her initial response was that her mother was right, she would never be afraid of hard work. However, after careful contemplation, the dissonance dissipated and she identified the disparity between the genders. A very bright woman, she had never gone to college. She said that she and her brothers never brought it up to her parents, so nothing was prepared. I asked about her two-year-old son's college, and she said she already had some $4,000 in his college fund.

The husband of one woman would go out with other couples and tell them false stories of sexual fetishes his wife supposedly liked. This was very embarrassing for her. As a "trophy wife" she expressed feeling her societal expectations were to "sit back and look nice" (her husband was an ex-jock).

One woman's husband (who was selected for her by her older sister) was a naval officer who could get violent toward her as well as her two children from a previous marriage (a marriage to someone I had had to institutionalize for schizophrenia). After some time had passed I convinced her to keep a suitcase for herself and her children in the trunk of her car so that when she did have to leave she would not have to come back for anything. (Eventually she did have to leave for good.) And after significant encouraging, she eventually told her mother to be ready for her to escape should she need it. Further encouragement eventually led to her visiting her mother, whom she had not seen in years at the direction of her older sister. Her older sister had barred her from seeing her mother because her mother is lesbian.

A week after this whole ordeal, this client proudly announced she had a new friend, one she could trust, and her mother's sexual orientation had nothing to do with how good a person she was or how understanding she was. She said stereotyped thinking was completely unfounded and she was elated to have her mother in her life again.

Her story is not uncommon; in fact, one in three women have been victims of some form of physical violence by an intimate partner within their lifetime (Black, Basile, Breiding, Smith, Walters, Merrick, Chen, & Stevens, 2011). Additionally, one in four women has been the victim of severe physical violence by an intimate partner (Black et al., 2011). One in seven women has been stalked by an intimate partner in their lifetime to the point where they actually feared for their life or their physical well-being (Black et al., 2011). Concomitantly, one in five women in the U.S. have been raped (Black et al., 2011). As we can see, the fear women experience is not unfounded; however, it is often downplayed, ignored, or these women are blamed for their own victimization.

Reference

Black, M. C., Basile, K. C., Breiding, M. J., Smith, S. G., Walters, M. L., Merrick, M. T., Chen, J., & Stevens, M. (2011). The national intimate partner and sexual violence survey: 2010 summary report.   Retrieved from http://www.cdc.gov/ violenceprevention/pdf/nisvs_report2010-a.pdf

12.

AFTERWORD

Henry V. Soper, PhD

We have taken a tour through many of the cultures we are likely to meet as therapists, but we looked at only a very small sample of each. This is somewhat like touring Europe, visiting one town at random in each country, and trying to draw conclusions about all of Europe. We would probably get an idea of the diversity in Europe, which is one of the purposes of this book, but it would feed us little information about any of the countries and how they fit together to make Europe what it is.

Although there will always be areas that could be covered and could help therapists help clients who do not come from their general culture, the array presented in the preceding chapters should give the reader a good idea of the range and diversity within cultures in terms of what can help and hinder therapy. The idea was not to create a dictionary of terms and scenarios but to give the clinical psychologist a flavor for what might be important in the mind of the client from a culture different from yours. I might add that the same is true for individuals who come from basically the same culture as you. The psychodynamics may be similar across cultures, but influences that the roles, cultural beliefs, and practices have on those psychodynamics can vary substantially within and across cultures and, importantly for us, across individuals within a given culture. Some woman in a culture may feel depressed because her husband's back injury has prevented her from having sex, which is very important to her. Similarly, a woman who has not been the same since she struck her head in a motor vehicle accident will slowly become more and more ostracized in her family for not being able to care for her children, but a similar woman in another family who understands the situation a bit better may receive extra help, supervision, and socialization to help her with planning and organizing her life and the lives of her children.

Knowing that the grandmother is in charge of the family, and bringing her into the solutions for a mother who does not take care of her son properly, can be far more effective than anything the psychologist can do alone. Knowing the gender roles in a given Hispanic community or a Jewish community can provide essential information that the clients may have difficulty producing, yet the therapist is able to work through the problem without embarrassing or blaming the client.

I have seen cultural exercises where several over-educated individuals attribute the difficulties the patients are having to various factors within their culture. Talk about pre-judging! To them, the difficulty has to be related to cultural differences between the client and the therapist. A hornet does not care what culture you come from; the sting will hurt just as much. People from any culture can become depressed or anxious. When one looks closely, the impression one walks away with is not the impression of the culture, but rather how similar we are. I remember someone telling me that I was the blackest White man he had ever known. When I asked him how many White people he had known, he said only me.

Cheddar Man, the oldest (10,000 years old) complete human skeleton yet found in England, is thought to be a member of a group of ancestors to about 10% of today's White Britons. Recent DNA evidence tells us that he had blue eyes, dark skin, and curly black hair (Williams, 2018). It seems incredible that a group of people could make such drastic morphological changes (from dark skin and curly black hair) to today's prototypic Briton, who does not look like that at all, and all within 10,000 years or, to put it another way, just some 400 generations. This is further evidence of the meaninglessness of using supposedly racially identifying morphology, such as dark skin and curly black hair, to make gross distinctions between peoples. To carry this a bit further, it may have taken a relatively short time for the Hottentots and Eskimos to develop their distinctive morphologies.

The best source of information, of course, for culture-specific problems, is the client, and often the lack of information is exacerbated by the client's trying to live in their native culture as well as the dominant culture. In addition, it would behoove therapists to be aware of the major incidents occurring during the life of their clients or just before. For example, a massive immigration from the Deep South to Detroit can have a major influence on those who moved and their offspring. Those whose parents lost many friends in the camps in Germany during WWII may well have this as a source of stress. Gender issues within a culture are exceedingly important. People who look as if they come from a different culture (e.g., look African American) can have problems not only as immigrants (e.g., from the Pacific islands), but through misidentification of others of their heritage.

Specific stresses such as disease can also cause problems, and how the culture of the individual takes care of these can play a role in mental health. There are two major groups of individuals, those who are born with the disorder and those who acquire it during life, often during adulthood. Most of the examples provided were of disorders acquired in adulthood, dementia perhaps being the classic example of people (relatives) changing who they are and requiring help from others. However, there are also families with stresses coming from children with autism, mental retardation, and Down syndrome, among others. Although there is a literature developing on how to be a caregiver for such individuals, many families have the feeling they are the only ones going through this, and they have difficulty not blaming the proband or the spouse ("I don't have any of this in my family, so it must be your family's fault"). The stresses can not only be bad for the proband and the caregiver, but also for the siblings and other relatives who have to suffer, or feel they have to, because of the child with the disorder. The interaction between culture and such stresses can be very important. For example, the roles that the grandmother or others are expected to play can have an influence on how disruptive the child is to his or her relatives and/or family.

We find it incredible how influential the concept of race is, even though quite clearly cognitively it is a meaningless concept. People feel they have to attribute factors to it based on incredibly small samples. Having heard such attributes since we were very young, it is very difficult for us to give up such beliefs. Let me give an example of how this can happen. Most of us were told by our grandmothers or someone else not to climb up in a tree and touch the chicks in the nest. We were also told that the mother bird would smell us on the chicks and throw them out. Wow! Even as a comparative psychologist I sort of believed this, but when you think about it, it cannot be true. Birds do not have much of a sense of smell (ever been in a chicken coop?). They tend to fly and look for food on the ground, not smell it out. And we also know that ornithologists swap birds from nest to nest with no ill effect. Also, many birds lay their eggs in the nests of other birds, to no ill effect. However, having been told this story when we were very young and not being in the habit of challenging such information, it remains unchanged in the lore of information we accept. Supposed racial attributes, told to us at the same time, can be very resistant to elimination and, even in the face of counter-evidence, they tend to remain strongly embedded in our knowledge and belief system.

Similar to the racial attributes, gender attributes have been impressed upon us since about the time we were born. The genders, right from the get-go, are treated differently. Somehow we can be impressed that a boy who wears pink can have some serious problems, but worse than that are the different roles and expectations of even young boys and girls. The chores given to each can be very unfair; the girls do the dishes after every meal and the boys cut the grass once a week. The sad thing is that many of us do not see the disparity. These roles can continue well into adulthood, and when someone steps outside their gender role, questions are raised. Here the concept of difference emerges—that is, difference from the roles expected or assigned. A woman who wants to take on a "male" job faces a lot of discrimination and questions about her identity. The same is true of men who take on traditional "female" employment.

It seems that many are able to accept that there are many Christian religions, but most are relatively unaware of the many Jewish religions. It can become absurd, as with a friend of mine who, upon announcing that he was Polish, was told that could not be true because he was Jewish, and therefore he had to be affiliated with Jerusalem, and not Poland. No amount of explaining could straighten that out.

This concept of diversity of culture is indeed very complex, and we have just scratched the surface. As we become more familiar with the peoples around us, the complexity emerges. It can be hard not to generalize what you have learned about one Hispanic culture and apply it to another, which can cause real problems. Confusing the culture of Havana and Guadalajara can cause serious problems and confusion. In addition, many who are tagged as being in the same culture have only language in common and there can be serious problems between the groups. Take a look at the Near East.

Reference

Williams, S. (February 7, 2018) DNA Analysis Paints New Picture of 10,000-Year-Old Briton. *The Scientist Weekly.* Retrieved from https://www.the-scientist.com/the-nutshell/dna-analysis-paints-new-picture-of-10000-year-old-briton-30307

About the Authors

Scott Curry, M.A. is a Ph. D. student in Clinical Psychology with an emphasis on Forensics and Neuropsychology. He obtained his Master's in Counseling and Psychology from Troy State University at Dothan in 1992, and began working with troubled youth immediately after his first practicum. He has worked as a therapist and probation officer for this population since then, and has had positions in the State of Alabama and the State of Utah. He has spent the last 10 years as the program coordinator for a youth mental health court in the 3rd District Juvenile Court in Salt Lake City. He was awarded his Master's in Clinical Psychology in 2015, and has most recently completed practica working with adult forensic patients and sex offenders. Scott lives in Salt Lake City with his paramour Kelli, and their rescue AmStaff, Jax. He has studied traditional Japanese karate for the past 38 years, and enjoys gourmet cooking, grilling, and barbecue.

Rachel Rugh Fraser, MA, MA Ed. is a graduate student from Fielding Graduate University who is currently completing her final neuropsychological practicum training in Southern California, involving the neuropsychological assessment of pediatric populations. She completed two year-long practica at UCLA; the first rotation a therapy-based training emphasizing CBT for the treatment of OCD and anxiety-related disorders, and the second rotation a neuropsychological and therapy-based training where she gained experience in neuropsychological assessment of both research subjects and outpatients, as well as experience providing cognitive rehabilitation for patients with dementia. She holds a master's degree from Azusa Pacific University and currently works as a behavioral coach for patients with anxiety-related disorders, and as a psychological assistant for a pediatric neuropsychology private practice in West Los Angeles, California. Rachel has been involved as a research assistant for a variety of studies, some of which involving OCD treatment outcomes, the prevention of Alzheimer's disease, and the most recent, an examination of the effects of a community arts program on abused children.

Samantha F. Hill, MSW is a graduate student at Fielding Graduate University who currently resides in Bakersfield, California. She serves as a full-time clinician for the State of California as well as on a non-profit board for a foster family agency. Samantha is passionate about working with individuals in the forensic system of care and has held positions within the state of Arizona Correctional System as well as the State of Washington. Her experiences working on the west coast have driven her to understand how culture can define an individual, as well as community.

Pavel Litvin, M.A. graduate student from Fielding Graduate University who is currently completing his pre-doctoral neuropsychology internship at the California Pacific Medical Center in San Francisco, California, where he spends more than 50% of his training at the Ray Dolby Brain Health Center—an innovative memory clinic for individuals with cognitive changes, early memory loss, or dementia. He is a licensed marriage and family therapist and completed two neuropsychology practica at UCLA, worked as a neuropsychological rater for Alzheimer's disease clinical trials, and engaged in research that merges his clinical work in anxiety with geriatric neuropsychology. He has recently matched for the 2-year Harbor UCLA neuropsychology fellowship that will provide exposure to a broad spectrum of neurological and neuropsychiatric disorders, in addition to providing opportunities for collaboration on research geared toward understanding the neurocognitive sequelae of traumatic brain injury via cognitive paradigms, standard neuropsychological tests, and neuroimaging.

Margaret Loo, Ph.D. graduated from University of California, Santa Barbara in psychology and received her Master's degree in Marriage and Family Counseling from Antioch University. She obtained her Master's and Doctorate degrees from Fielding Graduate University in clinical psychology. Her areas of focus are diversity, transgender and gender perceptions, and mental healthcare. Her thesis was entitled Transprejudice: Personality traits that predict anti-transgender attitudes. She has a background in geriatric psychology, severe mental health and transgender support. Margaret is a native Angelina and currently lives in Southern California with her husband, daughter, three dogs, and two cats and enjoys yoga and rock climbing.

Angelina J. Prince-Jeffers, M.A. is a graduate student at Fielding Graduate University who currently resides on St. Thomas in the US Virgin Islands with her husband and daughter. She serves as full time faculty in the Psychology Department at the University of the Virgin Islands and is currently conducting neuropsychological and psychodiagnostic testing in practicum. Angelina is passionate about assisting families and children. She has spent the past 6 years working with the non-profit Kidscope, Inc.; an organization that provides holistic trauma informed care and forensic interviewing for children who have been victims of trauma, sexual abuse, and maltreatment. Angelina's research interests include exploring the impact of trauma on neuropsychological and behavioral outcome. She previously completed training on providing interventions to individuals with severe mental disorders and substance use disorders. Her educational background in psychology and communications prompted her interest in understanding how elements of culture influence the human experience. She has a vested interest in exploring culturally diverse populations and in exploring how to improve the delivery of mental health care services to diverse and underserved populations.

Whillma Quenicka, M.A. was born and raised in West Java, Indonesia. She migrated to the United States in 1998 just after graduating from high school due to political turmoil triggered by monetary crisis in South East Asia. She earned 4 Associate Degrees with Honors in Business Administration, Economics, and Liberal Arts within 2 years of her study at St. Barbara City College. She then received her bachelor's degree in psychology with College Honors from UCLA, Masters of Science in Clinical Psychology from CLU, and Masters of Art and Doctorate degree in Clinical Psychology from Fielding Graduate University. She is also a certified addiction treatment specialist, CATC. She has an extensive background working with adolescence and adult from diverse ethnic backgrounds who suffer from complex developmental trauma and substance use disorders.Outside Psychology, her life is centered around her husband and son. She is spiritual, loves reading, traveling, and exploring world cultures through culinary experience. She is a traditional Sundanese dancer, plays organ, and is aspired to invest more of her free time engaging in her long lost passion for creating water based abstract painting.

Laura Rieffel, Ph.D. is a neuropsychologist with a thriving private practice in Louisville, Colorado, who conducts neuropsychological evaluations and treatment with individuals suffering from a range of neurological disorders, many of whom are Spanish language dominant. She completed her undergraduate degree at Emory University, her master's degree at Georgia State University and her doctorate at Fielding Graduate University. She has been practicing in the field of psychology/neuropsychology for 30 years with individuals ranging in age from preschool to geriatrics. She is passionate about many areas of psychology, but in particular enjoys working in the areas of clinically diverse groups, mood/bipolar disorders, and neuropsychology.

Iya Ritchie, M.A., a native Ukrainian and Pepperdine alumni, resides in Beverly Hills, CA. She found her professional calling in a role of a clinical neuropsychologist, with her interests falling at the intersection of neuropsychology, psychopathology, forensic and health psychology. She underwent a broad range of academic and training experiences in assessment, empirically-supported intervention, and consultation. Iya continuously challenges herself with research and philanthropic projects. These projects are aimed at evaluation of brain-behavior relationships, psychological restoration, as well as education of the public on the prevalence and destigmatization of mental illness. She systematically volunteers with severely mentally ill, homeless, underserved, formerly incarcerated, or at-risk for offending, individuals. Iya is completing a doctoral program in clinical psychology at Fielding Graduate University, where she is leading a student chapter for the Association of Neuropsychology Students in Training (ANST)."

Heather Sorensen spent much of her childhood and adolescence on indigenous First Nations, "Native American" reservations/rancherias in the central California area, specifically Picayune Rancheria of Chukchansi people, Big Sandy Rancheria of Mono people, North Fork Rancheria of Mono people, Cold Springs Rancheria of Mono people, and Table Mountain Rancheria of the Chukchansi band of Yokuts and Monache tribe; although her personal lineage is with the Lenca tribe in Honduras. After her secondary education she worked as a clinician at the Sierra Tribal Consortium Inc. "Turtle Lodge", providing prevention services to youth on the aforementioned Rancherias and residential treatment services to federally recognized indigenous First Nations adults with co-occurring substance use disorders and mental health conditions. Then she received a degree in alcohol and drug abuse counseling, became a certified Alcohol Drug Counselor (and three years later she was certified as an Alcohol Drug Counselor – Clinical Supervisor). She then received her Baccalaureate, cum laude, from Brandman University, in psychology. She is currently working toward the doctorate in clinical and neuropsychology at Fielding Graduate University.

About the Editors

Henry V. Soper, Ph.D., has a B.A., Yale University (awarded Normal Hall, 1965; and Robert R. Chamberlain Awards) and M. A. and Ph.D. from the University of Connecticut. He received two NIH Postdoctoral Fellowships (ADAMHA), (NIMH), was Chief Fellow, Neuropsychology, University of California, Los Angeles; Wilmont Sweeney Juvenile Justice Award; Reviewer, Perceptual and Motor Skills Psychological Reports, Editorial Board, Applied Neuropsychology; The Encyclopedia of Neuropsychological Disorder. Fellow, National Academy of Neuropsychology and Psychonomic Society. He has published over 150 abstracts, papers, chapters, and books in the neurosciences, neuropsychology, medicine and psychology.

K. Drorit Gaines, Ph.D., received an academic excellence scholarship to UCLA and completed a Bachelor's Degree in Business Economics and Accounting. She received her Ph.D. from Fielding Graduate University in Clinical Psychology with specialization in Clinical Neuropsychology and completed post-doctoral experience in neuropsychology at the Veterans Affairs of Greater Los Angeles and UCLA Longevity Center. Dr. Gaines received awards from the American Psychological Association, Society of Nuclear Medicine and Molecular Imaging, Veterans Affairs of greater Los Angeles, and Fielding Graduate University. She serves as an expert on the Criminal Panel for the Los Angeles Superior Court, Principal Investigator, Clinical Faculty, vl., at UCLA, Adjunct Faculty, past Secretary and Board Member of the National Academy of Neuropsychology Foundation, Journal Reviewer for Applied Neuropsychology, and CEO of Neuro Health, Inc, supervising a clinical group. She is the first neuropsychologist to air a radio show in *Neuropsychology & Wellbeing* on several networks.

She authored *Combating Dementia in Thirty Days*, and co-authored *Fractioning the Frontal Lobe*.

About Fielding Graduate University

Fielding Graduate University, headquartered in Santa Barbara, CA, was founded in 1974, and celebrated its 45th anniversary in 2019. Fielding is an accredited, nonprofit leader in blended graduate education, combining face-to-face and online learning. Its curriculum offers quality master's and doctoral degrees for professionals and academics around the world. Fielding's faculty members represent a wide spectrum of scholarship and practice in the fields of educational leadership, human and organizational development, and clinical and media psychology. Fielding's faculty serves as mentors and guides to self-directed students who use their skills and professional experience to become powerful, socially responsible leaders in their communities, workplaces, and society. For more information, please visit Fielding online at www.fielding.edu.

www.ingramcontent.com/pod-product-compliance
Lightning Source LLC
Chambersburg PA
CBHW031500270326
41930CB00006B/179